THE
SPIRITUALLY
CONFIDENT
MAN

PIONEERING A
NEW FRONTIER
OF CO-CREATIVE
MASCULINITY

Zeus Yiamouyiannis, Ph.D.

Published by Phoenix Transformation Media

Cover design by Korrine Holt
Typesetting by Ekow Addai

ISBN-13: 978-0-9893203-3-7

THE SPIRITUALLY CONFIDENT MAN

PIONEERING A NEW FRONTIER OF CO-CREATIVE MASCULINITY

Contents

CHAPTER 4
Cultivating The Fruit—The Emerging Man
103

CHAPTER 5
Pulling Up The Weeds—The Patriarchal Man
143

CHAPTER 6
Bringing Home The Harvest—Raising Men And Boys; Opening To Women And Girls
199

CHAPTER 7
Lighting The Fire, Providing The Feast—Developing Spiritual Confidence
247

EPILOGUE
Wholeness
299

To Phoenix, who has been my greatest teacher, and Regina who is the heart of my heart and the soul of my soul. The masculine challenge of my son and the feminine support of my wife have helped make me a far better man.

Acknowledgements

THANKS, IN THIS BOOK, go first and foremost to my son, Phoenix, and my wife, Regina. Phoenix taught me to fight for him in the face of harm. When my anguish over my son's harm threatened to consume me, it was Regina who drew me past my fatalism and helped me remain steady, strong, and open-hearted. It was a community of men who stood by me and encouraged me never to give up, that helped me through a long road of struggle and triumph over despair. It was a community of feminist women who helped me become aware of the intense harms of patriarchy and initiated my desire to fight for the dignity and worth of all people on this earth, men, women, girls, and boys. It was my mother and father and my family who taught me to stick up for the underdog and to never quit in the fight for justice. Thanks also go to Sandie Sedgbeer for her editing help and for introducing me to Regina. Korrine Holt deserves mention for designing a splendid cover for this book. For all these teachers, champions, and friends, I am thankful. Without them, I could have never gathered the awareness, persistence, and conviction to write this book.

Opening The Portal

What is a man today? Where is masculinity going? Wage-based masculinity, where worth is rooted in paid work, is fading as men's jobs become automated. Virtual reality masculinity, where young men and boys boost their sense of heroism through video games, holds no promise either. Both of these options leave men, quite literally and metaphorically, sense-less.

What if developing masculine identity was a bold, creative experiment instead of a slavish duty or escape into fantasy? What if a new spirit of life came upon men, and challenges gave rise to curiosity rather than fear? What if men opened themselves to feel again rather than walling off the world?

For the first fifty years of my life, I was misplaced. In this half-century of time, I have experienced every condemning and promising form of manhood that I describe in this book. I have been a Toxic Man, a Striving Man, a Responsible Man, a Retreating Man, a Confused Man, an Equal Man, a Despairing Man, a Searching Man, and a Spiritually Confident Man.

On this journey, I have found that manhood, at its best, is a fundamentally creative endeavor. It is not about holding abstract ideas, following easy formulas, or kowtowing to cultural expectations. Vital manhood instead emanates and advances from the very spark of life given a man when he is born. Male personality is forged in aware engagement.

In the course of my life, I have experimented, tested, and failed with more versions of masculinity than I can count. I have accepted and left vocations both satisfying and unfulfilling. I have entered into romantic relationships that transformed what I thought a man should be. However, none of these adventures ever really defined me. I learned firsthand that there is no easy place for a man in today's world. Male prerogative is slipping away, forcing men to re-create their own identities or else destroy themselves and those around them in resentments and resistance to change.

My own journey into masculine rebirth did not originate in some academic or professional interest. I was thrust into this pathway by a near-death experience at the age of three and a half:

> *I was edging around the rim of the pool, holding on to the sides when I slipped. Suddenly, I was below the surface looking up at the sun. Instead of panicking, I felt an overwhelming sense of peace. I floated outside my body and watched myself being pulled from the pool. In an instant more, I was back in my body looking up at a ring of concerned faces against the contrast of a deep blue sky.*

I am not sure exactly what happened in that timeless out-of-body realm, but I came back with a keen glimpse into the powerful potential of human life. I became strongly aware of the extraordinary capabilities all human beings possess and express in individual and completely original ways. This unique "something" is what I call "divine genius." My experience catapulted me into the world with a deep desire to unleash and connect our divine gifts in a turbulent world that more than ever needs practical spiritual capabilities.

As a result, my own identity has become a matter of exploration, of questioning and finding out what human and masculine is, rather than adopting and asserting a package of "male" characteristics or conforming to social expectations. As a boy growing into a man, I became philosophically, emotionally, and spiritually receptive. I was drawn to develop my awareness so I could make sense of what I was feeling. At the same time, I became very physically involved in sport: in track and field, wrestling, football, fencing, and rowing to name a few. I saw no contradiction between the life of the mind, the life of the heart, the life of the spirit, and the life of the body.

In the strange lands of male identity, I did not meet with idealistic archetypes of masculinity seen in so many books; instead, I encountered three real types of men:

- **The Animal Man**, driven by effort and survival, defined by a sense of resistance, a will to succeed, and desire for victory.
- **The Social Man**, attracted by ease and belonging, characterized by a sense of flow, will toward peace, and need for acceptance.
- **The Co-Creative Man**, constituted by elevation and thriving, evoked by a sense of interaction, will to give, and commitment to transformation.

I am a blend of the three—the survival aspects of the Animal Man, the belonging aspects of the Social Man, and the transformation aspects of the Co-Creative Man. I experience these states as distinct, but intensely interconnected, elements of my being, and it is with this sense of integration that I write this book. In my boyhood and manhood, this interconnectedness has been developed further by conversations with the wisdom of Nature and engagement with the intelligence and intuition of women.

This creation of a new man does not follow a singular, heroic storyline. It arrives one step at a time and one choice at a time. Creation of new masculinity follows the more mystical path of a stranger in a strange land in which the minds of men themselves have concocted most of the monsters and demons. I have found, for instance, that stereotypes around man-hating feminists are largely the fabrications of misguided men confronted by the legitimate challenges of women.

The real battle of a man is within himself. Can he step up? Can he show up? Can he be present, transparent, and open in all that he is? This is the new learning edge for men, and this book, *The Spiritually Confident Man*, will push this learning edge into new lands and territories.

CHAPTER 1

Exploring a New Frontier

Where might we find the soil, sun, and water for a newer, healthier, transformed masculinity? So many of the standards of masculinity from across different political, economic, and cultural backgrounds have proven inadequate.

It is time to take steps toward a new frontier for masculinity with new operating principles. As with any exploration of the unknown, this means risk, challenge, and discovery. It is in the essence of a man to push the boundaries of exterior achievement and limitation. Yet when it comes to their inner frontiers, most men seem reluctant to apply the same pioneering spirit. In this chapter, we take a certain courage and adventuring spirit past the edge of the known masculine world and into a beckoning wilderness of new ideas and possibilities.

A different age calls for a different man

What does it mean to be a vital man in a world of change, in which old definitions of masculinity have collapsed? What is spiritually and practically needed for men to answer the challenge of transformation?

Old answers are not adequate. Men cannot turn to dominance, because doing so destroys the earth and those they love. Men cannot turn to acquiescence because doing so dissolves them as men. The Animal Man who seeks dominance and separation is as bereft of viable masculinity as the Social Man who seeks approval and absorption into the people in his life.

Heaven and earth both cry out for a new kind of masculinity, a spiritually confident Co-Creative Man, who passionately develops both the core of his masculine energy and dynamically embraces a distinct, reciprocating pole of feminine energy in the service of spirit in the world. What might this look like?

> *What does it look like for a man to walk into the refining fires of change and be so transformed as to exalt rather than perish in those flames? What does it look like for pride and pretension to be burned away in a man, and curiosity and courage to emerge? What new sources of authority guide him? What supports him in his journey through and from the fire?*

As human beings, we have exhausted the scripts of the past and find ourselves in an elementally creative age requiring a new kind faith in the future, in ourselves, and in possibilities greater than ourselves. No longer can we base our notions of the good life solely in dreams of material riches and technological progress. We are necessarily moving from owners of the world to participants within a much vaster dance of the universe.

Our blinders are being taken off, and we are invited to see, taste, and know in new ways. Men can no longer plausibly retreat to the unthinking self-certainty of their own power. It does them no good, and in fact, makes the crisis of masculinity that much worse.

> *Men's old ways no longer hold up in the light of the future even as these old ways attempt to extend and preserve themselves through inertia.*

Enter the need for a spiritually confident man to create amid the turmoil, a presence to walk forward calm, daring, and intrigued by the challenge and opportunity to engage without the net of his past habits to fall back on. He honors the staples and stories of male history and tradition. He realizes that they inform and equip him, *but he does not rely upon them to guide him forward.*

He has a larger faith than the lore dictated from his past. He realizes that for too long men have relied upon male archetypes, gurus, mentors, and father figures to provide the path, and now he must listen deeply to his own spirit and choose for himself where he will venture.

He has awoken to the necessity of reaching out of his tradition and engaging other wisdoms from a self-assured place. He senses deeply that he offers something of value, but also that he receives essential value from others.

> *He is no longer on his own, no longer solely calling the shots. He is the radically generous co-creative provider of the feast, not the controlling ruler on the throne.*

He asks, "How do I meet the future as a man, and respect this woman and these boys and girls as spirits-in-the-world?" He reflects upon Teilhard de Chardin's famous comment: "We are not human beings having a spiritual experience. We are spiritual beings having a human experience." He wonders, "If this is so, what does it mean to be a spiritually *confident* human being in a world in which so many human changes are occurring? How do I authentically meet an age that invites me toward a fundamentally new basis for identity and interaction?"

The spiritually confident man accepts that change is happening around him, within him, and between him and others. He welcomes this change as an opportunity. He vaguely senses the grinding nausea of his old ways competing with the thrilling vertigo of his new path, yet he is drawn forward, motivated by a desire to engage transformation as an invitation to a life of extraordinary experiential richness. He looks forward to considering and experimenting with new modes of masculinity in the spiritual and practical realms of becoming, being, choosing, and acting.

The spiritually confident man realizes that neither separation from, nor sameness with, other energies, ultimately work for him. He holds his male friends close in his heart, and the energy of male camaraderie in his gut, but just as strongly feels the need to offer and exchange this energy with those outside his male sphere.

He realizes that for him to renew, he must both give of himself and learn how to receive from feminine energies and wisdom. He learns that vulnerability requires courage and that emotional permeability is a strength rather than a weakness. He knows with certainty that feminine energy is both qualitatively different and intrinsically necessary for the healthy development of the men of this age.

He also knows with almost alarming clarity, that if he were to cut himself off from engagement with other energies, he would devolve into something that is neither a giver *nor* a receiver, but rather a *taker*, a Patriarchal Man, an imploding self-server.

The spiritually confident man knows in the fibers of his being that strict independence can only be an illusion. He depends wholly upon that which gave him his life, that which emanates from beyond this world. He remains interdependent throughout his life. He came interdependently into this world through the womb of a woman. At birth, he suckled from the breast of his mother.

> *He cares, and ultimately is cared for, as he breathes his last breaths. Knowing he will die, he knows to ask one important question, "How will I live?"*

Foundational principles for the spiritually confident man

This book, *The Spiritually Confident Man*, is a journey. It does not seek to instruct, nor to give formulas for what it means to be a man. It is an experiential keyhole, a prophetic story, through which to glimpse masculine possibility and invite discussion, experimentation, and greater understanding about an emerging kind of maleness not yet formed and not capable of being formed in the mind of one man. It is a shared enterprise that requires the leadership of spirit and the openness, talent, and input of a community of men, within a larger community of life that includes women and children.

This book departs in many ways from typical books on spirited masculinity. It does not assume that men can solve their own problems but must instead open themselves to a wider and deeper wisdom. At the same time, it recognizes that men have something crucial and unique to contribute and that they cannot simply imitate past models of manhood or abandon their masculine imperative altogether.

> *Men must be men in the most generous and*
> *daring sense of the word, as co-creators, developing*
> *and drawing from their unique energies and contrib-*
> *uting them to a movement of human flourishing that*
> *is much bigger than any gender ideal can capture.*

So, what are the new foundational principles of this vibrant and inter-connected spiritually confident man?

Principle #1: The spiritually confident man does not confine his masculinity to heroic images and stories. He trusts the heart of his spiritual character to empower him beyond his limitations.

Too many books on masculinity rely upon archetypes, ancient, noble, and mythic images and stories to tell men what they can be. This may be helpful in revealing hidden powers and facets of male potential, but they do not and cannot supply a blueprint for contemporary manhood. Vital manhood does not simply rest on the uptake of given mental representations, traditions, or formulas. It relies more so upon active openness, courage, intuitive sense, and experimentation with being.

Male archetypes of the warrior, the king, the poet, the magician, the jester, and the lover serve as ancient reminders of time-honored aspects of male identity. However, they are still derivative, largely conceived in abstraction, and almost always formed in isolation from the essential archetypes of women. Many of these archetypes pretend toward rugged self-sufficiency and do not adequately engage spiritual and feminine energies that transcend the masculine sphere.

To less enterprising men, old-worn archetypes invite a kind of imitative behavior and mental laziness: "That archetype fits me; I think I will role-play the warrior." Archetypes, poorly understood and used, dumb down men, breaking up the organic, complex, and multiple nature of masculinity into simplistic roles and boxes. Similarly, other ancient practices like drum circles and sweat lodges may be powerful rituals to bring men together, but something more spontaneous, improvisational, and faithful is needed to bring out the heart of an individual man.

Principle #2: The spiritually confident man recognizes that strict independence is an illusion. He knows he is ultimately connected. His existence is always interdependent.

As stated earlier, there is not one moment in a man's birth, life, and death where he is truly independent. In other words, there is no such thing as the "self-made" man. He was given life from beyond himself without his merit. He incubated and came into this world through the womb of a woman. He continually relies on others to survive in the world, including relying on plants to provide oxygen so he can draw each breath. He relies on his family and friends to care for him and send him into the after-realm upon his death.

Independence understood as resourcefulness, freedom from mindless conformity, or resistance to oppression is a commendable human quality. We recognize this in phrases like "financially independent," "independent thinker," and "The Declaration of Independence." However, the spiritually confident man recognizes that his choices and his life itself are always contingent. Independence, for him, does *not* mean rugged, self-sufficient separation.

The only way humans can even conceive and assert independence is in reaction to an imposing force. This imposing force is itself formed by the false "independence" of disconnectedness taken to the extreme level of separating from others, asserting superiority over others, and dominating others. (This is important for masculinity because much of the arrogance, competition, and militarism of men comes from twisted, oppressive forms of "independence.")

> *All healthy independence is a form of interdependence.*

Positive, creative "independence" proceeds from our inherent original relationship with spirit, the interdependent meeting of divine inspiration and the mind, heart, body, and soul of a unique male or female being. A man who does not pretend independence is much better able to both receive the wisdom of women and the inspired energy of the divine.

Principle #3: Masculinity is not primarily about "consciousness" but the active cultivation of spiritual energy and human elevation. The spiritually confident man aims to thoroughly embrace the flow of spirit.

Spiritually confident manhood is total. It is not a merely intellectual enterprise. A spiritually confident man grows as a man by committing all of his being, not merely part of it. Such a man transcends himself not merely by establishing goals from his present mind and reaching them, but by opening himself to a wisdom greater than his current mindset and allowing that greater influence to transform him.

> *Men are so accustomed to seeing the worth of their identity in terms of "doer" or "master" that many men fail to recognize the absolute spiritual necessity of being mastered by a larger intelligence.*

The mature spiritually confident man recognizes that he is a participant in a larger deed, under which "doer" is simply one role. He is impregnated with possibility, and *then* he acts. Without this fertilization, he acts from small purposes, and he remains small as a result. Being committed to the fullest expression of his energies means opening himself beyond himself.

The spiritually confident man, then, is an explorer and a learner. He learns about who he is and develops himself by engaging who he might be from the depths of his uniqueness. His way is one of engagement and conversation with the world and with others, allowing that conversation to draw out and activate the latent miracles and talents of his being.

Principle #4: A spiritually confident man is a master only of himself. In all other interactions, he is a beginner.

There are few things more aggravating than a man trying to assert his mastery. It is the nature of true mastery to show itself. It is the nature of anything that is true to demonstrate itself.

> *Mastery and truth do not need provers. They need manifestors.*

They need men who can exemplify spirit in the world, rather than endlessly bray, "Look at me and how wonderful and amazing I am!"

> *The only helpful "mastery" for a man is mastery of himself, including mastery of his impulses to enlarge himself or mistake the pretensions of his ego for "vision."*

The spiritually confident man exerts reign over his immature desire to prove he is at the top of the heap. Until he does, he is not free to learn and work toward the kind of excellence that surpasses his own expectations and the current limits of the world.

The spiritually confident man, in other words, *wants to go higher than the heap* by example and not simply by words. Any energy he uses outside of his own example and performance to "prove" he is the best is wasted energy, detracting from his potential. The best mindset for a spiritually confident man is a beginner mindset; this allows him to take in everything, notice important elements, use his tools, hone his skills, and learn from the ground up how to advance his performance.

The spiritually confident man doesn't have to ally himself with sports teams for an adrenaline shot of self-esteem. Instead, he actively participates in sport himself, admires and learns from the athletic talent of good teams, and suffers with those who have long championship droughts.

He doesn't brag about himself to impress others but asks others questions about themselves and their lives because he is fascinated to learn more. He realizes that the beginning mind is a flexible mind, an absorbing mind, and a strong mind. He cannot become excellent until he opens his heart, cultivates the resources upon which excellence is built, and serves and waters the seeds of his own active genius.

Principle #5: The spiritually confident man embraces life. He is epitomized by gratitude. He is ecstatic to be living and breathing and shows it by daring to live life to its fullest.

A spiritually confident man understands that all men die, including him, but that only some men truly live. Given the inalterable fact of his death, he knows, therefore, that his own survival can never be his ultimate purpose. A man's purpose is given in the quality of his life, not in the number of his years, nor in his "legacy".

He is not concerned with establishing his alleged immortality through fame and accomplishment in the minds of others. This is a sign of insecurity, not confidence. Rather, the spiritually confident man is driven by his peculiar and powerful life passion. By sharing and developing this passion, he aspires to make the world more vivid and possible for others.

The spiritually confident man does not hide, but rather openly shares his grief and failure. He accepts his partiality, and he is grateful for the help of others and his own spirit. He displays honesty of being. He is not stoic. He radiates and embraces his feeling.

> *He allows himself over and over again to be broken open so that he can shed the shells of his limitations and move past hopeless or fruitless endeavors.*

If he is bored and uninspired, even if he is succeeding in the eyes of society, he plots his moves toward a vocation with greater correspondence with his spirit. He realizes that vulnerability is necessary for greatness, for only in a vulnerable state can one learn and recognize a larger truth. *Only when he is permeable to a greater destiny can he become a greater man.*

Today, for many men, we have the worst of both worlds, a man who boasts about his greatness (takes credit) and a man who complains when he does not get what he wants (resents life). This weak masculine character, built upon self-glorification and entitlement, is the opposite of the spiritually confident man's character. The spiritually confident man strides into the unknown; he does not believe his hype nor confines himself to his own image. The spiritually confident man builds; he does not expect the world to be built around him.

The nature and flow of this book

It should be evident by now that this book, *The Spiritually Confident Man*, is not just another communication across the sexes/reviving the wild man/pleasing your woman/typical "men's studies" kind of book. It does not simply seek to accept traditional forms of manhood and then tailor these forms to new realities. Rather it aims to help men transform at the base level toward something higher and beyond what human society has assumed about men.

This book is dedicated toward unleashing the spiritual potential in men as new life experience and activity. It does not give formulas for what to do or how to be a man, but instead offers insights and experiments into *finding out* what it means to be a man.

> *This is the true and daring adventure for a man—not knowing who he is exactly, but curious and strong enough to find out who he can be.*

This book accepts that masculinity is a continually evolving, creative state of being. There is something unique about growing from a boy into a fully-fledged man. This process is distinct from, yet eminently compatible with, growing from a girl into a full-fledged woman. Therefore, this book embraces male uniqueness as positive and promising. It believes that personal originality and social benefit can rise up from masculine character.

The Spiritually Confident Man does not rely on ancient myths and archetypes to drive its challenge. Instead, it invites men to find and trust themselves at a deeper intuitive, spiritual level. By this trust, men can "learn by doing" and discover what they might be. This book clears up destructive myths about male identity and forwards healthier ways to enter into relationships. This book does not cater to a desire to be an entirely enclosed "rock-ribbed" man. It invites men into interdependent learning and formation of masculine character.

After spending many years amid institutional analyses of gender, ethics, psychology, philosophy, history, anthropology, sociology, and feminism, I came to the conclusion that the way we traditionally approach masculinity and femininity doesn't really allow for heart- and experienced-based conversation, experimentation with new approaches, spirituality, or collaboration. Too often, understanding about identity is dominated by left-brained, abstract, and largely irrelevant academic conjecture on one side and non-reflective, overly self-certain practical formulas on the other. This tends to fragment and separate out people and issues. New masculinity has to be *felt and experienced* and not merely thought about or acted upon thoughtlessly.

The Spiritually Confident Man redefines assumptions around purpose, accomplishment, time and space, treatment of women, masculinity, relationship, sensitivity, strength, and touch, authenticity, and commitment. It offers new ways to look at and enact traditional and non-conventional masculine character traits. It comes mainly from my location as a heterosexual male but addresses and embraces principles and examples that will be instructive to gay and bisexual men as well.

So, let's take the dare. Let's start the new journey. Let's step through the door.

CHAPTER 2

Examining The Seeds—The Animal Man, The Social Man, And The Co-Creative Man

We have entered the wilderness and absorbed its primal challenge. We have begun to explore the reaches of this new land. Now we arrive at a clearing. What psychological, cultural, and spiritual "seeds" have given rise to us as men? How have these seeds been reflected in our ideas of men and women, boys and girls? What new seeds or sources of growth might present themselves?

T IS TIME TO peel back the cover of male identity to reveal three current versions of masculinity: The Animal Man, the Social Man, and the Co-Creative Man. The first two, the aggressive and competitive Animal Man and the receptive and cooperative Social Man, comprise the two conventional extremes of manhood. The third version, the interactive and collaborative Co-Creative Man leaps outside this continuum and represents a dynamic, non-conventional emerging version of masculinity.

Picture these three kinds of men as points on a triangle. On the bottom line, you have the two endpoints of the Animal Man and the Social Man with a continuum between them. On the upper point, you have the Co-Creative Man.

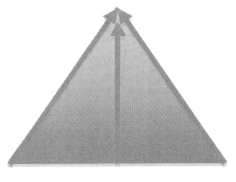

Co-Creative Man
Interactive, collaborative

Animal Man
Aggressive,
competitive

Social Man
Receptive,
cooperative

Many sincere men have been struggling between the poles of Animal Man and Social Man to find a more mature, compassionate, creative, and courageous third way to express their manhood. The Social Man emerged in modern times out of a recognition that Animal Man's aggressive and competitive tendencies can produce conflict and harm. However, the Social Man's desire to be accepted to the point of passivity, tended to take the substance and the active "oomph" out of masculine energy, leaving men feeling weak or disoriented and women feeling underwhelmed.

The Animal Man is the "thesis," the yang, the raw energy of masculinity that produces *effort* or initiative. The Social Man is the "anti-thesis," the *ease* that calms the Animal Man when he runs too hot or too wild. The third force of masculinity, the Co-Creative Man, is the "synthesis," the *elevation*, the fusion, transformation, and refinement of the Animal Man and Social Man.

> *The Animal Man (the traditional version of manhood) and the Social Man (the modern version of manhood) have largely played themselves out. There is still a need for men to draw from their energies and wisdom, but these models of manhood can no longer serve as guiding metaphors for male growth and contribution.*

Continued swings between their extremes are likely to produce exhaustion and very little illumination. By themselves, and even together, they remain too fragmented and underpowered for emerging challenges. Both fail to be adequately holistic, and both fail to sufficiently include the wisdom and power of the feminine.

The Co-Creative Man (the post-modern version of manhood) includes and transcends both the Animal Man and the Social Man. On one hand, it recognizes the productive aspect of gender *polarity*, that men and women, boys and girls, should develop and offer their distinct male and female energies. On the other hand, the Co-Creative version encourages sharing, exchange, and *equal respect* for these energies. Thirdly, the Co-Creative version embraces the diverse development of maleness and femaleness unique not only to each sex but to each person, understanding that every person has a nowhere-else-in-the-universe character, a *divine genius* to offer.

Therefore, in accordance with the Animal Man, males and females can be *distinct*, that is "men can still be men" and "women can still be women." In accordance with the Social Man, men and women, boys and girls, can still share and respectfully *exchange* their masculine and feminine energies. In accordance with Co-Creative Man, all individuals, whether male or female, have something *diverse and unique* to them to be developed and contributed to the flourishing of life on this planet and beyond.

Three Ways of Being

It is important to note that the Animal Man, the Social Man, and the Co-Creative Man fold into each other. They are interactive. They can work together; they *do not* have to be oppositional. They represent *ways of being*, as well *models of seeing*, of what it means to be a man. These ways of being are not unique to men, though their expressions can be strongly flavored by gender. In fact, the Animal mode, the Social mode, and the Co-Creative mode are universal to the human race and are associated with the evolutionary areas of the complete human brain, the "reptilian," "mammalian," and "human" (neo-cortical) regions proposed by Dr. Paul MacLean.

What is different about these modes of being for men, women, boys, and girls are their particular *expressions*. The Animal mode is associated with the "reptilian" area at the core of our brain, responsible for automatic functions of the body, "fight, flight, or hide" responses, physical desire and appetite, primal assertiveness, and territorialism. The Animal mode expresses *desire* in its most basic form, as desire for *survival* as well as sexual initiative. Taken to the extreme, without balance, the Animal mode can result in war, impulsive behavior, and in other actions that are destructive to the self or others. However, without the Animal mode, there would be very little passion in human life, very little fire or driving energy behind our purposes for living.

In a man, this Animal mode of being, by itself, might come out as a domineering personality in the workplace or it could come out more constructively, in interaction with the Social mode, as a desire to protect family. For a woman, the Animal mode might express itself as the "corporate supermom," protective mother bear, or the "tiger mom" severely intent on making sure her kids are the very best at everything. For a boy, it might be expressed by pulling girls' pigtails and for a girl by asserting herself as the reigning queen of the schoolyard.

The Social mode of being is associated with the "mammalian" brain area, which is wrapped around the reptilian region. This brain area expresses the desire for group *belonging*. The Social mode includes human tendencies for approval, cooperation, altruism, and conformity. Taken to the extreme, without balance, the Social mode can result in slavish obedience to social norms and a persistent anxiety about fulfilling conventional expectations. However, without the social mode, interpersonal and international cooperation would be quite difficult, and personal or cultural pride might overwhelm the ability to enjoy and respect other people.

In a man, this Social mode of being, by itself, might come out as being a "pleaser," a passive and amenable personality in social and interpersonal environments. Merged with some of the fire of the Animal Man, this same man might work well as a social justice organizer or someone who can host the perfect party. For a woman, the Social mode of being might express itself as delight in a "girls' night out." For a boy, the social mode might involve going down to the river to skip stones or play video games with friends. For a girl, the social mode might express itself in being there for friends who have lost loved ones.

The Co-Creative mode of being is associated with the large neo-cortical or "human" brain layer wrapped around both the mammalian and reptilian regions of our brains. This brain area expresses the desire for *beauty and love*, as well as higher artistic, emotional, and intuitive desires, which do not necessarily serve any immediate practical individual or group purpose. This area is responsible for "left-brain" logical and analytical reasoning, allowing us to design our environments and anticipate our future. The Co-Creative mode also includes "right-brain" creative and transformative capacities, integrative abilities, and intentions to serve higher principles.

> *The Co-Creative mode is where meaningful and reflective learning happens and is connected to insight, imagination, thought, and consciousness.*

Taken to the extreme, without balance the Co-Creative mode can lack grounding and stability. The Co-Creative person tends to take off and keep going, jumping into thrilling connections and openings without pausing to rest, consolidate, and situate ideas in the world. The Animal and Social modes help the Co-Creative person to bring their ethereal inventions and visions back around to the physical and human planes. The Co-Creative person's sense of creative adventure is complemented by the Animal person's personal pragmatism and the Social person's ability to apply insights to help others.

In a man, the Co-Creative mode, by itself, might express itself as pure invention, idea after idea about how to solve world problems or make money or create some ingenious little gadget that will save people time and effort. He might talk to others avidly about his discoveries, and even incorporate the ideas of others, but his challenge comes in manifesting his ideas. For a woman, the Co-Creative mode might express itself when she takes her experiments with home baking into an online business. For a boy, the Co-Creative mode might involve writing and illustrating his own comic book. For a girl, the Co-Creative mode might take the form of a social media campaign to save wounded horses from the slaughterhouse.

Again, in the best situations, these three modes of being (Animal, Social, and Co-Creative), and the three brain areas with which they are associated (Reptilian, Mammalian, and Human) are *interactive*. What we know of as "love" in its healthiest and fullest form would likely be a combination of all three areas: a deep sensual or physical desire, mixed with a deep desire to bond, combined with a cosmic or spiritual desire for the well-being and full flowering of one's beloved.

In fact, it is when these modes of being become *fragmented, ranked, and non-interactive* that they become ineffective and even dangerous. This leads to a very important point:

> *Many of the problems of men and male identity today can be traced to the men's tendencies to compartmentalize and rank their different modes of being as oppositional to each other.*

This creates a fatal incompleteness in identity, which comes out as belligerence, confusion, and a host of other incoherent states.

Frequently men will swear allegiance to a particular way of being oftentimes along political, cultural, and personal preference lines. The conservative or traditional man tends to attach to the model of the Animal Man. The liberal or modern man tends to cling to the model of the Social Man. The progressive or post-modern man tends to emphasize the Co-Creative Man. In the following sections, we will flesh out these conditions and their regressed, transitional, and evolved forms as well as discuss ways to bring these important and integral aspects of manhood together.

The Three Types and Nine Forms of Manhood

In summary, there are three basic types of manhood, each having three forms, for a total of nine, corresponding to the regressed, transitional, and evolved states of these types:

- **The Animal Man**, which includes the regressed *Toxic Man*, transitional *Striving Man*, and evolved *Responsible Man*.
- **The Social Man,** which includes the regressed *Retreating Man*, transitional *Confused Man*, and evolved *Equal Man*.
- **The Co-Creative Man**, which includes the regressed *Despairing Man*, transitional *Searching Man*, and evolved *Spiritually Confident Man*.

I will describe each type and form of manhood, providing examples from popular culture and my own life, and discuss the implications of each form for work, play, fatherhood, and romantic relationship.

However, before I discuss these, I offer a caveat: These types and forms needed to be treated as a collaborative whole and not in isolation from or opposition to one another. When isolated or opposed each of these types of men and their associated forms remain fatally incomplete. This partiality erodes masculinity by diverting male energy toward compensation rather than creativity.

The ideal state for creativity is wholeness.

For example, a Co-Creative man like Steve Jobs, of the mega-company Apple, might accelerate human evolution by drawing from his pragmatic, competitive Animal side to bring brilliant ideas into impressive fruition in the technological realm. However, Jobs had a reputation for being quite abrupt and harsh on the interpersonal level. Even a man of his stature could have incorporated Social Man attributes to mitigate impatience and enhance broader service.

If a man acts solely on the competitive and aggressive instincts of the Animal Man, he will likely seek to dominate another person. If a man acts solely from the cooperative and passive habits of the Social Man, he will likely erase himself. If a man acts solely from the innovative, transformative orientation of the Co-Creative Man without including the passionate individual desire from the Animal Man, and regard for others from the Social Man, he will likely lead a less passionate and connected life. Wholeness unites these conditions in a mutually informative and enhancing way.

> *The evolution of manhood from Toxic Man to Spiritually Confident Man does not mean any particular man leaves behind his other "stages" or kinds of manhood, any more than we, as human beings, "leave behind" our primal lower chakras or energy centers as we meditate and lift our primal energy upward.*

The motto for a maturing man is "Incorporate and Elevate": "Incorporate"— inclusively honor, be grateful for, and retain the best energy and insight of what has come before, and "Elevate"—keep growing into more refined, wiser, and more powerful expressions of what it means to be a man.

So, imagine the three types of man and nine different forms of manhood inclusively and non-competitively. One type or form of manhood no matter how low or lofty informs the others. Each type and form of manhood has its own energy to contribute to a more complete man, and the problems of manhood have less to do with what "type" men are and more to do with how well they have been able to integrate and grow beyond one particular "stuck" type of manhood.

The Animal Man, the first type of manhood

The Animal Man is driven by a desire to survive and to succeed on the concrete, practical planes of human existence. His abilities and personality characteristics emerge from this desire. He is "animal" in the fact he adores physical power and its extensions—social sway, political influence, and economic strength. *Emotions* guide his existence. Typically, he is a competitor, striving for dominance, and seeking fame, money, and glory as his mark, thinking that such achievements will give him a kind of immortality.

In his more evolved forms, the Animal Man is concerned with the survival and support of his family, tribe, or nation, but he still expects to be given credit and held in high esteem.

> *He believes not so much that life is a gift given to him, but that he is a gift to life.*

Thus, he expects to be appreciated and praised, even idolized, and frequently condemns those who would call him to a higher accountability. The Animal Man can contribute a certain charm, charisma, and "animal magnetism." However, conceit and a tremendous insecure need for obedience and exaltation govern the Animal Man when he is alienated from other aspects of manhood.

The Three Forms of Animal Man

The Toxic Man ("Life is a conquest")

Within the *Toxic Man* (the regressed form of the Animal Man) lies a propensity for dominance-seeking and arrogance, yet also the energy of animal magnetism and charisma. There is indeed something "virile" and involving that emerges from animal expression in sexual play, for instance. Yet the growing man is not satisfied with simply conquering women (or other men if he is gay). Such an endeavor becomes empty and faceless after a time, so he moves on to a new challenge if he is to grow at all.

On the level of self, the Toxic Man believes the entire universe revolves around him. His motto might be: "The world serves me." Other people are merely actors and objects on his stage. This gives him a kind of bald audacity to pursue whatever feeds his whims. He is concerned only about his own profits and costs, regardless of the cost to others. When his disposition is coupled with political, cultural, or economic power, this Toxic Man believes he has the mandate to be and do anything he wants without restraint or reflection. No amount of decency gets in the way of even his most outrageous impulses. When confronted with the harm his actions cause others, he pleads ignorance or makes excuses. Responsibility on any level is not in his plan.

Perhaps this type of man is best demonstrated by the disgraced movie mogul, Harvey Weinstein, who allegedly sexually harassed hundreds of women in his multi-decade power binge. *Time* magazine on its October 23, 2017 cover did not even mention his name, choosing instead to have a roguish, unrepentant black-and-white full-page photo of Weinstein with the title, "Producer. Predator. Pariah."

Weinstein's comment in *Time*'s article underscores the mixture of animal arrogance and boyish willful ignorance that so typifies Toxic Men: "I just didn't know any better, this is just how we did things in the old days." In other words, "People are there for me. I'll take what I can force. If you don't like it, it's up to you to force it in another direction or say "no." ("Of course, I might fire you if you do, but, hey, those are the perks of power; take it or leave it.")

This kind of black-and-white clarity can be very seductive to people looking for direction, holding out for a promise, or asking to be told what to do. Toxic masculinity can look like overwhelming confidence because it is not beset with any uncertainty or healthy self-doubt. With the Toxic Man, there is no need for negotiation, consideration, or conversation. The Toxic Man wants what he wants and desires what he desires. If he wants to use his power to feel up a woman's "pussy," he feels he is simply entitled to it on the basis of his will alone.

Sometimes these men are romanticized as brash "enfant terribles" and sometimes in the same breath described as "creeps." The unapologetic deafness of a Toxic Man to any kind of mutual respect, allows him to simply make a splash, make a mess (for others to clean up), and move on, whether it is a business relationship or a romantic relationship. Toxic Men dupe people into investing in them, declare bankruptcy, and congratulate themselves on their cleverness. "Take the money and run!" "All's fair in love and war."

This "lean and mean" perspective (ironic since so many Toxic Men seem to be big-bellied) reduces the world and life itself to a simple battle of dog-eat-dog. Toxic Men have a simplistic goal and an even more simplistic worldview: They aim to be the top dog by any means necessary. Toxic Men have no brakes. They are "effective" only insomuch as they are not dissuaded by morality, convention, good taste, or any impediment to self-interest.

They are not introspective in the least, nor do they ever aspire to be. To them reflection is tantamount to self-doubt, self-examination is equivalent with disempowerment. This also means that Toxic Men are not largely bothered by guilt, shame, or anxiety, yet they are continuously dogged by insecurity and the compensatory need for the next show of force to outdo the previous.

> *This is the Achilles heel of the Toxic Man—the use of force, charisma, and charm to cover up primitive disregard for others and a primal insecurity with the self.*

Even spirituality itself is seen as a weakness, an excuse for failing to conquer the physical world and the minds, hearts, and bodies of others.

It should be no surprise that such a Toxic Man is horrible in relationships. A woman married to one will likely be an expendable accessory or a convenient servant to take care of his home base while he ventures out to build his own empire of the ego. Some women will agree to be with a wealthy Toxic Man, trading on economic security and the role of arm candy in order to exist in upper social echelons. A son of such a man will likely either follow his father's ways or bow out of the empire altogether. Since there is no room for another personality to thrive, one has to decide if he or she will be a bird in a gilded cage or simply fly the coop. To the Toxic Man, work is a contest of one-upmanship. Play involves self-satisfied and materialistic self-gratification.

As a regressed form of the Animal Man, the Toxic Man ultimately breaks down and becomes fragmented. His narcissistic ego is too much in control of his being. As a result, he is neglectful of others. He does not admit he is wrong. He does not apologize. He does not care if he is feared and hated. In fact, he takes a measure of pride in the loathing he elicits. He excuses abuse as "tough love" or "survival of the fittest". The regressed Toxic Man is a legend in his own mind and almost always a scourge in the minds of others. He is his own god and his own kingdom.

The Toxic Man feels he is answerable to nobody. Perhaps this is why he is often called "jerk," "asshole," "tyrant," "misogynist," or the somewhat dated "macho man." As a result of his actions and overreach, the Toxic Man can become, like Harvey Weinstein, a despised pariah. This social pressure may lead the Toxic Man into the realm of the Striving Man, where ambition is directed not as much with hoisting himself *over* the world as proving himself *against* the world.

The Striving Man ("Life is a race")

Within the *Striving Man* (the transitional form of the Animal Man) lies ambition to prove himself against the world. No longer satisfied with (and trapped by) sexual conquest, he seeks to enlarge his domain. Now he wants to show his larger capabilities, his attractiveness, his cleverness, his savviness, his "chops" in a wider world of business and social status. He may strive after a high-paying, high-status position in work. He may engage in hyper-intensive physical training.

On the level of self, the Striving Man believes himself the ultimate competitor and gamesman. His motto might be: "Everything is a contest." This attitude is embodied in the quote, "Winning isn't everything; it's the only thing," a phrase originated in American football by UCLA coach Red Sanders and popularized by Vince Lombardi, celebrated coach of the Green Bay Packers. For the Striving Man, worth and value involve perseverance toward victory with a mindset to match. Unlike the Toxic Man, others are to be acknowledged as people, rather than simply objects, but only on the basic level as competitors. If the Striving Man loses, he becomes like the muddled masses, undistinguished, worthless, and lowered. Transcendent importance, as well as immortality, are wrapped up in victory.

As a boy, dwelling in the shadow of my competitive father, I often embodied this Striving Man. My worth was wrapped around success. My dissatisfaction with myself and with others often had to do with whether or not I won even in the smallest arenas. I had to be right about some political issue or some petty factoid (or hide/minimize the fact that I was wrong). My self-esteem became tied to what I did, rather than who I aspired to be. Success equaled worth. Failure confirmed insignificance. When I felt that the playing field was not level, as it wasn't under my father's roof, I sought to excel in other arenas, such as school. And excel I did, finishing first in my high school class academically and reaching the state finals in track and field.

> *However, no victory could confirm my own personhood. I became alienated and besieged, as many Striving Men do, by the constant contingency of my worth on accomplishment.*

It was as if I did not exist in the eyes of others and myself if I was not succeeding. Failure loomed as a kind of annihilation of existence. This had the effect of making me far less creative and far too attentive to conventional authority, structures, and rules.

Looking back, I now recognize that chronic competition, and

the quiet desperation it inspires, wore down my being and gradually replaced it with expectation, a neurotic and endless "becoming" that never really went anywhere new. I compensated for the felt necessity of this striving life by developing a very active imagination, in which I was free to do as I sought, free to learn as I chose. This imagination would later serve to keep the flame of spirit alive in me until I could gain the power to act upon those deeper desires that had been undermined by the rules of competitive living.

What I began to realize is that no amount of winning, even if I were to become champion of the world, could ever establish my worth or give me lasting value precisely because it lacked authenticity and a creative contribution from my own sensibilities. I was just cleverly responding to and mimicking other people's expectations as if they were my own. I was, in essence, a highly functioning fraud.

This same sense of fraudulence is epidemic in the "gifted" kids I have taught. It is the same existential angst that leads some young people to suicide when they do not get into a choice college or fail to live up to expectations on an entrance exam. Tragically, the Striving Man's worth is *contingent*, never to be assured, always in doubt, always conditional. There is no spiritual or emotional foundation upon which to rest your being when the metaphorical sands of worth are always shifting under your feet. Combined with the imperative to constantly win, it is no wonder that many Striving Men become control freaks (as I was for an extended time) to maintain some kind of mental stability.

It should also be no surprise that such a Striving Man is hot-and-cold in relationships. Someone close to a Striving Man may find him elated one moment and depressed the next, depending upon how things have gone with a professional venture, adult-league softball game, or any other competitive test in life. A woman married to one will likely feel she is irrelevant to his well-being, playing second fiddle to his accomplishment.

In work, the Striving Man will tend toward perfectionism and workaholism. In play, he cannot simply have fun with a pick-up volleyball game. He has to spike the ball "in your face" to feel he is having a good time. He also has to win every game and will likely resent those laggards who are not taking a team game seriously enough.

As a father, he will likely be "that" parent who screams incessantly at his son to hit a home run in baseball, yells at the umpire for making the "wrong" call and chastises his son for striking out. Extreme Striving Men are not all that fun to be around, and will often end up as loners, as people tire of their competitiveness. Other people want to be able to relax and not be tested all the time, especially in leisure situations like a friendly backyard game.

It is this fatigue, alienation from others, and constant vigilance that can induce the Striving Man to look for a basis of identity that is not simply rooted in himself and his accomplishment. The Striving Man pushes and exceeds his limits, and that is a good thing, but also *not* an end in itself. A man *stuck* in striving becomes hopeless, because there he can never enjoy the *culmination* of his efforts. He becomes merely a spinning wheel.

So, if he is healthy, a man must move on from the Striving Man, retaining the vigor, activation, desire, and effort but leaving behind the hopeless, endless addiction to activity. He begins to look around for a more solid foundation to his being, something involving serving others, rather than just himself, and acting upon principle rather than acting from self-compulsion. This is where the Striving Man may find himself moving toward the Responsible Man.

The Responsible Man ("Life is a duty")

Within the *Responsible Man* (the evolved form of the Animal Man) is a certain forbearance and maturity. His motto might be: "Do the right thing." He can provide, protect, sacrifice, and serve, but he still does so more out of duty than out of love. The traditional Responsible Man can be committed, enduring, constant in his presence, but also quite stoic and alienated emotionally. Because he sees his life necessarily as a role, he can become cut off from the joy and spontaneity of life. He can become dour and strained. He may retain the prediction and control of the Striving Man. He may die early of heart-related problems. Yet amidst all of this, he is a man proud, in its healthy sense, of his family and his ability to provide a "roof over the head and food on the table." If he is too busy at work to attend every soccer game, he still is happy to come home to dinner and see his household doing well.

The Responsible Man combines the traditional man's penchant for authority and structure with the conveniences and leisure created by modern life. He likely came of age as part of the World War II generation, confronted by the horrors of war at a young age. This fueled the Responsible Man's desire to create a scaled-down paradise, a little Eden of a nuclear family and home in the post-war suburban oases and job opportunities created by the G.I. Bill. This was the reality of a *Father Knows Best* world both literally and metaphorically. The Responsible Man is "king of his castle," a (mostly) benevolent patriarch who expects his cocktail after a long day's work, just as he expects his children to be well-composed extensions of himself.

The Responsible Man is not simply a historical anomaly, however. There are younger men, who grew up in largely conservative households, who continue to be the bearers of this type of Responsible Man masculinity. They will be the ones still going to church regularly and engaging in other traditional institutional aspects of community life. They may still take the time to go hunting and address others as "sir" and "ma'am." They may not have the same outright prejudices of older conservative men, but they still may reject the supposed unnaturalness of women taking on men's roles in the workplace and may express open discomfort for public acceptance of homosexuality.

The Responsible Man generally longs to re-awaken the era of "when men were men" and did not have to ostensibly apologize for their lack of sensitivity or validate their "caveman" routines of locking themselves in their dens with football on the television and chips and beer by their side. To the Responsible Man, these characteristics and routines are merely the fulfillment of a tacit deal, the compensations and perks for a long and bruising work week.

My Greek grandfather, my dad's dad who passed away in the 1990's, was typical of the Responsible Man. As the owner of a high-end East Coast restaurant, it was not uncommon for him to arrive there by 4 am to bake the day's bread and desserts and return home just before midnight—a 20-hour day. This structure and work ethic, common in so many European immigrants to America, had its admirable qualities and its costs. My grandfather provided well for his family, was a high-ranking member of fraternal organizations, and was known and respected in the top social echelons.

Yet he also used alcohol to cope with his demands and pressures and could explode emotionally and violently at the drop of a hat. He and my grandmother seemed locked in a perpetual battle of will and words, but when my grandmother (14 years his senior) died, he was not long to follow her. I particularly remember speaking to my grandfather at length after my grandmother died. He told me of working as a stateside cook for the U.S. Army during World War II and how he would save and sneak food to starving families. It was in conversations like this where I could clearly see and deeply feel his vulnerability, compassion, and kindness obscured by the stoicism that attended his daily obligations.

> *It is this obscured sense of loss that often besets the Responsible Man.*

The disgruntled Responsible Man is a common sight in today's world. He can often be seen complaining that the world is going to "hell in a handbasket," looking to incendiary talk radio or television to reinforce and support his pessimism. His discontent lies in his perception of a broken social contract: He has "followed the rules," and yet is not given the same kind of appreciation, authority, or opportunity of men of past generations.

He may find himself arguing against Affirmative Action policies that give women or minorities "unearned" (in his mind) chances to rise through the ranks of profession and society. He considers himself "self-made" and, therefore, seems unable to conceive that the "rules" were stacked against others and that this new leveling is not taking something away from him but rather, is extending opportunities to others. He also seems unaware that extending these opportunities to others could *enhance* his masculinity as a Responsible Man because it supports an *expanded* notion of family to include not just relatives but all of humanity.

The structured life of the Responsible Man has its benefits and costs. It should be of no surprise that a Responsible Man is some-what rigid in relationships. Someone close to a Responsible Man may find him a generally stable and reliable partner, but perhaps a bit too predictable and patterned. A woman married to one will likely feel she is honored in a traditional sense but also sidelined in terms of intimacy and equality.

In his work, the Responsible Man tends toward sensible jobs that provide for his family and offer good benefits. Again, there is this trade-off between predictability and adventure. In fact, his legacy is his family, and the family is his main life project. It is hard for the Responsible Man to loosen up and simply play. On a road trip, he is likely scheduling the stops, thinking about the logistics of loading up the car, and deciding upon the time to be spent in one location or another. As a father, he likely is quite strict and strait-laced, expecting his son to carry on the family legacy and represent well the family name.

Clearly, a man committed to growth sees the problems in the Responsible Man. So wedded is the Responsible Man to prediction and control, he can demonstrate a crippling lack of spontaneity and improvisational learning. However, a man committed to strong growth in his masculinity would do well to emulate and retain the Responsible Man's commitment and constancy, while perhaps discarding the harsher aspects of this form of manhood. A long and happy life requires a balance of responsibility and serendipity. Joy and seriousness need to be balanced; else a man will be consigned to a shorter and grimmer life.

The Social Man, the second type of manhood

The Social Man tends to be a less combative and more receptive team player. In his regressed forms, the Social Man is "diminished" in the fact that he shies away from challenge, responsibility, and the exercise of power of any sort. Feeling power itself to be evil or that he is not up to the task of exerting himself, he is continually reactive and needy, expecting others to act for him and provide for him. In his transitional forms, the Social Man is conciliatory, striving for an illusory "civility" where everyone can get along. He is just trying to make it through life with as little trouble as possible. He is not a risk-taker. He does not tend to initiate action, and he lacks a driving purpose for his life.

The Social Man, in his evolved forms, is purposeful, congenial, cooperative, and quite pleasant and non-threatening to be around. He is generally reliable, a responsible parent, and an interesting conversation partner.

> *Since he has nothing to prove and takes joy in family and friends, he can be a good partner in business and relationship.*

In short, this evolved Social Man is able to see, experience, and serve something beyond himself and can feel personal fulfillment from engaging what is beyond himself.

In all forms, the Social Man is not without a certain sensitivity, laid-back attitude, and willingness to listen.

The Three Forms of Social Man

The Retreating Man ("Life is an overwhelming challenge")

Within the *Retreating Man* (the regressed form of the Social Man) lies a certain reaction and desire to be a boy again. His motto might be: "Life owes me, big-time." He is retreating from the grinding responsibilities of the Responsible Man, knowing their costs and damages, but he does not yet see the joys and adventures inherent in the vital responsibilities of parenthood and committed relationship. To strip away his obligations, he may romanticize a minimal existence living out of his car. He does all this to reject an arrogant, ambitious, or even "responsible" life that comes at the cost of authentic expression and freedom. The Retreating Man is likely to be a sampler of life including a sampler of people. This helps him gain an appreciation of variety, but does not dispose him to focus, stand ground, and choose a particular direction.

> *The regressed Social Man, the Retreating Man, is governed by his need to be liked and taken care of.*

He has limited ego strength and capacity for resilience. He falls apart without constant reinforcement. Even a small criticism or helpful suggestion can be taken poorly, setting off a defensive reaction or a nasty remark. Whereas the regressed Animal Man (the Toxic Man) is overly *inflated*, the regressed Social Man (the Retreating Man) can come off as overly *deflated*. He is lost and expects others to find his life and provide meaning for him. Perhaps this is why he is known by terms like: "weenie," "weasel," "sensitive new-age guy," "slacker," "loser," "Peter Pan," and "mama's boy."

In short, The Retreating Man, cannot be relied upon to "show up and step up." Unfortunately, this makes him an atrocious model for fatherhood, perhaps second worst only to the Toxic Man. Where the Toxic Man is present in all the wrong ways to his son, teaching him bad habits, the Retreating Man is *absent*, allowing no lessons to be learned. The Retreating Man's son is essentially the mother's responsibility while he looks for different ways to tilt at various windmills and fulfill his own needs.

The son of a Retreating Man is unlikely to be able to feel himself. He has no father figure to mentor him or to rebel against. His stronger emotions of anger, wonder, and angst find no sounding board. This lack of interaction and meaningful engagement produces a kind of default shallowness of being and uncertainty of identity. The passions and dislikes of a Retreating Man are not allowed a medium in which to form themselves, so the Retreating Man passes on his legacy of insubstantiality to his son.

This lack of guidance may lead the son of a Retreating Man toward a mentor outside of the family (in the form of a respected teacher, for instance). If he is not so fortunate, the son of a Retreating Man will become a Retreating Boy, gravitating toward the fantasy world of video games, to an immature gang of other boys, into depressed solitude, or into the arms of a manipulative woman who will prey on his desire to be substantial.

Many mothers I have talked to describe, to their great concern, Retreating Man sons who have cut themselves off from family and who seem to drift in a parallel universe, rarely communicating, yet nursing a desire to be powerful in the world and recognized in the eyes of another person. These Retreating Sons have lost the capacity to choose and decide for themselves.

This can lead Retreating Men into the arms of a Toxic Woman looking simply for a lap-dog and an accessory to her own ambitions. The rites of passage and masculine sources of support in modern society have become so muddled and confused that they present very little help to young Retreating Men who may, in fact, need guidance and structure.

This lack of support for initiative leads to the now common phenomenon of "failure to launch." For the Retreating Man, the deep care for others, necessary for the evolved form of the Social Man (the Equal Man), has not yet found a foothold in practice, so he stumbles around looking for someone to care for him. Because he cannot validate himself inside, he looks for validation outside.

This is also why most women are particularly averse to the Retreating Man as a partner. To such women, the Retreating Man shows himself to be a non-entity and a drain on their reserves because he seems to be asking her to take over the role of both woman *and* man. She is being asked to provide the financial and emotional support for the relationship, without much in exchange from the Retreating Man except his company.

High achieving women who are lonely will sometimes accept this deal for a time, but they tire of becoming a second mother, rather than a respected and equal partner to a person who cannot seem to make clear decisions or embark on a fruitful, sustained path. Because he insists on "authenticity without responsibility," the Retreating Man never really *has* to make a decision or contribute. He is free to "just be himself." The good and free life for him is one of infinite options and zero accountability.

It should also be no surprise a Retreating Man is the opposite of a Responsible Man in relationships–infinitely flexible and irresponsible to the point of flightiness as opposed to rigid and dead serious. Someone close to a Retreating Man may find him to be boyishly reassuring and non-threatening, but ultimately too unreliable and unsupportive. A woman married to one will likely feel she is pulling the entire load of the relationship and any family obligations tied to it.

In his work, the Retreating Man tends toward endless invention and re-invention in the realm of fantasy that never quite makes their way to the real world. The Retreating Man rarely settles on one job for very long if at all. Again, there is this other side of the trade-off between predictability and adventure. At play, the Retreating Man can be quite fun but rarely predictable or stable. He may cruise out of town (or even out of a relationship) on a lark because his some "voice" is calling him away.

The Retreating Man is caught in "everywhere and nowhere," and should he desire to grow, he will leave the trappings of solitariness and variety behind (while retaining the need for authenticity and freedom) for a more compelling life of relationship and commitment. This happens more often than one might suppose. After "crashing and burning" in fantasies and relationships that cannot sustain a workable life, Retreating Men can pop out the other side, first growing into the inquiring Confused Man, and then eventually, as his identity and experience solidify, into the Equal Man.

The Confused Man ("Life is an enigma")

Within the *Confused Man* (the transitional form of the Social Man) lies a constructive disorientation. His motto might be: "Can't we all just get along and figure this thing out?" Either he is coming out of his self-imposed shell and looking for direction without a compass, or his compass is spinning from the magnetic pulls to the various parts of his being. He may backpack around South America, indulge in extreme sports, or live a semi-monastic lifestyle. He is exploring, experimenting, risking new experiences and frameworks, and yet he still comes off as a bit of an adolescent.

> *The Confused Man wants to see his life as epic and meaningful, and he looks to exterior adventure to give him interior clues to who he might be spiritually.*

He impulsively thrusts himself into relationship commitments and just as impulsively decides they are not for him, sending what looks like mixed signals to his prospective romantic partners. All this is done to "find himself." He continues to shake off the patriarchal programming of his society with only partial success. He still wants to be acknowledged and adored, but he can no longer stomach the imperious trappings of presumed authority and identity.

As a pro-feminist man in college, I found myself squarely dwelling in the experience of the Confused Man. I rejected the entitlement of men and men's poor and dismissive treatment of women. I no longer believed nor cared about men's ostensible authority to "call the shots" in society, so badly have men messed up their responsibility to be carers and contributors. I was sickened by men's endless military wars on the social level and endless self-aggrandizement on the personal level. As a man, I was over men and their outworn and isolated notions of masculinity! At this time, I looked to learn from women how to more deeply care and even decide for myself whom I might be as a person. I knew sensitivity and caring were deep parts of my being, yet at the same time, I wanted to express myself powerfully and impact the world.

It was at this time that I began my life-long love affair with writing, poetry, and philosophy, and a dedication to supporting women and children as full and valued participants of this world. I found myself drawn to poems and philosophies illuminating the nature of healthy relationship. I read and was influenced heavily by Martin Buber's *I and Thou*. I left my job as a lab assistant in a physiological chemistry lab to travel to Switzerland to become a boarding house assistant and tutor at an international school. I biked with my brother around central Europe and Greece. I came back as an educator at a hands-on science museum in Ohio. I followed my muse and applied to graduate schools in Philosophy of Education, choosing Syracuse University.

At Syracuse University I worked with a wonderful mentor and graduate advisor, Emily Robertson. I collaborated with an engaging community of graduate students over "What does it mean to educate children to be valuable members of a valuable society." I learned what it meant to be a valued member of a group rooted in my own unique contributions and talents. I continued to take advanced classes on feminism and read up on men's studies. From this experience in conversation with my identity struggles, I wrote a dissertation on developing self-esteem from an interpersonal standpoint in which the wisdom of children is given due respect from an early age.

I tried marijuana for the first time, went through many romantic relationships, took up with a young artist and hung out with her friends, and I learned to grow past my own prejudices, control freakishness, and over-obedience to authority. For a guy as unconventional as I was (and still am), I still had a peculiar fear of breaking any rules and ruining some self-imagined perfect record.

Yet there I was on an idyllic late summer day traveling with my girlfriend and her friends by van to an area where we could swim and wade. The driver parked the car right next to a sign that said, "No Parking." We then proceeded down a path past a sign that said, "No Trespassing." We arrived at a most splendid and beautiful clearing with water running over these meter-high ledges that created a whole series of mini-waterfalls. I climbed under one of these ledges to experience a curtain of water pouring in front of me. I stuck out my hands and felt the glorious power of this private waterfall. Here, I could feel Nature herself coursing through me and recalling me to my life roots.

Then, I heard a police siren. At this point, I had committed myself to this experience and did not care if we were kicked out. The sirens came nearby, and then they faded. It was simply a cop or ambulance going to some other place. All this amazing natural wonder, I noted to myself, had been kept from me by *my own* choice and obedience to an artificial authority with no interest in enjoining my deep needs as a man. Finally, I could feel myself. This is what has been kept from me by patriarchal programming, by the misspent messages and training I had received about what it meant to be a man—to kiss up to power and deny my humanity. I was now a man *with* rather than *against* nature and all she represented. I was a man liberated to express my admiration for the feminine and my own unique embodiment of the masculine.

It should be no surprise, from my examples, that a Confused Man places a high degree of value on self-exploration and community. Without parental figures or adequate models to figure out a healthy identity, the Confused Man gravitates toward small groups to find and feel the various aspects of himself as well as try out different ideas and relationships. Someone close to a Confused Man may find him to be an enigma, not unstable per se (like the Retreating Man) but apt to change and flow with new situations.

A woman married to a Confused Man will likely feel she is living with many men, each one showing up on a particular day. This can certainly make life interesting if a bit unnerving at times. In his work, the Confused Man tends, in the same manner, to sample various jobs, trying to hit upon one that resonates more deeply with him. At play, he is open to a spontaneous road trip, a dance lesson, a new restaurant, or any experience that might promise some new way of seeing or feeling the world. As a father, a Confused Man will careen between intense interest in his kids' lives (because they show him the world and reveal aspects of himself in his close relationships) and what looks like apparent disinterest as he focuses upon himself and his thoughts and feelings.

It is this fertile time of exploration and community, well-engaged, that can move a Confused Man, with his focus on inward care and outward experience, to an Equal Man, with his focus on outward care and the beginnings of inward experience. Many women do not understand this aspect of manhood in general, because they often start from a ground of relationship first and work their way back toward individuality.

The Confused Man must find it within himself first to become a man, and then to engage in relationship. Since a Confused Man finds out who he is largely through relationship, it can look like he is all over the place. But such is the chaotic, if not spasmodic, way of men's development. *Do not be distracted by men's indoctrinated pretense that they already know before they have learned.* Do not be dissuaded by their "me-first" habits. The important thing is to support authentic exploration and focused commitment once such a man strikes upon aspects of his becoming that resonate with his deeper being.

The Equal Man ("Life is a collaboration")

Within the *Equal Man* (the evolved form of the Social Man) lies acceptance and rebirth. His motto might be: "Together we can make this work." The Equal Man has come to an insight and a decision point that now permeates his life: He must choose and commit to an equal relationship that has room both for his joys and those of whom he loves. The Equal Man perceives his ends as joined with those of others. He sees the not only the possibility but the advantage of developing and growing with someone else.

He may compromise on the little things, personal preferences, for instance. However, he acquires a much greater gift—companionship in his journey of life— someone he can share his joys and sorrows with on the concrete level, rather than on the abstract level of his sole estimation and imagining. This sharing includes not only his mate but his children, should he decide to have children. The Equal Man can now learn from something other than himself or his solitary adventures. The world is opened and giving, and in gratitude, he opens and gives back. Perhaps he gives himself to marriage or parenthood. He learns to care and to attend to something other than himself. He learns to share the chores of life and benefits from its joys.

My friend, Dexter, in Portland, Oregon provides an excellent living example of the Equal Man (and a good dash of the Co-Creative Man). He works a responsible but socially progressive job as an "energy technologies" research analyst for a company interested in developing global markets for renewable energy. With this job, he is able to write grants and telecommute part of the time from his home in a nice residential section of Portland as well as share in the child-raising duties for their young daughter and son. I met Dexter in the Philippines where he was working on and monitoring a technology that used the mechanical pressure of water running downhill to pump water to remote rural villages. As is typical of Equal Men, he and I were able to develop a collaborative bond, which made competitive energy irrelevant. We started to meet regularly to support each other in the books we were writing. His writing was about Millennial Generation activists, and mine was about new ways to conceive and develop learning.

Dexter's wife, Amber, owns an art studio catering to 1 to 10-year-olds based on "uninhibited play and exploration through the process of making art." The philosophy of the art studio also seems to express the parenting philosophy that she and Dexter share. The process of creating art (and life) becomes more important than concentrating on the finished product. "Imagination and sensory fun" that honors a child's more delighted developmental process and natural desire to learn, take precedence over the more traditional emphasis on regulated behavior.

When my wife, Regina, and I went to visit them, this supportive and rich approach did not seem to have any untoward effects on the discipline and behavior of the children. They were happy, active, and enterprising. Amber and Dexter worked together to share household duties and make regular family time to go out to eat or play at home. Both Dexter and Amber were very community-directed as well—looking to buy up the surrounding houses in their neighborhood with other young families to create an informal cooperative where the backyards could be joined. Their commitments did not prevent them from spending time with each other and with adults. Their flows of life seem like ocean tides washing in and out of the various spheres of their daily realities.

What seems so evident in Dexter's example of the Equal Man, and in his life as a husband and father, is this notion of *balance*.

> *An Equal Man can balance the various aspects of his life and take joy in integrating his various roles rather than separating and allowing his different interests and relationships to compete with each other.*

Dexter did not see his family chores, nor his parenting, nor his date nights with his wife, nor his alone time to be mutually exclusive, but as part of an ecological web of life. There is a certain acceptance and relaxation in this more connected existence. This doesn't mean that "ease" always predominates as any parent of young children can attest. *There is still a lot of work, but the strain of competition between aspects of life is largely removed in the commitment to share and collaborate.*

Also, Dexter was able to incorporate many aspects of the evolved Animal Man, the Responsible Man, into his progressive attitudes. He and his wife are married, own a house, hold productive jobs, provide healthy examples for their children, and serve as solid community members. Again, I bring this up as a way to point out that various forms of manhood described in this chapter do not have to compete or be mutually exclusive. Men can incorporate the lessons or the good from each form of manhood and choose to leave the less helpful or less useful aspects behind.

It should be no surprise, from my examples, that an Equal Man places a high degree of value on service to family and society. With strong support and good models upon which to develop a fulfilling identity, the Equal Man gravitates toward jobs that allow him to make the world a better place and toward community relationships and activities that make him a better man and father.

Someone close to an Equal Man may find him to be an open and engaging, if busy, individual trying to do many things while balancing the various aspects of his life. The Equal Man is a man immersed in the world and its relationships, like a sailor at sea managing the waves, monitoring the wind, tending to the sails, and guiding the rudder of his ship. A woman married to an Equal Man will likely feel she has a good partner in life, and looking around to the other forms of manhood, she will likely appreciate his steadfastness and respect for her. At play, the Equal Man is into camping or a spontaneous family outing; anything meant to invite relaxed joy. As a father, he will be there to both provide for and enjoy his kids.

So why don't we simply stop with the Equal Man? For many heterosexual women, the Equal Man may look like the ideal man. To this, I would say, "Then why do so many men, with satisfying, stable, and healthy family lives go through mid-life crises?" This is where men may differ from women. *A man usually cannot rely upon relationships to give him meaning in later life. He has to continue to "make himself" for his life to continue to have vibrant meaning.* There is a certain *necessary independence* in a man who makes (and remakes) himself and, from there, makes his mark.

It is not enough for a man to direct himself toward his job and his family. As his children grow older and this relationship with his spouse or significant other matures, he is left with more time and a greater imperative to look at his larger creative contribution. A man is not just a Little League baseball coach or a romantic partner in the world, but a spiritual individual with a larger purpose in the larger cosmos. As children leave the nest, and a man moves firmly into mid-life, there is a call for a different kind of man, what I have called the Co-Creative Man, one who realizes and works on his "divine genius."

The Co-Creative Man, the third type of manhood

The Co-Creative Man is the interactive giver and receiver. He is "co-" in that he is interconnected, inter-conscious, collaborative, and consummately learning. He understands that creativity is the highest human and masculine activity and that love is the highest form of creativity. He knows that his life is a gift he can only repay forward into his contributions to life, to the world, and others. Therefore, the Co-Creative Man is committed to bringing spiritual insight and transformation into earthly reality.

In the regressed form of the Co-Creative Man, co-creativity is disrupted by disconnection from other people and disconnection from spiritual depth. He has a vague sense of a divine purpose but, achingly, few tools and little faith to manifest that purpose. He cannot go back to a romanticized masculine role, but he lacks the strength and insight to go forward. Thus, the regressed Co-Creative Man is in existential crisis. Should he reach the bottom of this crisis, he encounters the opportunity to break out of his solitude and into a renewed type of learning.

The transitional Co-Creative Man breaks open from his self-imposed shell of despair and *knows he doesn't know himself.* Instead, he sees the world and others as an invitation to experiment and discover who he might be. He is thus liberated from his pessimism and gloomy assumptions toward a renewed birth and possibility.

> *The evolved spiritually confident Co-Creative Man devotes himself to a deeper life and service.*

He realizes self-inflation is a distraction from excellence. To him, ego is a servant, not a leader. He is willing to give everything to the creative act, and the divine desire called love. He flows and fuses, rather than regrets or retrenches. A higher call for creativity emerges in him. Gratitude governs him. Love grows in him, retaining the best of the past to equip him for the present and future.

The Three Forms of Co-Creative Man

The Despairing Man ("Life is hopeless")

Within the *Despairing Man* (the regressed form of the Co-Creative Man) lies the winter of a man's soul. His motto might be: "What does it all mean? (Life is short, and then you die.)" He experiences an undeniable and intense sense of his mortality. This man may have kids who are grown or decided to have no kids at all. He is left with himself. Job success and ambition have run their course. His life roles have played themselves out. His youthful adventures have largely receded. He is brought back to himself and his unvarnished interior. No crutches or distractions can shoo away this insistent certainty that his body is built to die, that his life to bound to end.

The Despairing Man is basically the existential "hangover" from imbibing a life in which masculine purposes have been largely pre-determined by family, marriage, and community, or by professional ambition and travel if he has chosen to remain single. Now it is the next morning. He can feel his mortality more acutely. Who is he now? What must he do before he dies to ensure his life's significance? Where will meaning and purpose come from?

> *The Despairing Man is not simply a malcontent. His disenchantment and underlying existential angst have been uncovered, rather than produced by, the loss of his social crutches.*

These crutches—a presumed life plan, his assumed superior status in society, and his personal entitlement—all create a kind of bubble around him. If a man is courageous enough to confront his mortality, rather than hiding in others' attention and care, he is forced out of his bubble.

These crutches have weakened boys and men to an extreme degree. Globally, mothers have coddled their boys, and given them a different standard than girls. Fathers have excused their son's dishonorable behavior under the rubric that "boys will be boys." Teachers have used phrases like "lazy but brilliant" with boys to pass off of their low achievement and subsidize to their alleged self-esteem. Societies everywhere in the world have largely conspired to create grandiosity over excellence in boys and men.

And now the payment for this societal weakening of men by unearned elevation is coming due. Men's privileges are eroding. People who were once silent are calling men out, as with the #MeToo movement, especially around issues like sexual harassment. Sitcoms, like *Married with Family* and *The Simpsons* portray men more as buffoons than paragons of the community. This is a necessary stage of growth for men but traumatic nonetheless. By and large, men have been allowed to keep themselves in a state of perpetual adolescence. Now they are feeling the accumulated consequences of a several thousand-year self-indulgent binge.

Again, this coming-to-terms is critical if men are to mature and rise, but we men have basically painted ourselves into a corner with very few tools and options. We have relied so much upon exterior status and position that we have eroded our ability for *interior affirmation*. Men have needed someone to tell them they are the best thing since sliced bread, but such pale affirmations only paper over men's mortality and their imperative for accountability.

Spiritual accountability enters the picture as men's unmerited praise dries up, age approaches, and they start to feel like the world, and even life itself has passed them by. Once the crutches of entitlement and status are removed, many men feel useless with no way out or forward. This unmasked reality can cause despair but also prompt honest introspection and grieving. The Despairing Man realizes he has staked his being in the temporary, rather than the eternal. His exterior accomplishments are merely sands that eventually blow away with the wind.

This is a critical and vulnerable "aha" moment for men and one that few men face squarely. Despairing Men are often distracted from existential challenges by the ready stock of personal and social avoidance mechanisms in our societies. You see men looking to reawaken their primal roots in ancient rituals or hyper-intensive training. You see others trying to seek meaning through fraternal organizations and other forms of "manly" bonding. Others divorce and marry a woman half their age. Still others rebel from the direction of the world and try to re-assert their superiority.

All these diversionary tactics ultimately fail, because they do not get at the core of men's malaise. We men have played at presumed authority, and we have not really known what we were doing. We have also messed things up on a grand scale with global wars, environmental destruction, and towering monuments to our insecure egos, and we *do* merit legitimate criticism for getting things wrong and being too self-involved. (How many buildings, for instance, do you see named after women?) Men need to face the music. Men need accountability, reconciliation, and learning from others.

It is at this cold-water-in-the-face stage that many men give up. They simply cannot handle the metaphysical challenge. They may romanticize cynicism or skepticism, or they may turn to the manic opposite, hyper-activity. They may attempt to turn to some fantasy of a life they "could have lived." They may reminisce about "the good ole days." They may seek to re-enact a former joy or go through a second adolescence. They may obsess over some new technological toy, instead of endeavoring forward toward a transcendent new spiritual basis for their lives.

In this, I have heard young men idealizing the homeless lifestyle after experiencing increasing pressure and decreasing opportunities. I have seen many embittered older men simply try to reassert their power and false confidence in ugly racist, sexist, xenophobic, and homophobic ways. I see other men hiding within the confines of their family just trying to lie low and do the right thing.

These diversionary attempts fail to admit the limitations and errors of masculinity, and, furthermore, to creatively learn from those limitations and errors. Yes, men *have* done some things wrong! Men have produced some great things and some disastrous things. It is the pith of admirable male character to face what this man ("I" not "society") has done wrong, admit error, remedy harm, and create a transformed new approach and basis for identity. *Men's self-worth cannot be so weak as to rely upon willful ignorance and imperviousness to learning.*

In a strong sense, existential disillusionment is to be welcomed by the Co-Creative Man as the sacred precursor to growth and spiritual truth. This is why the Despairing Man, though regressed, is still elemental to the Co-Creative Man. A substantial man needs the rite of passage created by deep despair to understand the stakes of his growth, to purify himself, to clear his metaphysical boards, and to launch him into a new incarnation not ladened by metaphysical and emotional regret

> *This Despairing Man stage is critical. It is where a man is being spiritually respected rather than disrespected. It is where a man is being honed to take the journey to the core of himself and relinquish worldly pride to give of himself authentically.*

Ironically, this despair is the place of opening, of new life, and of "no turning back." It is the end of one road and the beginning of another. The Despairing Man has only the memories of his former life. He exists beyond pretension, striving, and proving. He must commit to *finding out* rather than pretending to know. He is no longer the expert, the master, or the authority. He must dedicate himself to apprenticeship to his own Higher Mind and the larger cosmos. He must move on to the learning life of the Searching Man.

The Searching Man ("Life is learning and discovery")

Within the *Searching Man* (the transitional form of the Co-Creative Man) lies a tremendous vulnerability. His motto might be: "Okay so I *don't* know. Let's find out!" He understands that he cannot rely on his own devices but must enter a certain larger grace and trust for him to proceed in the arc of his life. He recognizes that what he once based his value upon as a man, what he socially aspired to, were largely delusions of grandeur. He now acknowledges the poverty of men's attempts to "enhance" themselves at the expense of others.

He realizes that so-called "world beaters" are doing just that, beating the crap out of the world.

> *The Searching Man may not know what exactly what he should do, but he is committed to the uncertain task of discovering what he might do.*

His vocation is no longer one of conserving or retaining, but letting go, surrendering his possessions and his power to something *beyond* himself.

The Searching Man discards even his image of himself along with the trappings of his life. Instead of buying a new red sports car, he is more likely to hike the Pacific Trail or spend time in an ashram. He finds himself drawn to poetry rather than pick-up lines. He is deepening. He is pregnant with a larger purpose, and he is going through labor pains. His mantra is: "Surrender the things of the self. Awake and grow."

The Searching Man begins to experience his life as not just about him. He begins to welcome a larger cosmic dance and the deeper insights that come from this intimate engagement. His spirit-in-the-world is maturing. He feels into things more deeply. Acumen and openness gradually replace self-consciousness and image-projection. Integration becomes his new mission.

The Searching Man enters the world of "both-and" rather than "either/or." He realizes that any life instance or choice is rich with simultaneous possibilities. He gains nuance. He notices injustice and strives for justice without the aid of labels. He knows that if he resides in truth and feels, thinks, and acts from inspiration, he shall make room for transformation beyond his limited perspective. The Searching Man, in short, allows himself to be called out of his bubble.

In this calling out beyond himself, the Searching Man learns important new truths. He learns of the temporary nature of the material world, and he seeks things of a more eternal nature. He becomes interested in the nature of the spirit. He ceases to look outside himself for meaning and validation and more toward his internal wisdom to connect him with others as well as the sublime aspects of his being.

The Searching Man asks, "How many times *can* I be top sales-man of the month before this striving starts losing its energy? How many ways can I blindly live for others before I lose a feel for myself?" The Searching Man knows that *the outer and inner must meet* in an engaged process of learning that transforms his very character. The narrow gives way to the deep. Professional obsession gives way to vocation or life calling. Black and white give way to a trillion shades of vibrant color.

The Searching Man realizes that his self—his personality, his unique divine genius, and his work ethic are actually *honed and evoked rather than watered down* by an aware, selfless service to others arising from his deeper talents and joys. I found myself learning this Searching Man lesson when I served as a math tutor for a college student who had been in recovery from a six-week coma suffered after a car accident. She had gotten a D- on her first midterm. After doing my diagnostics, I determined it was the university's teaching disabilities rather than a slow-healing brain that were causing the problems.

Under my tutelage, she received a B+ on her next midterm exam, and an A- on her third. I was all set to help her with a comprehensive review for the final exam when she phoned me to say she didn't need me for that review. She felt confident that she knew her stuff. My first reaction was one of betrayal: "How could she leave me when I had helped her so much!" As my pride receded and the Searching Man won out, however, I had a different insight: "Of course, this is what I want. Others should not be taught to depend upon me; they should use my help to make themselves more capable, self-sufficient, and able to contribute."

The Searching Man realizes that it is not just "me" conducting an interaction. As a tutor to that young woman, I was a participant in an evocative, co-creative mutual action that drew out deeper capacities in her. It was her capacities, not mine, that helped her learn. The Searching Man similarly operates as a facilitator in a creative deed "leading out" the gifts and abilities of another person. This is an evolution from pressing himself on others as master, savior, or tin god. (Incidentally, the Greek root words of the word "education" actually mean "to lead out.")

The Searching Man thus pursues a new model for manhood as a generous, caring, and giving learning partner. He is a facilitator, coach, and mentor, rather than a boss or a king. This filters across the professional spectrum. He could be a doctor who supports the holistic health, awareness, and education of this patient rather than paternalistically "curing" them with some drugs that simply cover up underlying fundamental issues. He could be an athlete that respects his adversaries for helping him raise the level of his game, rather than trash-talking them.

You will find many philanthropists and activists among Searching Men. The founders of Ben and Jerry's ice cream, after they sold their company, for instance, organized politically-oriented campaigns to divert military spending into social causes. The genuinely committed Searching Man has gone through an evolution from "me vs. we" to "me *and us*."

For the Searching Man, the small kingdom of self, based on singular, material achievement, is surrendered to a larger sphere of social service and metaphysical exploration. This brings about a certain kind of catharsis, as individual expectation replaces exaltation in the places where spirit meets the world. With this embrace of something beyond him, the Searching Man ironically encounters deeper parts of himself he never knew existed—proclivities, intuitions, senses, successes—which bring him closer to his spiritual uniqueness. He is on his way to becoming a Spiritually Confident Man.

The Spiritually Confident Man ("Life is creative engagement")

The *Spiritually Confident Man* (the evolved form of the Co-Creative Man) is broken open to the eternal nature of his being. His motto might be: "Unleash the spirit!" Within him lies the universe of possibility meeting a universe of creativity. The Spiritually Confident Man realizes he has nothing to lose. Life has been given him. Now he must give himself fully and deeply to life.

> *Therefore, the Spiritually Confident Man no longer possesses himself but is moved by a possessing spirit to express what constitutes him at a profound, high, and clear level.*

The Spiritually Confident Man realizes that he is neither his body nor his reputation, for these things, if they have any value at all, serve something that outlasts his own life—Love. Love is his only legacy, the only thing that lasts. He is freed from fear of death by this realization, and he is freed to leave despair behind and activate his spiritual core.

The fiber of a Spiritually Confident Man is active faith in his spiritual core. He needs nothing of an urgent nature, so he has all to give. He desires the world, instead of fighting against it. He longs more deeply for his romantic partner instead of wondering if there is something better out there. He moves and is moved. He sees and expresses life in a new beauty, depth, and universality.

The Spiritually Confident Man knows he is an essential yet microscopic part of the universe. The energy of his atoms is freed to do its work. He has nothing to lose because he has already surrendered himself. Life, then, becomes a boundless richness. His being overflows. He can radiate pure essence, kindness, and a peculiar kind of courage born of curiosity. He has been readied and quickened. The Spiritually Confident Man is a quantum man walking forward into the already-and-not-yet world.

These are the outlines of the Spiritually Confident Man. I have devoted the next chapter to the Spiritually Confident Man, as well as the title of this book, so I will not go into greater detail in this chapter. Suffice it to say that I believe there is lasting and crucial value for this form of manhood to emerge in our time.

The Spiritually Confident Man includes and incorporates the lessons and experiences of the previous forms of manhood. He has within him a unifying basis, a compassion and focus that allows him to join together past masculine aspects and serve as an inspiring example of a healthy and strong masculine future. This is the critical direction that the Spiritually Confident Man takes and the crucial decision he makes—toward vivid truthfulness, wholeness, and rebirth.

The Undivided Man: From Fragmentation to Wholeness

In my late 20's, I was very far from being a Spiritually Confident Man. I had become so expert at compartmentalizing my feelings that I could not access my own emotions. I felt then, and I still feel today, that no amount of pain could match the hell of not feeling anything at all. My life and mind were being run by my Animal Man impulse for prediction and control. Authentic and spontaneous feelings in relationships with others were not predictable, so they needed to be stoically resisted and cast to the side.

This Animal Man predict-and-control tendency stood at odds

with my other desires to passionately and spontaneously engage the world, so I found an outlet for my desire to feel by taking risks on my inline skates, going down extremely steep roads. I remember feeling an odd (somewhat twisted) joy in crashing on those skates. One day, my skates flew out from underneath me in a particularly tight and fast turn. I scraped the skin on my forearms and thighs bloody, but at least I could feel the triumphant pain of this daring move.

Most women would consider this close to insanity, but almost every guy will relate to this example in one way or another.

> *We men cut ourselves off from unpredictable feelings in dealing with other people, and then compensate for this by producing individual feelings (even feelings of pain, anger, and aggression), which gives us back some spark of what it means to be alive.*

A woman might say: "Why not simply learn to be okay with accepting unpredictable feelings, and treat your relationships as adventures?"

Good point. Often a man will not think in that direction because he has taught himself to pay attention only to those things that are under his control. It is clear at this time in history that men are being challenged consciously to transform themselves toward integral and interactive beings. We are all being called to expand and deepen ourselves beyond our current assumptions. By contrast, animal tendencies, especially if they are unconscious, can turn themselves against us and those we love.

This is not to say that men have always walled themselves off from positive passionate and sensitive interactive feelings (empathy, generosity, affection). In my younger years, I allowed myself to openly feel my spirit in nature and in my own imagination but not so much in relationships. Occasionally, I would selectively share this private world with a close female friend or romantic partner. Perhaps I did not feel other people would be able to understand or want the undeveloped "me."

Spiritual growth demands that we learn sharing, confidence, communication, and self-understanding. Masculine myths assert the opposite-- that men have to *already know* and assert who they are. As a boy, I had to pretend to be an expert before I learned. This is just one of a myriad of failed circular logics that hamper men today. It is better to learn *by* doing, not *before* doing. Maybe this is why men are largely poorer at multitasking than women. Good multitasking is inherently an interactive, "learning by doing" skill.

Understanding and unifying different spheres of manhood

"A man divided against himself and others cannot stand. A man united within himself and with others can do anything."

It is the fragmentation and opposition of different aspects of masculinity, that give rise to problems in men's development, relationship, and identity. Men who adopt a "divide and conquer" strategy to take care of their problems end up creating more unintended problems. Even books promising to grow men's masculinity often make this mistake, setting their new-and-improved model of masculinity against the old and obsolete ones.

> *For a man to be whole, he must recognize and, at some level, embrace all of who he is, who he can be, and who he has been.*

My intention in this chapter has been to honor each condition and form of manhood for its necessary strengths and contributions and to challenge each condition and form of manhood for its significant weaknesses.

The Spiritually Confident Man is not simply an evolved form of manhood but an embracing one, which includes, appreciates, and at the same time transcends other forms of manhood. The spiritually confident man does not hold any form of manhood, even the Toxic Man, in contempt, because he is driven by compassion and a desire to learn from his flaws. He recognizes that he has inherited and has within his constitution and grasp a whole range of male development, from the ugly and primitive to the beautiful and refined.

> *In other words, the Spiritually Confident Man takes no joy in being "right." He is interested in being good, helpful, and more aware.*

A man who chooses one way of being a man over another will remain divided. If a man is to be whole, he cannot allow himself to be reduced to "his" formula versus that guy's formula. He must constantly choose and grow, experiment and flow with his life and relationships. A living man is not a stereotype or even an archetype; he is a chooser, a learner, an engager of challenge, and a lover of life. He meets things as they are, rather than what they "ought" to be, and brings about a healthier reality by revealing what things "can" be beyond his small inclinations, petty prejudices, and limited individual imagination.

It has been the purpose of this chapter to show the strengths and flaws of different types and forms of manhood as a collaborative endeavor. This discussion seeks to integrate the energies and insights of different forms of manhood, rather than proving one type or form of manhood superior. Its theme is inclusion, not exclusion. Here, challenges are helpful rather than threatening. Here, contrast helps a man to assemble a more vibrant and complete understanding of what it means to be a man in the emerging world. Here, difference is treated as a blessing. And here, uniqueness creates synergy, and connection creates purpose.

Now we move on to the Spiritually Confident Man, a man who appreciates and integrates what he has been, what he is, and what he might be. We elicit the possible behavior and sensibilities of one who can embody, appreciate, integrate, and transcend the different forms of manhood.

CHAPTER 3

Tending The Garden—The Spiritually Confident Man

Having looked at the long-term growth of masculinity as reflected in different past and present forms of manhood, we now come face to face with a newer, vibrant form of masculinity—the Spiritually Confident Man. What does this spiritually confident masculinity look and feel like? What advantages does spiritually confident masculinity offer and how does it differ from past forms of masculinity? What capacities and care does it require, especially at its beginning "sprouting" stages? What social and cultural perspectives might help men grow, understand, and learn into spiritually confident masculinity? How do we till the rich soil of the creative spirit and supply the nutrients of the higher self to spiritually confident living?

YOU CAN SENSE A spiritually confident man more than you can see him. He does not dabble in the obvious signs of manhood. He has a certain, perhaps subtler, grace of movement and mood. His kindness and openness give rise to both his expression and assertiveness.

He is neither a braggart nor a doormat. He welcomes the world and the people in it. Where is this mysterious creature? He likely dwells in your midst, sometimes working an ordinary job, but filled with an extraordinary passion and curiosity. He is brimming with creative desire for life.

His spirit and intuition guide him. He will engage in a conversation with a stranger because he wants to know that person's story. He will interrupt his routine and his normal routes because these actions promise to reveal something new about him. He will listen and feel into the pulse of a situation or interaction. He is, as they say, hiding in plain sight.

You may or may not find a spiritually confident man in the conventional "enlightened" places like yoga studios or vegan restaurants, where the vast majority of the clientele are women anyway (or women who have brought their men). It is best to start by learning to see confidence itself differently.

The qualities of spiritual confidence: What does spiritually confident masculinity look and feel like?

There are plenty of pretenders out there who are quite willing to broadcast their alleged sensitivity to get into a woman's heart and/or her pants, just as there are wannabe Don Juan's who will say anything to get what they want from a potential target of their lower desires. There is hope, however. There is emerging a masculinity, based in spiritual confidence, which is as powerful as it is open, and as receptive to new possibilities as it is passionate about acting in the world.

Spiritual confidence and desire can be demonstrated in the "back-rub test." How many guys out there actually desire to give a back rub to someone they love without wanting or needing something in return? How many men can simply rejoice in the feeling of spiritual energy coursing through them into the body of their beloved without expecting some kindness or sexual response in return?

> *A spiritually confident (and competent) man desires for himself the ability to give calming and healing touch and desires for the other person nourishing, liberating energy.*

This kind of spiritual confidence roots itself in cultivated capacities. Spiritual confidence does not simply arise automatically because a man is "a good guy." It is something that can and must be learned.

Practically speaking, a spiritually confident man *directly responds to life*, rather than projecting, evading, or posturing. Life is a blessing, not a threat. Therefore, there is no need to conquer life. *Fruition*, rather than finality, draws the spiritually confident man. He does not make excuses or skirt the edges of uncomfortable realities about himself. *He knows he is art in progress.* If he has hurt someone, he apologizes. If he has erred, he corrects his error. If he feels a bolt of joy, he expresses it and shares it.

Emotionally, a man displays spiritual confidence by intense curiosity and creative engagement. Creative engagement draws him so strongly that he cedes control-freakishness, cookie-cutter achievement, and eventually even conventional notions of success to ply his own horizons. This is vibrantly active and experiential. Spiritually confident men let go. They feel no preemptive need to withhold, intellectualize, or theorize. They feel no need to stay in a seaport dreaming of the rolling waves when they can sail the open and unpredictable oceans of fortune.

Perhaps a spiritually confident man will proffer his heart without knowing how it will be received. Again, responding directly to life, he may grieve if his heart is rebuffed, but he still admires and expresses gratitude to life for being able to feel at all. He affirms himself for pursuing something or someone he intrinsically cares about, regardless of the result. He is not bound by regret. The old world is gone, and the new one is before him.

> *Metaphysically, masculine spiritual confidence is demonstrated by vivid presence.*

When the existential going gets tough, a spiritually confident man does not tail away but leans into and learns into the point. "Okay, so I have lost my job… now what, so what, and for what?" Instead of balling up or detaching, he *connects,* inquiring *into* his situation. In so doing, he finds that every failure presents a learning opportunity to dissolve his pride and liberate himself to new heights. He engages in *active* contemplation, moving beyond placid regard into dynamic knowledge, inspiration, and transformation.

In quality after quality, a spiritually confident man chooses the organic flow of noticing, intuiting, gaining insight, learning, experimenting, reflecting, and transforming. He *begins to know* what and who he is spiritually and uniquely through a conversation with the world. Since he is a spirit at play *and* work in the world, this comes with a certain sense of humor as well as focus. He is not simply playing a role, though he may choose to *take on* various roles and experiences in the course of his life.

Spiritually confident men are spontaneous, rather than calculated. They aim at unpredictable, rather than predictable, excitements. For the spiritually confident man, interest is developed less by exterior variety and drama than by interior complexity. Novelty can be triggered simply by candidly meeting new people, places, and experiences. This creates a heightened ability to notice and *feel into* the world rather than impose upon it and attune the senses and listen rather than toot one's own horn.

A spiritually confident man notices the infinite elegance in things. The petals on a rose, for instance, exhibit a compelling mathematical pattern unified with exquisite texture, color, and aroma. This regard for the beautiful around him leads to his own refinement.

Spiritual confidence is intrinsic versus extrinsic. Males, trained toward tasks, solutions, and objects, often find pride and worth in being the master of some exterior process— "I was able to sell my start-up business for millions of dollars!" Yet, it was an interior creative idea meeting outer opportunities that gave rise to this successful enterprise in the first place.

In college, I was part of an eight-man rowing team at an invitational competition. We won a nineteen-minute race by a mere one second. In fact, the top four boats were within six seconds of each other. What stood out was how in sync we were in the last 100 meters of the race. Had we been even a little off, we would have come in fourth rather than first. It was a sense of connection that gave rise to our win. And it was that lesson of connection, not the thrill of victory, that I retained.

> *Whether one is composing a hit song, finding a new teaching technique, or developing a more efficient way to do an ordinary task, real magic lies not in extrinsic acclaim but in the intrinsic, generative energy that gave rise to the success.*

When an instrumental desire for outer "success" dominates his generative energy, a man loses his mojo. He is now cut off from his creative source and coasting on his reputation, a business formula, or other people's desires to be with that "cool guy." I've noticed this happen so many times with tech gurus who assemble a "tribe" based on some semi-inventive insights and then peddle book after book, program after program, saying the same things in slightly different ways.

Spiritual confidence requires social courage and a willingness to stand apart in pursuing one's deeper purpose. None of us are truly like other people, but few of us are willing to admit that inherent distinctness and follow their uniqueness into some original passion. That passion can take on any form—like restoring old cars, as with my wife's father. It does not have to be monetized, but it has to be engaged consistently over time. Spiritual confidence is not about living on the margins of society versus selling out. A spiritually confident person may keep his or her day job but commit to a deeper productive joy. This requires discipline though. You may have to pass up that social invitation to tend to your creative obsession.

Spiritual confidence involves openness. There are so many ways that men get closed off in our post-modern societies. I have already talked about spontaneity as an aspect of openness, but there are other related qualities—the ability to understand nuance instead of casting every issue in black and white, the ability to embrace holism instead of compartmentalizing life, the ability to be flexible and permeable instead of hard and resistant, collaborative instead of go-it-alone, intuitive instead of linear, and restorative instead of punitive.

All these qualities have an air of mercy, grace, and acceptance that may feel to many men like giving up or ceding sovereignty over their lives, being "surrender monkeys," as the pejorative phrase goes.

Nothing could be farther from the truth. A spiritually confident man possesses himself by having the courage to relinquish himself of his vanities. A man becomes whole by accepting the inclusive truth of his interdependence. He gains, rather than loses sovereignty, by having mercy on himself and extending mercy to others. We all need one another. Our choice now is to *want* one another.

Men have been taught to construct their lives in ways that set people apart, over, and against each other. In this devolved frame of mind, openness is an invitation to competition and abuse. However, this fear is based on a lie. In truth, separateness is sheer delusion. We men did not make our own lives. We were brought into this world by grace and spiritual choice, so we are called upon to give as we have been given.

That is spiritually confident masculinity in a nutshell: Creatively give life as you were given life.

The difference between spiritual confidence and social, professional, or romantic confidence

Almost all people find confidence, in general, to be attractive. However, there are different kinds of confidence and different ways of expressing confidence. The spiritually confident man has a different orientation and focus than a typical socially, professionally, or romantically confident man.

> *Spiritual confidence is universal and embracing, quieter, more oriented toward connection with others and one's path of service in the world.*

A spiritually confident man is less task-directed and less self-directed. He is neither ambitious nor lazy. He is neither a control freak nor a stoner. He does not rely merely on his will or lack of will. He is looking to connect with something larger and deeper than his short-term aims. Thus, he naturally resists stereotypes and easy characterization.

Social confidence

Male social confidence as we typically understand it in Western contexts revolves around successful public status and positioning, which, in turn, relies upon signifiers of worth. Are you able to hobnob with powerful people? Are you wealthy? Do you take the time to dress sharply? Are you the life of the party? This is not unlike the animal kingdom where the king of the herd struts his stuff, reinforced by a certain social muscle. Social confidence seems to require an odd combination of emotional self-sufficiency and desire to soak up attention. The skilled socially confident man may revel in controversy. At the same time, he gives off the air that he does not care about what other people think.

It *is* pleasurable for most men to be the "big man on campus," the king of his workplace, or his family, or simply the chief of his own "man cave." I am not criticizing that pleasure, but rather, pointing out that such indulgence can also confine a man. Being a big fish in a relatively small, exclusive pond does not lend itself to truly confident social exploration with different groups and types of people.

Maintaining status diverts creative energy into image control. Before he knows it, a socially confident man's polished life is running him, rather than the other way around. Every interaction becomes a potential loss of esteem or positioning. Social "confidence" (accentuated by social media) becomes about looking good and radiating success even when you are feeling depressed and fraudulent. Who needs that kind of constant pressure that misleads others and creates constant anxieties for the self?

Spiritual social confidence involves taking off masks, rather than putting them on, radiating magnetism, rather than selling charisma.

Spiritual confidence dispenses with all social pretense, including the banal lies that a man is master of his domain or an expert about something he knows little about or a thousand other conceits that detract from his authentic interaction with the world.

Authenticity is of supreme value for the spiritually confident man: You don't have to "fake it until you make it." You don't have to pretend to be more successful than you are. You don't have to pretend to be more sensitive than you are. You don't have to pretend to know the directions when you are driving in a car. Dropping pretense frees up interaction, learning, and eventually true excellence.

Professional confidence

Typical professional confidence centers around expertise, skill, and proving oneself. It tends to be proportional to the salary one makes. Spiritual confidence centers more around conversation, the art of improvement, and discovering new things rather than asserting old authorities. Again, note the dynamism and movement in cultivated spiritual confidence. It elicits trust in the journey and in the self. It does not derive its worth from extrinsic promotion up the corporate ladder, for instance, (as nice as that can be for one's salary) but rather from intrinsic improvement and refinement.

Spiritually-focused professional confidence is more reflective and can be a big time and money saver in practical terms. How many times have ambitious people, climbed the ladder of professional success only to find their ladder leaning on the wrong wall! History is littered with people (you may be one or know one) who just got burned out by a "successful profession" that did not feed their souls. Ultimately you will lose a fight against your higher self, and if your lower self happens to "win out" over your higher self, you lose anyway. A hollow life of empty pleasure and disjointed existence awaits you. This is no substitute for labor of love. Real confidence of any sort requires *integrity*, the correspondence of your aspiration and conviction with your deepest desires and the highest parts of your being.

> *Success is different for the spiritually confident man. He directs his focus, courage, intelligence, and energies not so much to accomplishment according to conventional standards but to unveiling deeper and stronger capacities in himself and more inventive possibilities in the world.*

You will not find many spiritually confident men trying to climb the corporate ladder, but you will find more than a few amid the artists, writers, travelers, entrepreneurs, non-profit leaders, and those men devoted to service. The spiritually confident man's assurance and stability has a different source, not so much the external structure provided by a high-status job, but an abiding conviction and inner resourcefulness.

Romantic confidence

Traditional romantic confidence is evidenced by charisma, charm, being a "good lover," and so on. Again, these qualities can be quite enjoyable. The purpose here is not to dismiss and put down other types of romantic confidence, but to expand and deepen them, and to situate them in the context of a more lasting, intimate notion of relationship. It's one thing for a man to be able to confidently approach a woman (or another man if he is gay), but another thing entirely to follow through into learning about that person, honoring them, and eventually committing to them if that direction is merited.

The spiritual romantically confident man plays in the fields of spirit, but he is not a "player" in its immature sense. He realizes that the world is already given but also, at the same time, not-yet-here, not yet fully formed. He does not draw people into his made world with his confidence; he steps out into their world, and a world *between* not yet created. He does this with eagerness, *desiring not so much to prove himself against the world but to find his best relationship with it.*

Spiritual romantic confidence does not show itself only in the courting stage but through a lifetime of growing awakening and attunement with other persons.

> *In short, spiritual romantic confidence is **delightfulness**—to be so intrigued and turned on by another person that you want to get to know him or her on a deeper level, have him or her know you on a deeper level (and thus know yourself at a deeper level).*

When I first met my wife, Regina, over dinner before she interviewed me about my book *Transforming Economy*, we concluded with a warm hug that lasted longer than it should have. This did not occur because she wanted to send me a message or for me to send her one; it was simply an expression of mutual delight and wanting to remain in that space together.

So many people become fascinated with another person and choose to absorb themselves into that other person's world, either leaving behind their own will or walling it off. This abdication of choice is created by a combination of fear of exposure, fear of rejection, and not wanting to intimidate or displease the other person. On the other side, some people simply want to invite another into their den of preferences and refuse to cross over to the sphere of the other person.

You can see this unsatisfying dynamic play out in the less than stellar sex lives of so many couples. The guy wants a quick release. The woman wants extended romantic foreplay. The guy thinks romantic foreplay is too much work. The woman thinks the guy has no sense of romance and does not care about her. The guy gravitates toward pornography to get what he wants. The woman gravitates toward romance novels or "chick flicks" to meet her needs.

Can you imagine what sex lives could be like if creative, exploratory *sensuality* were allowed to have free reign rather than stereotyped gendered notions of sexuality? What would it feel like to have the unknown wonderland of another body, mind, heart, and spirit touched sensually rather than groped? What would sexual play look like without a man's insecure desire to prove himself? What would sexual pleasure be like without a female's reluctance to communicate her desires?

Spiritual romantic confidence is about joining up rather than impressing. The *beauty* of desire replaces the *politics* of desire. Every passion and naivety becomes a source for wondrous or humorous revelation rather than anxiety.

The advantages of spiritual confidence

We have touched on some of the advantages of spiritual confidence in preceding passages, but let's delve more deeply into these advantages. There is a hazard when speaking of higher states of being that some people might see them as too demanding or too lofty. *It is important not to turn spiritual confidence into some kind of unattainable ideal.* Spiritual confidence is actually fairly accessible, ground*ed*, and ground*ing*. For spiritual confidence to have real-world value, it should logically help make your life simpler and truer.

Spiritual confidence works by taking the load off, rather than putting more pressure on. Spiritual confidence is *not* about being more complicated and "enlightened" to the point you are doing contortionist yoga, bowing and praying eight times a day, or living like a monk. Workable spiritual confidence removes burdens and replaces them with opportunities and responsibilities. These responsibilities, are exactly that—response-abilities, a greater mental, emotional, and spiritual ability to engage the world. Spiritual confidence empowers a person by emphasizing a receptive and enterprising disposition over a façade of expertise and "been-there-done-that."

> *The main difference between traditional signifiers of confidence and spiritual confidence is that traditional confidence pretends to know and spiritual confidence desires to find out.*

Spiritual confidence approaches, rather than retreats, opens rather than closes, communicates genuine warmth rather than throws up barricades and false signals. Spiritual confidence shows up, steps up, lets go, and strips away the inessentials. Gone are the things that do not serve any more. What a relief this can be! No more pretending. No more holding up what should have long ago collapsed. No more lying and feeling like a fraud. People romanticize these insecure activities as signs of our inherent collective imperfection and vulnerability.

Stand-up comics have a field day with them. "Hey, everyone, we're not perfect. Deal with it!" These tendencies, however, are not real vulnerability and imperfection. They usually involve childish impulses or calculated game playing. They are mistakes, which we, for some reason, keep repeating.

Spiritual confidence is the courage to be seen for what and who you are. What would a graceful man look like, who does not misrepresent himself? A typical man would probably be far more interesting and less insufferable if he replaced his controlling mind and pick-up lines with abiding curiosity. Exploration would give him value and enjoyment rather than posing a threat to his façade. He would dare to leave the familiar and feel the edgy thrill of a new frontier. That sounds like a far more exciting existence than attempting to play out a retreaded fantasy in the real world. Primal risk *is* an inherent male need, but why not meet that need through emotional adventure in addition to extreme sports?

Spiritual confidence also has the advantage of unifying a man amid his fragments. Alleged confidence, based on separation and control, fractures a man. "I will be a certain man to my wife, another to my boss, another to my mistress, another to my kids…" Such a fragmented life is exhausting. Trying to keep all the scripts separate, and then trying to play all the parts. Why not just be yourself, and learn where you can? If other people are looking for perfection or a certain "you" that you don't really offer, leave them to their own devices. By contrast, if someone believes in you and offers you faith in your higher abilities or self, take them up on it! If they are not doing it for the wrong reasons, and you sincerely try, there will be progress rather than disappointment. Let the givers get with the givers, and let the takers stay with the takers.

> *There is spiritually confident benefit for a man who feels and acts directly from his own spirit rather than playing a role he cannot fulfill.*

The higher spiritual pleasure of joy involves more intense, full-hearted, full-body feelings. Lower pleasures of control and domination bait a man into a prison of emotional insecurity. He does not just *get* to rule; he is forced to! He is now a slave to his own expectations and pretensions of superiority. He now has to put other people down, even if they are better than he, to maintain his delusional status. He will breed resentment when the world will not do what he tells it to do. What a horrendous life! No! We do not have to agree to our own slavery. Deeper manhood is deeper offering, *not* reinforced selfishness, ignorance, or immaturity.

With spiritual confidence, you can get rid of junk psychology. Every Tom-Dick-and-Harry seems to be offering the magic bullet that is going to make your life instantly wonderful *if* you just attend *his* program or read *that* book. Spiritual confidence starts with recognizing that you are not missing something essential that must derive from another person. You have what you need in the very life given you, and in the unique divine genius that you offer the world. You simply need to *manifest* that spirit in the most vivid way possible. There is no need to prove yourself. There will be far more challenge in the creative realm than in the realm of pat expectation.

> *Spiritual confidence stimulates mercy—allowing things to be as they authentically are without our intervention and fixing—and grace—inviting wider help.*

With mercy and grace, we have no need to chastise ourselves and others emotionally. Therefore, we do not have to compensate for this brand of emotional brutality with self-indulgent excesses like empty-calorie foods, drugs, and alcohol, which make us even more removed and unhealthy.

This is an especially relevant point, given that humanity is still emerging from habits pounded into them by the Industrial Age (the second Dark Ages) where men were treated as either machines or animals, and women and children were given an even lower status. Spiritual confidence shows that oppression degrades humanity for all people, oppressor and oppressed, by reducing all concerned people to objects. Spiritually confident openness and creativity, on the other hand, elevate humanity by imbuing people with *subjectivity*.

Spiritual confidence requires far fewer physical and financial resources. From a material point of view, spiritual confidence is lower maintenance! Because spiritual experience relies almost entirely on shared, non-scarce, non-material "goods" (like learning, love, and levity), it does not require a lot of money to develop. What it does require is courage, compassion, and creativity. In terms of *character*, however, it is *higher* maintenance. That is the trade-off. Some people spend tons of money proving themselves to others or indulging themselves. Others would prefer to exchange energy in the form of opening up to a friend, sharing a hike, or volunteering for the library.

Spiritual confidence also encourages emotional range and intellectual vitality. For the spiritually confident man, things are not always black or white but can be multicolored, gray, or even black *and* white at the same time. He lives amid fruitful contradiction and is not troubled when opposites exist together. The spiritually confident man can talk about "life, the universe, and everything" one day but can still arrange to take the kids to the doctor's appointment the next, without thinking it too mundane or domestic.

In fact, the spiritually confident man is intrigued by productive opposites. That is the reason why he can take in and develop feminine energy along with his masculine energy. He is interested not only in exploring possibilities but developing creative and deep relationships, including healthy and strong relationships with the women in his life. This spiritually confident man commits to the universe and enjoys participating in the grand unfolding of life. He is an adventurer and a learner, experiencing this world for the first time. He brings his active, creative understanding to his vocation, to his relationships, and to the possibilities in the world.

How does spiritually confidence exhibit itself in wider social, cultural, and psychological realms? What are the more specific signs and indicators of the spiritually confident man in society? Though I talk about relations between men and women in much of this discussion, the principles of spiritually confident men apply to any sexual orientation or style of relationship.

Spiritually confident treatment of women

There is perhaps no better indicator of a spiritually confident man than how he treats women, regardless of his sexual or gender orientation. Even gay men have mothers, and the old adage about knowing how good a mate a man will be by looking at his relationship with his mother is largely true. Typically, males are task-oriented. Romantically, they tend to like the "chase," the clichéd "thrill of the hunt." Many men are taught to see romantic love as a conquering game, winning the desire of an intended quarry.

However, very few men know what to do once they have caught

their quarry, and precious few have learned to question why they started the hunt in the first place, much less why they decided to pursue this or that particular person. Usually, the reason for pursuit is less than profound. In short, few men know what they are looking for in their heart of hearts, because few have explored and shared what is going on in their hearts. Their motivation lacks conscious intent and falls easily into a habit of garnering good-looking, supposedly "high class" people, to bolster their reputation and self-esteem.

This understanding, fortunately for both men and women, is falling out of favor. Women, who are now developing careers in the world and social spheres apart from men, are not interested in merely being an object or adjunct of "their" men. No longer do we say, "Mr. and Mrs. Charles Smith," but rather Mr. Jake Rosetti and Dr. Kate Porter. However, this emerging independence of women and equality of genders does not mean there is no longer a leadership role for men to exert in their relationships with women. A man is not there merely to figure out what a woman wants and to provide it for her.

> *The spiritually confident man welcomes reciprocity, that is, he accepts the desirability of a woman initiating and asserting her own needs, but then engages in a conversational banter, an enthralling dance of support and challenge that engages and mixes his talents and initiative with hers.*

He, as she, has a right to say "no," to negotiate or offer new ideas, not from a place of resistance but to enter the stream of the relationship with his or her authentic take on things. This is not about compliance or control but rather *interaction* in which the conversation or relationship between persons supersedes the individuals. Women, especially strong women, do not want a compliant "wet noodle," nor do they want a control-freak. What they want is a life partner.

The spiritually confident man is just such a life partner, in any relationship—friendship, familial, romantic, and so on. He is an empathetic sounding board and advocate for the deepest aspirations of the women in his life. He wants what is best *for* her from the best *of* her. Thus, he takes time to listen and to find out who she is and what she needs at a deeper spiritual level. What is *her* calling? What does she care most deeply about?

He is not aggressively, nor passive-aggressively trying to get something out of her. He derives pleasure from his support, challenge, and interaction in the service of her higher self. This just so happens to be a good way to turn a woman on, and not only romantically. In brief, the spiritually confident man does not try to win or conquer a woman, nor base his identity upon fulfilling her desires, but instead strives to find out and respect who she *is* at her most authentic.

The spiritually confident man then interacts upon this knowledge with curiosity, openness, humor, generosity, learning, attentiveness, enjoyment, and love. Again, he does not have to know everything or pretend he knows nothing. He is motivated by discovery. What are the things about his beloved that inspire, intrigue, or fascinate him? It may help you to pause right now and reflect how often and well a man does this with the women in his life, and to what degree women can receive this kind of opportunity in their relationships with men.

Again, this dynamic and reflection holds not just for romantic relationships, but also with co-workers, mothers, daughters, fathers, and sons. If you find yourself "playing an angle," or expecting something

from your own projected desire, whether this is sex or expecting someone to do your work for you, then you have some learning to do. If
you find yourself ceding your decisions to the other person in your
life, then you have some maturing and strengthening to do.

The spiritually confident man does not have all the answers, but he
is passionate about asking questions and pursuing possible answers, as
opposed to pursuing possible targets. He desires to share this journey
with a willing and interested co-explorer.

Spiritually confident maleness

The spiritually confident male retains and develops his masculine energy.
He is neither overly proud of it nor ashamed of it. He is neither a
testosterone-laced he-man nor an endlessly amenable "sensitive new
age guy." He realizes that women need character and fiber in a man
as well as openness. The spiritually confident man also realizes that he
desires a woman to retain and develop her feminine energy.

In spiritual terms, this understanding is about retaining and developing *polarity* between the sexes and genders.

> *The spiritually confident man embraces the
> healthy, constructive, and creative tension between
> maleness and femaleness, without ladening it with
> stereotypical opposition and "battle of the sexes" rhet-
> oric or tailing away toward to a generic androgyny.*

In this embrace, male and female dispositions absorb the wisdom and
energy of each other in a way that balances masculine and feminine
forces but also enhances, by contrast, the knowledge and expression
of what it means to be a man and a woman.

Spiritually confident men and women experience the best of both male and female worlds. Another way of saying this is that real men need real women, and real women need real men. This is true regardless of relationship type or sexual orientation. A spiritually confident man is, if not femin*ine*, thoroughly femin*ist*, in the sense of reliably and fiercely advocating for the empowerment of women.

> *To empower women is to enhance the spiritual confident man's masculinity by strengthening the polarity of feminine energy in his relationships.*

This is not a theoretical appreciation or commitment. It means that the spiritually confident man strives for the equality, dignity, and integrity of women in pay, power, respect, intimacy, decision-making, gratitude, love, and joy in the world.

The spiritually confident man also generously offers his masculine energy to the feminine energy of the woman or women in his life. He sees this not as a duty or an obligation but a high adventure, and a commitment to healthy challenge and possibility. He sees this giving as a way to become a better man.

In addition, the spiritually confident man is not worried about whether he "fails" or succeeds with a woman. He understands, as surely as he is born, that there are multitudes of classy and beautiful women that are simply not for him. He realizes that his particular relationship with a particular woman is about deepening connection, not "winning" a fight for her heart.

On what basis does a man usually fight for a woman? Most likely, he fights from his ego or some overweening sense of competition. This motivation comes from a small imagination geared toward a shallow and short-term end. One so motivated uses the woman and plays with her affections rather than respecting her desire to find a connection that honors her deeper needs. The spiritually confident man, on the other hand, complements rather than conquers.

> *The spiritually confident man also pro-actively welcomes and enjoys difference.*

If he is a heterosexual man, then gay men do not threaten him nor his masculinity. In fact, he sees friendship with men of differing gender and sexual orientations as an indispensable benefit. He realizes that to allow himself to be hemmed in by traditional notions of masculinity is to cede his vibrant manhood to a two-dimensional cartoon of himself.

The spiritually confident man is an engager who seeks learning, genius, and beauty in everything he meets, even the difficult and the ugly. That is what makes him an adventurer. That is what allows him to know who he is, even when he is not sure exactly where he is going or where life will take him.

Spiritually confident relationship

Two people interested in each other can be high-quality persons with shared beliefs, but for some reason, the spiritual or emotional chemistry does not work between them. Few people, however, let this insight come to the forefront of their consciousness, because they worry about being liked and not being rejected.

This is wasted energy.

> *We are not the center of the universe. We cannot choose for someone else or make them feel something for us. We can choose to recognize who we are on a deep level, express, and experiment with our spirits, and share that spirit with someone who has some desire and ability to resonate with us.*

A man's spiritual relationship confidence is not simply about waltzing into a room full of women (or other men if he is gay) and believing that he can get anyone he wants. If this is his motive, his decision is more likely based on superficial attributes and first impressions. Even if his eyes meet someone across a room and there is magic between him and that other person, this is no guarantee of a long-lasting, abiding life partnership.

> *A spiritually confident man does not want just **any** person, no matter how impressive his or her attributes, but one that is right for him.*

He is not looking for a good "catch" or to be considered a good catch, for this is simply a form of objectification. At a party, the spiritually confident heterosexual man is far more likely to follow his intuition and strike up a conversation with a smart, funny, original, cute, slightly nerdy, quirky, or punky female, than pursue a woman whose classic physical beauty and perfect grooming command attention. If he is fortunate, he may find a woman who is both beautiful and original in *his* eyes, who radiates a great attitude and carries a gleam of adventure in *her* eyes.

Bottom line: if a man succeeds in getting the most attractive woman, but there is no fit, then he has failed. The man takes home the prize of the most beautiful woman. The woman takes home the prize of the most financially successful man. The relationship becomes quickly contractual, not spiritual.

> *In a non-spiritually based attraction, a fateful precedent is set: "What can you do for me?" rather than "How can we learn from, support, and serve one another?"*

With this precedent, the man begins to feel roped in, and the woman learns to be valued for her exterior qualities. The man complains that his wife keeps running up the credit card. The woman complains that her husband keeps ogling other women. This is no big surprise, given the shallow and selfish basis of the relationship.

To ward off the disaster above, the spiritually confident man knows that his own deeper heart and spirit are his compass and comfort. "Opportunity" is not about "making a play for" or even "getting" this or that hottie. Opportunity is a kind of grace, opened when a man trusts his vulnerability and heart. This is not merely a naïve endeavor, though there is always an inextricable innocence and risk in this endeavor of the heart.

Opening to another, however, does *not* require giving your heart over to another person completely and immediately. It is about being honest and authentic and letting the conversation and actions in the relationship *show over time whether there is a growing fit between you and someone else.*

Spiritual confidence is neither desperate nor defensive. It is relaxed, poised, assured, open, and curious. It wants to know the truth. It wants to discover and explore. Spiritual confidence does not try to edit out uncomfortable or off-putting information but courageously brings these observations up for discussion. Spiritual confidence does not involve being a cheerleader for the other, nor a critic, but rather, rests on a desire to simply know and experience someone else on a real human level.

We humans live inside ourselves and come to know ourselves in relationships from the "between" spaces. Other people's choices cannot truly be ours unless we bring them inside ourselves in a way that meshes with our spiritual natures and authentically connects to theirs.

A self-respecting spiritual man wants to be evoked rather than ego-stroked in his relationship with a woman. For all the "nice men" who feel women have ignored them, what about the "nice women" that have been ignored by men? Is "niceness" itself a true quality or simply another play? Too often it is simply a personality stance in a dating game. Conversely, who wants to end up in a relationship with a high-maintenance supposedly "classy" woman? Pedestals are for statues, not for people.

Men and women are living, breathing, feeling, aspiring human beings, and yet, too often, we operate as tin gods, steel machines, and silicon computers. We allow ourselves to be programmed, rather than choosing to step into the chilly but invigorating waters of the infinitely creative spirit. This stepping out and into vulnerability, in strength, sensitivity, and touch must be the compact of the spiritually confident people in relationship.

Spiritually confident strength, sensitivity, and touch

The spiritually strong man does not seek his own advantage but is still willing to put his life on the line physically, mentally, and emotionally for that and for whom he cares. He senses the world around him with wonder and lets this wonder come through his body and his touch.

As a result, his touch and his presence are soothing, calming, healing, and reassuring. In love, he does not simply make a case for sex because he is feeling frisky or because he has had a long day at work. Instead, he sees physical intimacy in much more nuanced and giving ways, being just as disposed to offer a back rub and conversation as to make an overture around sex.

Strength

Strength, for the spiritually confident man, is assertive, not aggressive. Again, he is establishing his presence *in* the world, not dominance *over* the world. He may have adversaries but treats even his enemies with noble respect.

Because he respects his own spirit, he can generously extend this respect even to other men acting like jerks. He keeps his cool. He walks softly and carries a big stick. The spiritually confident man stands up for his spirit and himself. Thus, he knows he is an example and witness to dignity and grace and does not let himself get pulled down into the gutter or kicked around.

The courage of a spiritually confident man involves a certain creative daring. He is not content to rest on his laurels or his reputation. Nor does he consume himself with self-striving ambition. He seeks what can happen when he throws himself into the flow. He perks up at the prospect that his creative river might be filled with rapids. The spiritually confident man sees vulnerability itself as an important strength and razor-edge prerequisite of adventure.

He is willing to go beyond his imagination, and indeed his ability, to test himself in the larger universe. He knows he will be supported and find help in strange, unpredictable ways, and thus, he is not afraid to ask for help. He is an extreme athlete of the mind and heart, and occasionally the body. He seeks new levels of unfolding and intimacy. He is constant in his dedication to a larger truth.

Sensitivity

The strong spiritually confident man requires a high degree of sensitivity, for what besides sensitivity allows a man to wisely and appropriately apply his strength? If I try to impress a woman with a dangerous physical stunt, and irreparably harm myself, I will incapacitate myself in ways that I cannot take back. If I insult a woman, by aggressively and suggestively commenting on her body, I likewise can harm my relationship with her in a way that cannot be taken back.

A spiritually confident man, on the other hand, absorbs, observes, learns, listens, notices, empathizes, and exercises patience so that he may apply his strengths in experimental, meaningful, and productive ways. A spiritually confident man realizes that a woman may be a challenge, but she is not a task, an object, or a problem to be figured out. The sensitive, spiritual man takes up the woman's challenge by taking up the woman in strength. He lets his masculinity meet her femininity. He feels no need to posture. He desires to engage.

The sensitive spiritually confident man is not some stereotype of a scrawny, sexless "wet noodle." If he is vegan (like me), he does so to develop, rather than deny, his masculine polarity and power. Receptivity to the feminine is different than a desire to imitate a woman. Women want to be seen in their own right and beauty. Heterosexual women do not need a metrosexual competitor. They need men who can receive and complement their uniqueness and desires.

There is nothing that requires a spiritually confident man to be constantly in a charged relationship. There may be times in his life where he steps back, consolidates, and simply pursues friendship or solitude, taking time to reflect without the activities of the world.

Touch

Even non-spiritual persons can sense when a spiritually confident and competent man touches them. A vital energy radiates from his fingertips. This man's touch has an intense giving that invites release. He does not need to signal a demand with his touch, considering such a move as a betrayal of his generous intent.

A spiritually confident man is an affectionate man, communicating playfulness, tenderness, warmth, and firmness through the mutuality of touch. His hands do not grope a woman or exert that little extra pressure that turns a supportive pat into a power play. His hands are instead a generous extension of his heart. His fingertips are tendrils of discovery and delight, inquiry and wonder, open, firm, and responsive.

The spiritually confident man can give a good, open-ended back rub or foot rub. This massage will take as long as the conversation of skin to skin dictates. The spiritually confident man makes love not from technique or eager-beaver excitement, but from presence, absorbing the energies and signs of his intended. The spiritually confident man desires to meet in ways both new and familiar.

Spiritually confident authenticity

"To thine own self be true." The spiritually confident man is a truth-teller in his heart, in his soul, and in his life. There is nothing he is striving for that is greater than the truth and creative miracle of life he has already been given. Therefore, he does not lie to himself or others, nor does he dishonor this gift to sell out to something lower than the full manifestation of his life. The power of life frees the spiritually confident man from the fear of his inadequacy. Service of this miraculous life become his aim and his creed.

If the spiritually confident man does not know, he says, "I don't know, but I am curious to find out." He says this because he values his growth more than his vanity. He realizes he is a work in progress, rather than a legend in his own mind or an ambitious "project" for his wife to build. *He is neither a "man's man," a "ladies man," nor a sad sack.* He is his own man in order to give to others. He is a questing, fascinated male human ready to see the humor and serendipity in things.

The spiritually confident man admits when he is wrong without fuss or self-consciousness, *not* because he is without conviction or advocacy, but because he embodies humility in the service of higher truth.

> *The spiritually confident man realizes that there is always something greater and deeper than himself.*

He does not consider himself an idol, nor strive to be one. He is something so much more: a servant of the divine, a compassionate warrior for the spirit.

The spiritually confident man aspires to full vitality, which he knows is identical with full virility. The spiritual confident man's humility does not make him falsely modest or cause him to draw back from challenges. He relishes challenges as a way to hone and invite his expression of spirit. What is life, if not an opportunity to test his capability? What is life, if not a possibility to know what he has never known, feel what he has never felt, and experience what he has never experienced?

He knows this is not found with another affair with a toy mistress, or another line of cocaine, or some other pseudo-adventure. These are all examples of diminishment and compensation, rather than truly new frontiers. Every man, even the non-spiritually confident man, knows this in his heart. Real life and real manhood are forever found in creatively engaging a universe of infinite love and possibility.

Spiritually confident commitment

The spiritually confident man makes a commitment to himself to devote himself to his spirit, to humanity, to the universe, and to the special others in his life. This commitment involves an agreement to express himself and see others for who they truly are. A spiritually confident man, therefore, knows not to play with the affections of others, even as he enjoys the art of good-humored flirtation.

Flirtation does not have to be a shallow art. It can allow maleness and femaleness share themselves appreciatively whatever the sexual orientation of the people involved. Flirtation crosses over into affection when the dance of appreciation becomes a desire to explore and share with someone more profoundly and seriously. Men know the difference between flirtation and deepening affection if they allow themselves a moment of honest reflection.

A woman wants to be embraced for who she is. Her heart and who she is *at* heart are the same. The spiritually confident man desires to get at the heart of his relationship with a woman as a place of grace and wonder (and this goes for gay and straight men, alike). This tender heart space is a very vulnerable place for a man and a woman both, and here they make a compact, to tread lightly, patiently, and empathetically.

There is plenty of room for exploration, but no room for manipulation. Both parties have to be inside, honest and vulnerable, and not outside-pretending-to-be-inside. This may mean ultimately finding out that you two are not a fit as romantic partners or even as friends, but truth, again, is more important than pretense. A spiritually confident man does not want everyone to adore him. He is looking for those important few who "get" him to truly get him. He does not scatter himself to the four winds, but is one-pointed, even as he considers all directions.

This mutual, honoring, spiritual commitment to shared vulnerability and growth is *not* the same as agreeing to stay together forever in practical terms, as with a marriage agreement.

> *Spiritual commitment affirms that you will stay true to yourself and that you embrace the truth of another to the best of your ability.*

Spiritual commitment means you will be utterly honest in all phases of existence and relationship. When you don't know your feelings, or if you have feelings for another person developing, you let your life partner know. If you have worries, concerns, and insecurities, you share them with your life partner and count on their honest engagement. This will require courage and compassion from both people.

There is a Celtic phrase for this sacred agreement between spiritual life partners—"Anam Cara," "soul friend." This covenant recognizes that "you" are not "mine" in terms of possession but in terms of the heart. "'You are a child of the universe, created in love, to create in love. I shall do whatever 'I' can to advocate for your divine gift to the world, even if it means forsaking sexual opportunities, and even if it means blessing you in a life separate from mine.

This takes real courage and selflessness, an expanded mind and an expanded heart. Looking back on relationships, romantic and otherwise, most of us realize we are not likely to physically or geographically end up together with the people we court on this journey called life, but we can stay supportive in spirit. We are also bound by spiritual commitment to reconcile our relationships with our deeper vocation in the world.

> *Our dharma, the spiritual work in the world we are called to pursue, is not for everyone, even those we love and who love us.*

This is part of the bitter sweetness of life. There are more than a few times where a sweet, and otherwise perfect couple will break up because one of them cannot go where the other's dharma calls them.

There are no excuses for the spiritually confident man with his spiritual commitment. There are no "boys will be boys" clichés to legitimize disrespecting a relationship. If you desire to openly and freely explore the world of women (or other men if you are gay), then declare it, be aware with your heart and body (because it is riskier with both) and learn who you are by your *breadth* of experience. Allow who you are to be refined by *depth* of experience and know that, as breadth leads to depth in this learning, you will find yourself narrowing your choices until you likely arrive at one person with whom to share your innermost thoughts and feelings, and indeed life itself.

For the monk or nun, this other "person" may be the Divine itself, but for most of us, this takes on the form of a life partner. Just as unthinking, unbridled sexualism is not an option for the spiritually confident man, neither is the hard-heartedness of stoicism or cynicism. If he has a deep concern or feeling, the spiritually confident man feels compelled to share it. If he has a deep aspiration, no matter how nonsensical, he follows it to its root.

If he has a true desire or motivation, the spiritually confident man communicates it, reflects upon it, and decides to act upon it. The spiritually confident man knows that he may fail, but that, more importantly, he will learn, so that even his practical failures are spiritual growth successes. In fact, if the spiritually confident man succeeds too often, he knows he is not challenging and stretching himself enough.

Therefore, he almost purposely challenges himself to a level where he will fail. This gives him both humility and motivation to try harder or try differently. He relishes pushing his limits and asking for help in doing so from his spirit and the spirit of others. He relies on relationships and friends to accompany him. He breathes into those relationships, and he inhales something greater than himself. The spiritually confident man thus emerges as a warrior in service to the spirit and the world.

This spiritually confident ability to learn and grow does not come to a man overnight. Spiritual and emotional growth for a particular man are often obscured and erratic. To help clarify this journey, it is helpful to look at examples of what I call Emerging Men, who have met challenges imperfectly but pointedly. In the next chapter I will use the medium of film to talk about the spiritually confident growth males can make as they meet the challenges of life. Men do not have to embody or even arrive at the ideals I have laid out in this chapter, but they are invited to "get real," test their virtue and heart, and experiment with what works in the face of opportunities to grow.

CHAPTER 4

Cultivating The Fruit—The Emerging Man

I live on a small satsuma mandarin orange orchard in the Sierra foothills of California. It is surprising to those outside farming, how much is involved in cultivating and harvesting fruit from trees as an intentional activity—fertilizing, mulching, weeding, trimming, harvesting, storing, and even marketing if you want to sell your extra produce. Cultivation is co-creation, not simply consumption. Yes, you might have an apple tree on your property that you leave alone, and it bears fruit. You think, "Hey what a bonus; I don't have to do anything, and I get apples in the autumn." But the apples are fewer and less full than if you had cared for the tree.

Conscious cultivation of the fruit of healthy masculinity has a higher demand. It requires a deeper investment of energy to co-create bountiful, healthy fruit. More vibrant, future-directed, sustainable masculinity is not something you can consume from a store or an uncared-for tree. It is necessarily an outcome of hands-on care and learning. This learning can be quite thrilling, interesting, and rewarding, but it requires a respect for truth and a committed investment of the self. In this chapter, we look at both the hard-won lessons and grace-filled ways men learn to become higher men. We look at how men might grow into greater spiritual confidence.

The Power of Truth and Love

Guiding principle: Nothing, including masculinity, progresses or transforms without truth at its core. Nothing is worth transforming without love at its core.

It is an odd strength *and* weakness of male character that men are brazenly willing to challenge the heavens while remaining willfully ignorant of realities which confront them on earth. Too often men skip over the truths which lie in front of them in their desire to pursue a mercurial dream or dubious immortality in accomplishment, fame, or money.

> *What is needed for a new, more truthful and loving man to arrive? Nothing short of the very best of men.*

It is a grave misfortune that the global standard for "best" in men has been so far lowered that many are bewildered and lost. Many men simply abandon their responsibilities. Some spend their wives' money on alcohol, other women, and gambling. Still other men lash out against women or "society" to place responsibility for their "injustice" anywhere but where it belongs— on themselves.

A man *must* be truthful with himself and loving with others for him to *be* a man in its noble, transcendent sense. This is a fateful choice for any person. A man can choose a comfortable lie about himself to keep up his alleged self-esteem and identity, or he can trust himself at a more profound level and experience challenge, growth and merit to refine his character.

> *Today's successful Emerging Man uses his available inner resources to grow, rather than outer power to create empires.*

He listens and learns deeply from women, children, animals, spirit guides, and any source which can put him in touch with the inner spirit and outer world. He knows the growth happens where the inner infuses and empowers the outer. For his inner deepest to meet his outer best, he chooses to drop any pretense and commits to being consistently and honestly transparent.

In short, the Emerging Man is a champion of vibrant, clear life. What does this mean? This means that he is growing, learning, and exceeding his own self-imposed cage of expectation. This means he is transcending limits within his own experience and venturing beyond his own imagination. This means he surrenders restriction, perfection, and the arrogance that he is some kind of god over the heavens and apart from the earth. This means giving rather than taking, expanding rather than contracting, deepening rather than remaining superficial.

We are all too familiar with the examples of failed men. Their inappropriate sexual behavior, their unwillingness to admit their failures, their resistance to learning, and their stunted mentality only reinforce enlargement of their power over others. Where, however, are the tender, redemptive, inspiring, and instructive examples of manhood? How might we as men learn to transform from the ignoble to the noble, from the fallen to the redeemed? What does it take to become and grow beyond a spiritually confident man?

Confronting cultural myths about men, including the myths that men hold about themselves

What men think women want: The White Knight

In her talk on shame, emotion researcher Brene Brown related the story of a man who came up to her and confronted her about the fact that she had only interviewed women on the topic of shame.[1] He began to relate to her the pressures he felt from his wife and daughters to perform in a heroic way, and the shame produced when he did not:

> You say to reach out and tell our story and be vulnerable, but do you see those books you just signed for my wife and daughters?... They'd rather me die on top of my white horse than watch me fall down. When we (men) reach out and be vulnerable, we get the shit beat out of us, and don't tell me it's from the guys and the coaches and the dads, because the women in my life are harder on me than anyone else. [2]

Being a researcher and a woman *outside* male experience, Brene Brown largely took this guy's challenge to heart as both true and tragic. However, to me, as a male *inside* male experience, this man's assessment struck me as intensely false. I do not doubt, this particular man honestly *felt* besieged. I do not doubt this is how many men feel. But does that feeling have its basis in the real situation and people men face? Would this man's own daughters actually prefer to see him die on a white horse than fall down? No, of course not. And do the women in his life really

---

1   https://www.youtube.com/watch?v=psN1DORYYV0
2   https://www.youtube.com/watch?v=psN1DORYYV0

have sufficient power to enforce their "white knight" expectations on him even if they held them? No, they do not.

What this man and other men are feeling may be real, but the sources and expectations of his feelings are misattributed. It is men in a patriarchal society, not women, who mainly originate, perpetuate, and adopt the stereotype of the white knight, the tycoon, the invulnerable world beater. One can observe evidence of this over and over again in the military, in school, in business, in advertisements and in nearly every social and cultural arena.

> *This "white knight" stereotype becomes accepted as social reality by sheer repetition, not by truth.*

What was at first a collective idealized *projection* by men as an expression of their power becomes *accepted and reflected* by women and girls and becomes, in turn, a social *pressure* upon men. Basically, it is an emotional boomerang returning to its launcher.

Yes, a particular woman may attach her own untruth to a man, insisting he be something that is inauthentic to his character. Women are not immune to delusion. However, a man does not have to choose to kowtow to this "white knight" image or any image a woman or another man may hold for him. If he does he is "locked into the lie" with significant others and he merely reinforces it. When a woman is security-driven, she often *will* place pressure on a man to be the hero. This can happen even if she has the main bread-winning job and the man is raising the kids.

One should ask, *why* is she disposed to hold this untruth? In many cases, it is simply subconscious historical inertia, the collective trauma and imprinting of women generated by thousands of years of patriarchal rule reinforcing women's economic and social dependence on men. A woman's survival has been, for a very long time, dependent upon not only allying with but *cultivating* a reliable male. This habit does not change overnight, and it is really equally up to men to break with *their* patriarchal past to break the hold of this dysfunctional arrangement. One of the best ways they can do that is to take responsibility, stop reinforcing dependence, and actually listen and learn from women, rather than projecting upon women patriarchal insecurities and fears.

What women actually want: The Vulnerable and Resilient Committer

As a man, I tire quickly of the various versions of men's whining and angst over women. Women are far less mysterious than men romanticize. The main problem is that men simply do not listen and learn from women. Therefore, very few of men's complaints about women are rooted in truth. Most often these complaints are self-serving, including this perennial gripe: "If women really want nice men like me, then why do they always go for the assholes." Well, what woman *would* want a passive, entitled, pseudo-sensitive "wet noodle" of a nice guy who does not take the initiative and thinks he should be adored simply because he thinks he is a great guy? Passiveness is not sexy. Neither is jerkishness. There are more options for manhood besides asshole and kiss-ass.

> *What women want more than either a glittery white knight or some guy who can't stay on his horse is a guy who falls at times and **gets back up** to try again.*

Such a man *commits* to a decisive action and then sustains his initiative past short-term results. This happens whether he be involved in a marriage, a friendship, a business enterprise, or a new hobby. In short, a woman wants a man who generates thoughtful action, tries his best, falls, gets back up, and listens and learns from his own failures, successes, and from the women in his life.

If you want to know what women actually want, turn to what women are watching. Women are watching the Starz channel series *Outlander*, a historical drama that involves a woman surgeon from the 20th century traveling through time and space to be with her soul mate, an intense and complex man from 17th century Scotland. I watch this series with my wife, Regina, and we discuss the iconic male lead character, Jamie, as well as his relationship with his lady love, Claire. This is somewhat excruciating research at times because I find the pace of the story somewhat slow and the tenor a bit melodramatic for my taste, but I do find reward in what the series reveals about women's views of ideal men. In addition, there are potent insights in this series about what it means to be a man alone as well as evocative themes that highlight recurring issues between men and women.

Part of the reason why Jamie can powerfully be what he can be is because Claire stands in her power too. The series shows that a powerful man can admire and appreciate a powerful woman. Neither is perfect. Jamie runs a bootlegging operation to fund his political rebellion and lies about his relationships with other women. Claire exhibits jealousy, fatalism, and overreaction. Yet both still stand up in courage and vulnerability to live a committed life of principle, passion, care, contribution, and skill. Claire has commitments as a healer and a mother. She has made her own sacrifices, which sometimes go unappreciated by Jamie, and Jamie has made his sacrifices as a soldier and rebel, which are not appreciated by Claire. However, it is the emotional honesty and mutual stepping up to risk between them that keeps their relationship strong and growing.

In *Outlander* Jamie experiences a good share of trauma, trial, and crushing humiliation. He is raped by another man. He is forced into hiding and into prison. He is left broken, grieving, and dissolute. He must live without Claire for some twenty years as she travels back to the future. But through it all and amid his own imperfection, Jamie remains resilient and open to his own growth. He remains strong *enough* to weather extreme tides of misfortune and trauma to come back to life and to be reborn essentially as a new man each time he does.

Why do women find *Outlander*'s Jamie so appealing? He demonstrates integrity, vulnerability, resilience, and a real desire that comes at a cost. Jamie's love for Claire has gravity. Jamie experiences isolation (as with many male roles) but he strives for connection. It is this alternation between challenge and triumph, between being down and getting up, that makes him a compelling figure not only for women but for men as well. This ability to bounce back is the real test of a man's strength, not cardboard machismo or fey sensitivity.

When Jamie was asked by Claire why he lied to her about another woman, he gives a straight-up, emotionally honest and intelligent answer: "Because I am a coward; I was afraid of losing you." How many guys do you know who would make that admission instead of making excuses and getting defensive? Now we begin to really get what women want: A man who gets real with himself, shares himself lovingly and honestly with her, and recognizes rather than denies his wrongdoing. He is a man who has integrity, and even amid his trials strives to embody the truth.

What men think other men want: The Heroic Loner

When I was doing research for this book, I came across a blog with a post about men in cinema written by Jeremy Van Wert, a therapist specializing in developing healthy masculinity.[3] His blog had some very surprising and even counterintuitive observations about how ideal male characters are depicted in movies. Far from depicting men as irretrievable goofballs *or* as wise men, the most commonly depicted characteristics of men in movies were those of integrity/trustworthiness and isolation. This may seem like an odd combination, but if you look more closely, it makes sense.

> *Integrity is what a noble man aspires to, and isolation is what he feels.*

Both of these can fuel his desire for truth. These attributes exist at the core of male experience and pull at him from both ends. Men *do* want to have integrity and be considered trustworthy (which are necessarily connected to community and relationships), but they also feel like they are "going it alone" in a world of rugged male self-sufficiency.

 (W)hat does this say about manhood? Well, that people love honesty in a man, we find it so appealing and engaging. A man has innate power in his presence. When that power hinges upon the common use of honesty and integrity, we feel instantly drawn in. When that power is shifty, untrustworthy, unkind, or unwilling to make a stand, we're less likely to feel intrigued or drawn to a man.

 Somewhere along the way the archetype of the isolated male crushed the learned ability of men to make and keep close friends. Vulnerability, the admission of faults, and men supporting other men in crisis became almost feminine. How many men do you know (that) have strong friendships they call upon in times of loneliness or need? How many men do you know (that) actually admit to needing help or feeling lonely? [4]

Men are still being trained by film and by other media to be heroic loners. The bombastic iconic leads like Bruce Willis's character from *Die Hard* or the stoic, brooding Batman played by Christian Bale send the same message: "No one really understands me. I've just got to 'man up' and do what I can to save the world alone." This suspicion of the world is an extension of the John Wayne era of "Don't touch my woman, don't take my guns, and don't steal my horses." Dirty Harry, the iconic detective played by Clint Eastwood has few to any connections to other women and men and is definitely *not* to be messed with. When relationships between men are brought up in movies, they tend to be portrayed as superficial and humorous. Men are sidekicks or pals out for a good time.

> *This isolation seems to be a response to male conditioning, not female demands.*

---

4   Van Wert, 2013 http://consciouslymasculine.com/blog/2013/4/8/men-in-the-movies-a-case-study-of-masculinity-in-popular-films

Women I know never romanticize the isolated male. Quite the contrary, they long for the connected male. So where does this isolationist type come from? Is it that men fear or have experienced violation by other men and thus long for self-sufficiency and isolation? Is it a reaction to men's internalized obligatory sense of responsibility to women and children which has no room for their own aspiration? I am not absolutely sure, but there seems to be a connection between how men are portrayed in films and how they learn to view themselves.

What men actually want: The Connected Adventurer and Learner

 So many men I encounter are thirsting for friendship. I have friends tell me, "You're the only person who reaches out to me. I don't have any other male friends I keep in touch with." It seems to have become a unique characteristic among males to keep a friendship kindled. How many of your male friends reach out to you just to see how you're doing? My guess is, probably not many. [5]

Men, at their best, want a chance to emerge in their own authenticity and uniqueness and share that journey with others. They do not want to be left alone. It is my experience that men usually pursue isolation (as opposed to healthy solitude) to protect themselves from competition from other men, to escape the perceived demands of women, or to provide a space to feel themselves and exercise their imaginations after being swamped by life demands.

---

5   Van Wert, 2013 "Men in the Movies"

Many men I know feel that sincere, consistent connection is unreachable because of how they have structured their lives. They incur felt expectations from others, and often place unreasonable expectations upon themselves. All too many men spend most of their existences living out some combination of socially prescribed roles. It is a rare man that is able to consciously take on his original transformation from boy to man, from ignorant to wiser, and ignoble to noble.

> *The ways men have been taught to gain value, especially in an industrial, patriarchal (male-ruled) society, militate against transformation and connection.*

Patriarchal conditioning teaches men to "already know" before they have learned, to proclaim before they have listened, to lead before they have developed the requisite leadership characteristics, and to control others rather than to listen to and support them. Clearly, these motivations and implicit training can never be the basis for healthy connection.

Conversely, there is a certain precocious joy that can come when a man decides to abandon his patriarchal privilege, or better yet, use his privilege to subvert oppressive relationships and empower those who have been kept down. It is a true Emerging Man that voluntarily and whole-heartedly *gives up* his conceits and images of himself in the service of a higher spiritual vision and his deeper divine genius. This man realizes that the present system works against him and others. It denies him his own feelings and faith, and it denies others opportunities to share their deeper joys and talents by forcing them into subservience.

Therefore, emerging men are being invited right now to confront their patriarchal training in the name of a higher connected integrity and to look toward examples of resistance, rebirth, and redemption. In this process, men are encouraged *not so much to fight or conquer selfishness, but to allow themselves to be freed from it by a certain conversion and grace of the heart, by deeper care and empathy that melts his shell of isolation and callousness and exposes his warmth and generosity.* This is not a touchy-feeling task but a challenging process requiring every bit of courage, strength, and moral fiber a man can muster. To be vulnerable, responsible, and faithful at the same time is not for the faint of heart.

A Man Reborn: The Emerging Man in Film

Films don't simply program men to be heroic loners. There are many wonderfully made films that speak directly to this powerful, latent potential in men to be mature, magnanimous, and marvelous. Cinema can show all of us through art made real, how men can be noble, how men can become nobler, and how men can break through the shells of their conditioning or the prison of their circumstances. Therefore, I have chosen in this section to take inspiring, educative, and positive cinematic examples and link them to the real lives, real examples, and the real world of men.

I have chosen to show how the forms of manhood I discussed in Chapter 2, the Animal Men, the Social Men, and the Co-Creative Men in their regressed, transitional, and evolved forms play themselves out in film and in the world. This provides as an entry point into a more powerful engagement with the challenges men face and the ennobling and emerging qualities men might develop.

Why am I choosing film to talk about developing healthy masculinity? Developing a more evolved male identity is an emotional, social, and experiential proposition. I have found as an educator that no real learning happens around unconscious gender habits unless a person *feels* it deeply, *shares* that feeling, and then *rehearses* a positive alternative to their present identity.

> *Mere intellectual learning will not and does not cut it. Such learning stays in the mind. Effective learning and real conversion are felt in the body and the heart.*

There is something about films that gets behind the filters of men and goes to the body and heart. Also, men can go to movies alone or with maybe one other person and still have a *common* experience that they can discuss with others. The larger-than-life experience of being in a dark theater with a big screen (or less powerfully on a smaller TV screen), allows men and boys to become emotionally *involved*, and open and empathize with a character. This creates an "end run" around stoic male training. Film amplifies and etches experience on male being.

In fact, I have noticed that all profound learning is experiential. One has to directly take on what one is learning, experiment, role-play, or be deeply affected by a story. A good movie, fiction novel, or even music can be much truer and more moving than the most rigorously tested research in psychology. As humans, that is just the way we "roll." By providing "lived" examples of culturally common experiences (or giving men an opportunity to experience these films if they have not watched them) we are given a *conscious* chance to understand what is at stake and a hope and demonstration of possible positive changes.

Obviously, the analysis of movies below will involve "spoilers," because they get at the arc of the development of the male character as well as the arc of the story, but I think it is worthwhile it to give away the plot so that you can pay attention to the development of the male identity as you watch the film over again or for the first time.

Redeeming the Animal Man

8 Mile: Emerging from impulse to discipline, from failure to triumph, from reaction to self-determination [6]

One of the most compelling, instructive, and redemptive portraits of Animal Man masculinity comes in the form of *8 Mile*, a movie starring the rapper Eminem based heavily on his own life. From the get-go Jimmy (the character played by Eminem) has certain cards stacked against him: He is a white working-class man living in a trailer park with an alcoholic mother and her abusive boyfriend on the border separating black urban culture from white suburban culture near Detroit, Michigan. He is trying to make it as a white rapper in a predominantly African-American dominated field. Although talented, he lacks self-confidence, and in his first real test in the movie, a rap battle, he freezes up and humiliates himself publicly.

At first, Jimmy is highly reactive. He seems a slave to his own emotional reactions and the bad decisions of others. He does not have a grip on his own sovereignty and self-determination. He gets into brawls with rival rappers and resents his friend Wink for promoting his rivals. Yet he improves his attitude and work ethic to the point where he is granted extra hours at a car factory, and he strikes up a romantic relationship with a woman, Alex, after she became impressed with him for defending a gay co-worker against a mean-spirited fellow employee. We see the boy becoming "man" enough to become responsible at work

---

6   https://en.wikipedia.org/wiki/8_Mile_(film)

and fight against injustice in his own way.

In the climax to the story, Jimmy engages the leader of his rivals, Papa Doc, in a public rap battle and bests him, teaching Papa Doc humility, and gaining a merited sense of self-esteem, which he directs surprisingly toward committing himself toward a responsible job and his own path rather than trying to be the next big rap star. A redeemed Striving Man, like Jimmy, has something to prove to himself and not to others. He now can make choices from a sense of sovereignty over his life, rather than being compelled by competition to thrust himself above others. The motivation he holds and the growth he pursues have an intrinsic foundation versus an extrinsic one.

Wall Street: Emerging from predation to principle, from greed to generosity, from selfishness to responsibility [7]

The Oliver Stone written and directed movie, *Wall Street*, has two very clear portrayals of the Toxic Man and the Striving Man. The Toxic Man, Gordon Gekko, played by Michael Douglas, proudly and famously proclaims, "Greed is good." This is a reflection of his pernicious toxic business ethic of cannibalizing productive companies through "corporate raiding," firing the workers and making off with the loot. His pupil is an ambitious young Striving Man, a junior stockbroker called Bud Fox, played by Charlie Sheen.

Gekko essentially grooms Bud to accept corrosive notions of manly risk and courage as having the "balls" to cut corners and skate along the border of the law. Bud allows himself to be taken into this scheme of masculinity and soon finds himself insider trading for Gekko to win his approval and to gain an advantage in market trading. As Bud

---

7   https://en.wikipedia.org/wiki/Wall_Street_(1987_film)

is led down the primrose path of moral, ethical, and legal corruption, he becomes more involved, spying on a rival company and setting up straw buyers for potential deals. He gets pulled into all the materialistic temptations and markers of success: a penthouse, a corner office, a beautiful "trophy" girlfriend.

Bud does not wake up until a corporate restructuring deal he brokers to access the overfunded pension in his father's company, Bluestar Airlines, is betrayed by Gekko. Gekko moves to make even more money by firing all the employees and savaging the company. In typical Hollywood fashion, Bud devises a switcheroo and colludes with Gekko's rival to manipulate Bluestar's stock, save the company, and ruin Gekko. However, instead of emerging the hero, Bud's Striving Man past catches up with him, and he gets convicted for insider trading. However, he is able to live with a clear conscience by turning state's evidence to take down a Toxic Man, stick up for the "little guy," and demonstrate sacrifice and truthfulness. In the end, Bud grew into the evolved form of the Animal Man, the Responsible Man, learning to place principle over ambition and others before himself.

Dallas Buyers Club: Emerging from prejudice to compassion, from self-concern to service, from opportunism to advocacy [8]

Fear of death can bring out the deepest survival instincts of the Animal Man. However, the man who learns to rise above this fear is ushered into a new life and a new level of awareness, depth, and compassion. Ron Woodroof, the main character in *Dallas Buyers Club*, played by Matthew McConaughey, is just such a man. He's a Texas good-ole-boy, an electrician, a rodeo cowboy, and a drug-user who is diagnosed with

---

8   https://en.wikipedia.org/wiki/Dallas_Buyers_Club

AIDS. Woodroof starts out in denial. He is abandoned by family and friends who think he is gay. He bribes a hospital worker to get him the experimental drug AZT, only to find it makes his health far worse.

In desperation, he goes to Mexico. An alternative medicine practitioner there helps him secure different and more effective experimental drugs, ddC and Peptide T. At first, Woodroof sees this fortunate turn simply as an opportunity to make money. He conquers his own initial prejudices to team up with a trans woman, Rayon (played by Jared Leto), who brings in clients for his new drugs. The two form the Dallas Buyers Club and become not only business partners but friends. Of course, the medical establishment gets wind of their profitable enterprise and tries to block it, even though their own drug, AZT, does not appear to work.

Woodroof becomes more radicalized, now understanding that healing is not the primary driver of AZT trials or the medical establishment but profits. His concern shifts from making money to providing the drugs for healing. When the medical establishment uses the FDA and law enforcement to prevent access to the alternative drugs, Woodroof sues them. However, even with a sympathetic judge, he is prevented from distributing the drugs because the FDA automatically made any drug it did not approve illegal.

Ron Woodroof lived seven years longer than his initial prognosis indicated. That may not have just come from the drug but from the power of his own human spirit giving him something higher and larger to live for. This story is instructive for men because it shows how *shared* suffering helps to generate truth and transformation. How else could a low-consciousness party boy develop a conscience and a purpose for living? In this story, men are opened and thawed by life challenges, rather than remaining stoically resistant to them.

Thor: Ragnarok: **Emerging from egoism to altruism, from self-preservation to protection of others, from materialism to principled purpose** [9]

The popular superhero film, *Thor: Ragnarok,* demonstrates the classic Animal Man anti-hero who makes the journey from a preening, self-involved, materialistic jerk, to a Responsible Man who is willing to sacrifice his very life to protect the lives of others. The movie opens up in Asgard (the mythological Norse heaven) with the anti-hero, Skurge, trying to impress a couple of beautiful maidens with the collection of weapons he stole from various dimensions. He gladly serves Loki, an impostor who duped the citizens of Asgard into believing he was Odin, their king. To spare his own life, Skurge agrees to be the executioner of innocent citizens who do not obey the evil Hela, an entity who conquers Asgard and insists others bow to her.

It would be hard to portray a man more craven than Skurge, a man only out for himself and his own survival. He will do anything it takes to stay alive, move up, and seize whatever power he can find. He starts out as an extreme Toxic Man with elements of an ambitious Striving Man. Skurge is also a coward and an opportunist. When the fight turns against Hela, and the people are fleeing, he disguises himself and boards a ship leaving Asgard.

It is only when Hela traps the ship and sends her minions to kill the people on board that Skurge finally has his moment of courage and truth. In one final spree before he is destroyed, Skurge leaps to protect the people, free the transport, and mow down the evil-doers with the two machine guns he stole from Earth. He is a Toxic Man and a Striving Man redeemed as a sacrificial Responsible Man.

---

9   https://www.cbr.com/thor-ragnarok-skurge-iconic-scene-walter-simonson/

There is something intensely satisfying and inspiring about witnessing the transformation and redemption of a man from a degenerate waste of flesh to one who makes his life count by exercising manly courage and care for others. You see this in Jackie Chan's character in *Drunken Master*, in Jean Reno's character in *The Professional*, in Edward Norton's character in *American X*, and in Bruce Willis's character in *The Fifth Element*.

In each case a man who was clueless, self-involved, or immature, a man who makes bad decision after bad decision through character weakness, a man who indulges in racism, sexism, cynicism, laziness, selfishness, and greed, who does pretty much everything wrong, still gets up, comes to his higher self, and eventually does the right thing. Sometimes he does this reluctantly, even against his own habits and wishes, *but he does it anyway*. Some element of the human spirit arises; some form of love, principle, coming to terms, inspiration, breaks him open and helps him change his ways.

Maturing the Social Man

Moonlight: Emerging from alienation to intimacy, from hardness to vulnerability, from living a lie to living one's truth [10]

One of the most potent and powerful films in the last decade about masculine formation is the 2016 Academy Award winner for Best Motion Picture, *Moonlight*. This film starkly portrays the acute tensions between hard-heartedness and intimacy in growing from a boy into a man. The film also powerfully renders the clash between the worlds

---

10   https://en.wikipedia.org/wiki/Moonlight_(2016_film)

of respect based on physical power and love based on vulnerability within a distraught African-American community.

The film was shot in three parts, each part poignantly representing the main character's maturation as a Social Man. In the first part, the main character, Chiron, represents a boyhood equivalent of the Retreating Man nicknamed, appropriately, "Little." Little is a withdrawn child, living with a drug-addicted mother, Paula, and hiding from bullies. He appears to others to be homosexual, drawing epithets such as "faggot."

In this part, "Little" strikes up an unlikely relationship with Juan, a drug-dealer with a sense of compassion, who teaches him to swim, to be okay with his sexual orientation, to make responsible choices in his life, and to stand up for himself. I was touched by the vulnerability and uncertainty of Little. He seemed to represent the boy in every man, trying to be himself and live his truth, feel himself, and protect his deeper self, while being battered by a warped patriarchal system, which strives to callous his sensitivity and drive him into submission.

In the second part, Chiron is an adolescent mirror of the Confused Man. He is still avoiding a bully named Terrel, but he has developed a close friendship with another teenager named Kevin. One night Kevin visits Chiron to have a heart-to-heart conversation about their futures on the beach near where he lives. They smoke some pot, and Kevin ends up kissing Chiron and masturbating him. This closeness does not prevent Kevin from being pulled into a hazing ritual the very next day led by the bully, Terrel. Caving to peer pressure, Kevin punches Chiron and watches him being beaten up by other bullies. Chiron strikes back by breaking a chair over the body of Terrel and getting taken out by the police.

Again, we see this male push-and-pull between close and intimate private friendship and the necessity of maintaining a "cool" and dominating public face. We also see the seething anger of many boys and men to strike back against the perpetrators of the violently sexist and homophobic status quo, and the consequences of doing so. The innocent gets sent to the prison house, while the victimizers go free. This is an evocative reminder of the need for men and boys to stand up for the truth and one another's dignity in the face of a bullying system.

In the third part of the film, Chiron is a muscled adult drug dealer in Atlanta nicknamed "Black" coming to know himself as an Equal Man. After a long absence, "Black" finally visits his mother, Paula, in a drug treatment center, and begins the process toward reconciling his bitter feelings toward her. She, in turn, apologizes for not being there for him and not loving him as a mother should. Chiron/Black initiates contact with his friend Kevin from his teenage years and visits him in Miami. Chiron learns Kevin has fathered a son with a former girlfriend and is now living by himself and working at a diner. Chiron reveals to Kevin that he was never able to be intimate with anyone else after his adolescent sexual experience with Kevin. They embrace, and the film ends with the implication that they will renew their relationship.

The inherent difficulties of two black men starting a relationship arise against the backdrop of not only ethnic homophobia but sexism. Male homosexual relationships in black society are often conducted on the "down low," because, to many, they connote feminization and emasculation of black men, a stinging and lingering legacy of slavery. However, this view of submission and sensitivity as "female" is itself a sexist prejudice.

Sensitivity and willingness to be humbled to love are not the enemies nor the cause of suffering. The enemy of an Equal Man (or any man) is violence against his authentic person and against his genuine feeling for another. It is incumbent upon men to claim their new power in a masculine sensitivity which is both powerful and truthful. This is a lesson for all men, gay or straight: Do not let callousness triumph. Exhibit the courage to openly share affection, including affection for other men.

Back to School: Emerging from superficiality to depth, from hedonism to commitment, from ignorance to knowledge [11]
Switching gears, one finds a hilarious portrayal of the Retreating Man coming to terms with his immaturity in the Rodney Dangerfield comedy, *Back to School*. In this movie, Dangerfield portrays Thornton Melon, a mega-successful businessman who sells "tall and fat" clothing for men, but who never completed high school. Thorton is a bon vivant who seems to enjoy his life but remembers his father's admonition that if he hasn't gotten an education, he's got nothing.

Thornton's son, Jason, is struggling with his university schooling and is planning to drop out. Dad, Thornton, convinces his son to stay in by agreeing to go to college with him. Of course, much hilarity ensues in this contrasting comedy of manners between a savvy, street-wise businessman and the stuffy, ivory tower academics. Thornton is initially an adolescent-minded partier and must learn to become a serious student. By contrast, his son, Jason, has to learn how to be more relaxed and confident and *less* serious.

What I found so compelling about this film is that Thornton really appears to be doing his best to be a dad and a responsible (if spontaneous) man. He demonstrates genuine concern for his son and attempts to give his son all the things he never had growing up, but he just

11   https://en.wikipedia.org/wiki/Back_to_School

doesn't know how to do it appropriately. Also, he, like many Retreating Men, pretends to know "what's real," tries to laugh off challenges, and attempts to hide some of his own insecurities and doubts about his manhood behind his attempts to be popular. Yet his love for his son, and his growing romantic interest in a female literature professor, Diane, give him the impetus to stretch himself beyond his own comfort zone.

Thornton finds himself finally growing up at an advanced age, studying intensively for, and eventually passing a comprehensive oral examination to avoid being expelled from school for paying other people to do his schoolwork for him. (In one of the most hilarious scenes, Thornton pays the actual author, Kurt Vonnegut, to write a paper on Kurt Vonnegut, which is flunked by Diane with the commentary that the ghostwriter of the paper doesn't know the first thing about Vonnegut).

This movie, in rollicking form, still manages to depict the bittersweet, tragicomic edge to contemporary masculinity. Men are in this bind, where they are taught to pretend to know before they have learned, where strength means not admitting weakness, and where worth is measured by the slap-on-the-back admiration of others. This non-reflective stance leaves little to no room for actual honest engagement of feelings, of aspirations, of nobler qualities to say nothing of listening and learning.

This kind of man is trying so hard to outshine others, create a splash, or leave a legacy that he forgets to live into and develop himself earnestly. It is only when something more important than his own pretensions calls to him that he makes the shift to mature manhood. For the Retreating Man, the trick seems to be: Find those "more important" people, challenges, and vocations and let them call you to a higher way of being.

Good Will Hunting: Emerging from defensiveness to sensitivity, from arrogance to respect, from self-certitude to growth [12]

The main character of *Good Will Hunting*, Will, is a Confused Man. The contradictions of his character (played by Matt Damon) lead him toward so many conflicting future paths that he uses his prodigious intelligence and sarcasm to cover up his paralysis over important choices. Will is a math genius who hides his gifts behind troubles with the law and a lowly job as a janitor at the Massachusetts Institute of Technology in Cambridge, Massachusetts.

He is the picture of a vulnerable man with great potential, falling back on his rough-and-tumble upbringing and "macho" notions of manhood to stave off confronting his higher destiny as a human being. Will is finally exposed when he is caught by an MIT math professor, Gerald Lambeau, solving an extremely difficult math problem on the bulletin board in a hall that Will is cleaning. This leads to Lambeau's desire to exploit Will's math genius and Will's desire to resist and "not sell out" but also avoid the responsibility of using his gift.

In the typical self-sabotage of a confused man, Will gets into a fight to avoid having to face his issues. Lambeau arranges for Will to work on math and get therapy in lieu of jail time. Will belittles the initial therapists with his quick mind and seems to have only contempt for invitations to develop deeper self-reflection, until he meets Dr. Sean Maguire, played by Robin Williams. A skilled mentor, Sean calls Will on his bullshit and invites him to be more honest with his feelings, at the same time revealing his own vulnerability as an emotionally shattered widower whose wife died of cancer.

---

12   https://en.wikipedia.org/wiki/Good_Will_Hunting

In an achingly affecting scene, Sean recounts to Will how he gave up a World Series ticket to be with his future wife, how deeply he loved her, and how he suffered no regrets in the relationship even after losing her to death. As their relationship deepens, and Will and Sean open up to each other (as a positive example of mutual growth between men), they help each other open to and contend with their respective emotional frailties. This helps Will to date a smart and attractive woman, Skylar, beyond the lowly station implied by his upbringing.

However, old habits and past patterns die hard. Growing into mature manhood is not easy for Will, especially as he is being invited to leave behind the familiar, including his gang of friends from South Boston. Will and his mentor, Sean, reveal to each other that they were both victims of child abuse. This abuse disables both of them in important ways—for Will, past abuse creates difficulties around committing to a romantic relationship and a responsible job utilizing his gifts, and for Sean, past abuse hampers his ability to live and love again after the death of his wife.

Sean helps Will accept that the abuse he received in childhood was not his fault and Will breaks open emotionally. Both men grow into new paths with Will accepting a mathematics job and Sean deciding to travel the world. Will later decides his relationship with Skylar is more important and forgoes the job to drive out to the West Coast to renew his relationship with Skylar (ostensibly also finding another job matching his talent). He leaves behind his friends and charts a new and confident course, liberated from the bindings of his habits and insecurities.

It is this theme of liberation and consolidation that allows the Confused Man to emerge as an Equal Man. In doing so, the newly-emerged Equal Man grows into a new purpose and adopts a new basis for self-esteem. He leaves behind boyish dares, isolation, and past programming. New adventure comes in embracing mature commitment and mutual relationship rather than simply following his own whims. This can be hard psychologically for the Confused Man-boy. He *does* have to give something up of himself to grow into something new.

Many a woman has shaken her head in bewilderment at the tattered tee-shirt her husband or boyfriend holds on to for nostalgic reasons. You can make a similar analogy for the Confused Man holding on to old male relationships that have gone past their due date and comforting habits that no longer serve growth. There is a nostalgic bitter sweetness in a man that can hold back growth, and a man must decide to let go and step forward.

I Love You, Man: Emerging from isolation to connection, from woman-centeredness to guy-relatedness, from predictability to improvisation [13]

I Love You, Man, deals with a very common and central problem of heterosexual men who have healthy and mutually-respectful relationships with the important women in their lives: They have no deep, lasting, or regular relationship with other men. (Perhaps, a comedy could be made which does the switch for a gay man who does not have significant female relationships!)

The main character, Peter Klaven, played by Paul Rudd, is an everyman and a good example of an Equal Man, who is good to his fiancé, Zooey, and has a responsible job as a realtor. One can certainly imagine him being a good husband and dad, sharing in household chores and childrearing. He is open and sincere, but he lacks initiative

---

13   https://en.wikipedia.org/wiki/I_Love_You,_Man

and closeness in his relationships with other men. He is isolated not, as with Will Hunting, because of his fear of connection, but because of his unintentional habits which do not make having a "guy-friend" a priority.

Typical of an Equal Man, he begins searching for a guy-buddy only when he overhears Zooey's women friends expressing concerns about his lack of male friends. Peter also realizes that *maybe* he is relying a little too much on his fiancé to have his needs met. The film then displays Peter's comedic failures to meet up with the right guy, complete with embarrassing gaffes, until Peter happens upon Sydney Fife. Sydney is that kind of hip, irresponsible friend that appeals to the boy in Peter. He has no problem picking up free food and available women with equal alacrity. So taken is Peter, that he impulsively loans Sydney 8,000 dollars.

Sydney asks Peter why he is getting married, and Peter does not have a good answer. When Peter shares this exchange with his fiancé, Zooey, she gets hurt and angry, which only accentuates her suspicions of Sydney. To make matters more turbulent, Sydney uses the 8,000 dollars lent to him to post outrageous ads on billboards, promoting Peter's realty business from pictures he took of Peter on an iPhone. This embarrasses Peter, causing estrangement between him and Sydney. However, because *I Love You, Man* is a feel-good movie, Peter reconciles with Zooey, and Zooey (seeing how down Peter looks) invites Sydney to the wedding as the best man, and they all end up singing a song by their favorite band, *Rush*.

This film adroitly raises the possibility that an Equal Man can lose a significant chunk of that desirable masculine "oomph." So committed is the Equal Man to family and girlfriend/fiancé/wife, that he often loses himself to his roles and relationships and fails to maintain a certain personal manly *fire*. Obscured behind his attention to others is the question, "What am I passionate about?" Importantly, the answer to this question not only creates a good basis upon which to revive personal masculine enthusiasm *but also to create meaningful, lasting connections with other men.*

Men do well to share their dreams and help each other attain those dreams. When my friend, Dexter, and I met for writing jam sessions to discuss and support each other in the books we were authoring, we learned a lot about each other *and* learned to appreciate the masculine aspects in ourselves as well. Men don't just need to *do things* with each other (though this is helpful too), but also *be* with each other, including being real about aspirations and helping each other develop those aspirations. This is an improvisational move, a co-creative act. The Equal Man is invited to grow into the Co-Creative Man.

Reviving the Co-Creative Man

Finding Forrester: Emerging from defensiveness to embrace, from defeatism to renewal, from pessimism to hope [14]

The title of this film has a double meaning. William Forrester, the main character in *Finding Forrester*, played by Sean Connery, is a famous writer, a recluse, and a Despairing Man. He watches young men play basketball below from an upstairs window, removed from the action. When the players below notice, they dare the other major character, Jamal, a young black youth talented in both basketball and writing, to take something out of Forrester's apartment. Forrester catches Jamal (played by Rob Brown), and, instead of punishing Jamal, strikes up

---

14   https://en.wikipedia.org/wiki/Finding_Forrester

a relationship with him. Forrester begins to find himself again in befriending Jamal. Forrester's initial gruff ways give way to a wise and warm, yet subtle, mentorship. *Finding Forrester* is an eloquent reminder of what small miracles can emerge across the boundaries that divide men, even the most unlikely of pairings, when men open to care for and learn from one another.

This is not an easy process, and there is an "initiation" of sorts. When Jamal leaves his backpack behind after breaking into Forrester's apartment, Forrester writes notes in Jamal's personal journals and drops the backpack in the street. This draws Jamal back to Forrester's apartment to have Forrester read more of his writing. Forrester instead throws down a challenge, demanding Jamal write a 5,000-word essay about why Jamal should "stay the fuck" out of Forrester's home. An unlikely partnership of respect develops in which Forrester agrees to help Jamal with his writing as long as Jamal does not ask personal questions and does not let others know where he is.

The two begin to open up to each other and develop sensitivity to each other's lives. Jamal has been recruited to an elite private school not for his writing but for his basketball skills. We find out that Forrester's famous book, *Avalon Landing*, is a fictional retelling of a tragic family life. Jamal takes on a challenge to rewrite some of Forrester's essays to deepen his writing craft.

This mutual generosity and openness are countered by the suspicion and envy of a professor, Crawford, at Jamal's private school. Crawford ascertains that Jamal's improved writing must be the result of plagiarism and attempts to force a devil's bargain on Jamal: He must prove he has Forrester's permission to use Forrester's work as an inspiration to his own original writing (thus breaking confidentiality with Forrester) or ensure the school wins the basketball championship (thus debasing himself for the school). Jamal refuses to do either. Jamal shows himself to be a Searching Man, looking for the spiritual courage and authenticity upon which to craft his own identity.

Forrester, after initially declining to help Jamal, shows up at a writing contest at the private school and reads Jamal's essay as if it were his own. After the applause, Forrester discloses it is Jamal's essay. All is made well, much to the protest of Professor Crawford. The Despairing Man, Forrester, is drawn out into purposeful care that transcends past trauma and reclusion. The Searching Man, Jamal, is able to exert his sovereignty as a writer for himself, rather than a basketball player for others.

We see the spiritual, emotional, and mental development that sincere, if imperfect, men can share with each other. We are brought to what it might be like, as men, to heed the whisperings of the soul and to conquer the cynical mutterings of disenchantment. This is the core of spiritual co-creation between people. It starts with a decision to exalt the spirit of life over the fear of death, and creativity over conformity.

The Lord of the Rings: Emerging from innocence to courage, from temptation to strength of character, from reluctance to embrace of destiny [15]

For a gentler and more jovial rendition of the Searching Man, we can turn to the main character Frodo from director Peter Jackson's *The Lord of the Rings* trilogy. Frodo is a homebody and a hobbit (a small and humble, gnome-like person) played by Elijah Wood. Frodo is unassuming, quite provincial, and innocent, yet he is open to new horizons, and he, with his companion, Sam (played by Sean Astin),

---

15   https://en.wikipedia.org/wiki/The_Lord_of_the_Rings_(film_series)

engage in a profound and daring adventure that is above their heads literally and figuratively.

Frodo is initially happy where he is amid the mundane, yet perhaps a bit restless. One senses a longing in him for greater things. This transformative longing for greater things and simultaneous hesitation with the greater responsibility that greater things entail point to a tension at the heart of the Searching Man. Too often, this tension is pseudo-resolved by insecure men presenting themselves in puffed-up ways not followed by action. The true journey is never really taken. To be a growing man, on the other hand, one has to put something on the line, and Frodo and Sam put their very lives and innocence on the line.

Both Frodo and Sam are beset by adversaries of all description, and Frodo, in particular, has to contend with guarding a powerful ring that gives him special powers, but that also tempts him to misuse those powers and give himself over to arrogance, feelings of supremacy, and paranoia of others. In this, Frodo metaphorically plays out the essential lesson of the Searching Man, namely, how to devote one's self to the spiritually-led higher character as true power, and forsake the attractions of worldly power.

At the same time, Frodo learns to have mercy on Gollum, the former owner of the ring and one of the monsters that attacked he and Sam. Frodo's thinking is becoming more nuanced. He notices that life involves contradictions, that he must strike hard bargains, and that life exists without guarantees. He is emerging from his naivety and struggling with the implications of a more complex world in which he is not necessarily the center. This struggle is the signature of a Searching Man. *He cannot go back, but he does not yet quite know how to go forward.*

Frodo and Sam's journeys lead them into a kind of "rite of passage," in which their combined and individual mettle are tested. The men they are and the men they can be emerge from their engagement. Frodo and Sam must also deal with Gollum's betrayal. They learn not to take just anybody at his word. It is revealed later in the trilogy that Gollum was actually at one time a hobbit named Smeagol, who let the power of the ring corrupt him into murdering his friend. Smeagol then devolves into the creature called Gollum and forgets his identity. We see firsthand the perils of choosing worldly power over goodness of spirit in the choices of manhood. As the trilogy progresses, Sam rescues Frodo, at great danger to himself, and the two move to throw the ring into Mount Doom to destroy its powers over the minds of men.

Frodo, however, finally succumbs to the power of the ring and seeks to keep it for himself, losing his finger, with the ring attached, to the Gollum, who falls into the fire of the volcanic Mount Doom and is destroyed along with the ring. These scenes portray the symbolic and practical contrast for the Searching Man. Either he must follow his lower mind to the ill ends of worldly power seduced by fancies of glory, or else he must follow his higher mind and heart to a greater cause, paying for his way in courage and sacrifice.

Gladiator: Emerging from brokenness to integrity, from enslavement to sovereignty, from suffering to spiritual courage[16]

Maximus, the main character in *Gladiator*, played by Russell Crowe, shows us the course of a Spiritually Confident Man following the higher mind and heart amid conditions of the world that invite corruption.

---

16 https://en.wikipedia.org/wiki/Gladiator_(2000_film)

We see through the experience of Maximus, what happens if a man refuses to compromise with the temptations, pressures, and threats of the world. Maximus's Spiritually Confident Man gives rise to a particular kind of living strength and principle that sustain him even in the face of injustice and treachery.

Maximus does not dilute his principles to make convenient or comfortable alliances. As a result, his life departs from the path of wine and roses, viewed by so many as the "good life." To be imbued with spiritual confidence is to be compelled to take on the high demands and responsibilities that comfort-addicted bystanders refuse. This is true leadership—leadership by moral example. Again, knowing he will die, the Spiritually Confident Man is set free to live his life to his highest and best, to offer up his mortality if need be.

The moral leadership and metaphysical maturity of a spiritually confident man are demonstrated in concrete ways, most notably when he meets unexpected challenge. This is his test of character. Who he is and who he can be are brought to the fore. In the case of Maximus, he has served his nation admirably and comes home to an appreciative emperor who decides to pass down the kingship to Maximus based on his merit, rather than to his own blood son, Commodus. Upon hearing the plan, Commodus murders his father and seizes the crown, demanding Maximus's loyalty.

Maximus demonstrates his integrity and trustworthiness by refusing to serve a corrupt king. Of course, he also suffers the consequences. He is consigned to be executed but kills his captors and escapes only to find his wife and son have been murdered. Maximus collapses in shock and grief and is found by slaves who take him to be trained as a gladiator. The Spiritually Confident Man may be strong, but he is also vulnerable, affected deeply by injustice, and even incapacitated at times by personal tragedy because he feels his relationships so deeply.

After Maximus wins a surprising gladiatorial contest in front of Commodus and the crowd at the Colosseum, his life is spared for the moment by the dictates of tradition. Commodus attempts to eliminate Maximus by setting him to fight an undefeated gladiator. When Maximus prevails, and furthermore, spares the other gladiator's life, he gains the moniker, "Maximus the Merciful." He becomes both a legend and a transcendent example of manhood, standing not as a victor over others but as a compassionate brother.

Maximus joins a rebellion against Commodus. Commodus finally challenges Maximus to a duel, weakening him with a stab wound before the contest. Maximus kills Commodus, but is mortally wounded, and in his dying breaths asks for democratic political reforms, the reinstatement of the rightful ruler, and for his fellow gladiators to be freed. To his last, Maximus is a man of honor, giving everything of himself and leaving his best efforts to the ennoblement of others, before joining his family in the afterlife.

We see the real challenges of the spirit in the world. For the spirit to exercise itself, a man must reach a kind of emotional nadir to feel at heart who he truly is. A man must come to his core and not simply rationalize middling compromises. A man must come to terms with his own mortality, and decide how best to dedicate his life, knowing it will end. A man must persevere. A man must rise and fall and rise again, a testament to the resilience and the indomitability of the human spirit. A man must meet his own fears and choose courage over pain. A man must express in his example a deep desire for life in all its glory, not just a desire to survive. A man must search himself and transcend himself through a faith greater than himself.

Art imitates life

> *In all men, not just spiritually confident men, there is a Creative Fire, an Original Passion, a driving desire that is his birthright and that cannot be taken away by anyone or anything.*

It is this Passion that makes him a man among men, a precious and powerful being among beings. This Creative Fire, however, can be covered over and forgotten by an individual man. It is art of all kinds that awakens his Fire and fans the flames. It is Courage that ignites this fire. It is Love that gives this Flame direction and purpose. There is much a man has to relinquish to let this Fire out of the box of his mind and body. As these films show, he must forfeit his conceits to forge his future. He must let go of his image of himself to be re-made in a higher, greater, and more profound image. He must cede the powers of the world to accept the powers of the heavens.

Cinema shows us, even among examples that emphasize the warrior, that any man must admit his blind spots and come to terms with his weaknesses to be true to himself. This necessary vulnerability is an evocative opening to a man's own growth, and it serves as an invitation to his true empathy and care for others. His own humbling imperfection encourages a man not to see himself as an end but as a means to birth spiritual strength, creative energy, and compassionate will into the world.

If you look closely, the most difficult challenges for men appear to be the subtlest—not the salutations of swagger but the difficulties of opening up, of hoping again, of breaking through the crust or shell of the self. Men's most daunting "dragons" involve emotional learning without physical dragons to kill. Vital manhood is a demanding art, not a war.

This subtle and demanding art of vital manhood has implicit rules and principles, as demonstrated both in movies and experiments in real life:

- **Stay in truth even when you can appear to be beaten by lesser men who have taken a moral shortcut.** Persist in truth. The truth wills out.

- **Metaphysical growth is harder to capture and takes longer to unfold than progressing up typical ladders of material success.** Do not let impatience, insecurity, and mere calculation get in the way of taking the risks you need to in order to fulfill your divine genius. Face reality rigorously. Note that a "successful" job promotion can often turn into a prison of overwork and underappreciation. What looked good turns out to be "meh" and what looked bad (getting fired) might spring you into your own business or a better opportunity elsewhere.

- **Do not give in to expedience.** For instance, attempts to eradicate evil through killing and other forms of reaction, often give evil greater power, because it reinforces lower frequency reality. Non-violent civil disobedience has been far more successful at creating lasting positive change because it introduces the higher vibrations and power of the spirit into the world.

- **Embrace the surprising, odd, unusual, or out-of-place.** Enhance and honor uniqueness in yourself and others rather than squash originality. Listen and be compassionate with someone different than you. This can only enhance your understanding of the world, and it cannot diminish you. This means your self-worth rests within your divine genius and what you have to give to the world, not in your position.

- **The more and bigger your setback, and the better you respond, the deeper will be your next success**. Failure and even trauma have a way of blowing open the capacity of one who is not crushed by it. This greater capacity allows for greater ability, stronger will, and greater desire. Responding well to setbacks creates desire, as it did for basketball legend Michael Jordan when he initially failed to make the varsity team in high school. One of the best rowers on my college team was a man who had experienced significant burns over his body earlier in his life. As a result, he had a whole new threshold of pain.

- **Care unites and completes individual desire.** Deep care is the ultimate giving up of one's self, the offering of one's self completely. No individual transformation is complete without care for another. This does not so much require a death of the ego, but the sacrifice of the ego's leadership. It is only under the leadership of love, based on compassion, that we learn to extend ourselves into something higher and larger than our own sphere.

Even the classical or conservative male values of "provide, protect, sacrifice, and serve" do not derive from a man being the end in himself. A man who respects himself is always, as well, a man for others. The fatal opposite of this devotion to the highest in the self and others is catering to one's own "godhood complex" understood as authority and control over others.

> *Men are not built to be chess masters. They are built to be catalysts.*

A man is to be an instrument of higher wisdom, not make others be instruments to his basest pretensions. When the ego rules as if it were God then no good can come. The ironic thing is that the higher spirit does not act this way at all. The higher spirit is patient. The higher spirit is giving and sharing and always wanting the best for the other. The higher spirit delights when others achieve success. The higher spirit collaborates rather than competes.

We have given fertile ground in this chapter to the Emerging Man. Now let's turn our attention to the kind of man that stands in the way of emergence: the Patriarchal Man.

CHAPTER 5

Pulling Up The Weeds—The Patriarchal Man

Like all cultivation in which we strive to bear fruit, our crops can have their share of weeds. Just because a man is illuminated and willing to grow does not mean he no longer has issues to work on. The weeds of past destructive or unhealthy masculine habits persist even within the best of men. A man carries low habits not only in his past training and present-day reinforcement but in the patriarchal inertia of history and the collective masculine unconscious. These perpetuate old inequalities, fears, and impulses to dominate and control.

The best way to address such patriarchal tendencies is to unmask them and devise courageous, effective strategies to bring them forward and upward. Call it "compassionate elevation" of masculinity. This elevation, however, starts with a rigorous and resolute "calling out" of those low aspects of manhood that not only fail to serve the healthy growth of humanity but stand actively opposed. What do men have to confront? What stands in the way of developing spiritual confidence?

WHETHER HE BE A hero, anti-hero, or an earnestly growing and imperfect male, the Emerging Man, and his Spiritually Confident embodiment have their opposite—the Patriarchal Man. The Patriarchal Man is the unrepentant and willfully ignorant male, the one with no interest in growing, deepening, and transforming, the one who would rather keep things as they are or, even worse, one who delights in the destruction and subjugation of the human spirit. The Emerging Man at every level, especially at his higher level of refinement (embodied here as the Spiritually Confident Man), will have to confront the Patriarchal Man, both in society and community *and in his own habits of heart, mind, and body.*

The Spiritually Confident Man is the giver and receiver, the "provider of the feast." His opposite is the Patriarchal Man, the taker, the "ruler on the throne."

Here are the two contrasting dispositions:

Spiritually Confident Man	Patriarchal Man
"provider of the feast"	"ruler on the throne"
Giver	Taker
Co-creator	Dominator
Open	Closed
Vulnerable	Stoic
Transparent	Secretive
Accessible	Inaccessible
Flexible	Unyielding
Embraces humanness	Operates as a tin god

Spiritually Confident Man	Patriarchal Man
Understands he must grow	Asserts he is complete
Has much to learn	Already knows everything
Accountable	Non-accountable
Responsible	Irresponsible
Transformative	Oppressive
Mutual	Unilateral
Interactive	Non-interactive
Listening	Unhearing
Loving	Cruel
Receptive	Callous
Joyful	Angry
Egalitarian	Authoritarian
Caring	Punishing
Expects to serve	Expects to be served
Virtuous	Vicious
Strong	Weak

The spiritually confident "provider of the feast" allows himself to be open to give and receive.

He leans into learning by embracing his humanness and incompleteness. He is joyful, interactive, and flexible emotionally, seeking to transform and build a better world for future generations. His consistent accountability to his higher self and his responsibility to the healthy support of others make him secure, virtuous, and strong.

> *The patriarchal "ruler on the throne," on the other hand, shuts himself behind a wall of invulnerability, non-transparency, and "no access."*

Driven by self-importance, he proclaims his mastery, solely follows his own authority, and tells others what to do. He is closed, stoic, and unyielding, seeking to replicate the old world and force it upon emerging generations. The Patriarchal Man's authoritarianism prompts him to exercise so-called "tough love" to prepare people for (and therefore perpetuate) a cruel and destructive reality. His fear of "losing his grip" on himself and others disposes him to be insecure, vicious, and weak.

Why is this the case? What gave rise to the Patriarchal Man, and what might support the emergence of a Spiritually Confident Man? It would be too easy to simply dismiss the Patriarchal Man as evil or diseased, something to be shunned and left behind. As I said earlier, the habits of the Patriarchal Man are woven even into men who sincerely strive for the good. The man who earnestly seeks to learn and do the right thing will still have to contend with patriarchal habits.

As men, patriarchal habits are woven into our world system, our training, and even our subconscious. Ignoring these patriarchal habits, and present-day influences will only give them strength. Patriarchy, as any devolutionary system, must be systematically confronted and dismantled, not ignored. *We do this by rigorously examining how patriarchal habits are formed and perpetuated. Then we move to transform these habits in the light of a higher truth.*

> *Patriarchy is defined as a "rule by men," but more accurately it is understood as a ruling mentality. Women can be patriarchs and men can be anti-patriarchal.*

Historically, men have been by far the more numerous in taking on patriarchal norms as their operating principles, hence the confusion of a ruling mentality (power over others, control, taking) with a gender (maleness).

Men have, no doubt, been more weak-minded and susceptible when it comes to the false virtues of separation, domination, and self-glorification. Perhaps this has something to do psychologically with males' need to separate from the womb. Perhaps this developed in reaction to some unnamed oppressive force. Perhaps it stemmed from men's inability to gestate earthly life and men's desires to create their own lives. Whatever, their roots, these destructive habits act against well-being and the reinforce reactive fear and resentment.

On the physical level, men cannot give birth to themselves, suckle themselves, or give birth to another. On the spiritual level, the opposite is true. A spiritually adept man can choose to give rise to his own inner life and even die and be reborn many times in this life. A spiritually aware man can nourish himself by listening to the whisperings of his soul.

A spiritually confident man rejoices in the fact that he *doesn't* look like someone else but offers a unique divine genius to others and to this world. A spiritually creative man can give birth to an idea, a work of art, or care for another.

> *Thus, a spiritual man is motivated to give rather than take, because his very identity and life are confirmed and developed through sharing. Without giving he is alone and uncompleted. With giving, he is a contributing and receiving citizen of the cosmos.*

It has always been this way. Men can contribute their divine genius as Spiritually Confident Men toward the elevation of humanity rather than as Patriarchal Men to its devolution. Men can and do create life, but it is a life of spirit and a life of community that men can create, not babies. We men are built to seed enlightened thought, egalitarian feeling, principle, and kindness into the world. It is this faith in the pursuit of and *providing of* the unseen higher that makes a man a real hero. It is his unwavering loyalty to the spirit of life that makes him a warrior. It is a Spiritually Confident Man's choice and ability to give himself that gives him real worth, a value more real and elevated than financial worth, political clout, or physical prowess.

Why, then, has the bonding blessing of shared spiritual power, power *with* others, been usurped by power *over* others over the last few thousand years? Why has the life-affirming higher spiritual path for masculinity been largely replaced by a devolutionary lower path? Why isn't the spiritual "good" seen and pursued clearly among men? Why have men allowed themselves to choose taking over giving and ruling over providing? Why did the Patriarchal Man emerge as a dominant model of masculinity, and what can we do to turn this around?

A deal with the devil: Men's fateful turn toward the physical world and away from spirit

First, we must understand, in terms of the development of the human spirit in the world, that humans are hybrid creatures of spirit on the one hand and body or matter on the other. Dimensionally, Earth itself is a hybrid of "light" and "dark." It is both a playground and a battleground of choice. In us are two resulting possible movements: *Elevation*, a movement to the higher spiritual self and mind, and *devolution*, movement toward the lower physical self and mind.

Elevation is less defined and less emotionally obvious, just as love is less defined and less emotionally obvious than hate. Lower existence has a denser, easier-to-grasp apparent reality. Higher existence means learning to feel and understand higher vibration, which is lighter and harder to see. As such, higher existence requires subtle senses, more focused attunement, and more developed intuition. It is also, in short, harder work.

> *In spiritual development, it is not so much the starting point but the movement upward or downward that counts.*

As we saw in the last chapter, even men with a history of bad choices, failures of character, and ill-treatment of others can, if the choice is made, redeem themselves through a change of heart that leads to virtuous practical choices and action.

Conversely, even the highest men can bring themselves low, if they viciously "sell out" their growth and make their own self-importance the idol of their lives. So, there is no inherent character of a man that ensures or prevents him from rising or descending spiritually. It is the *choice* of a man to learn and transform to become heedful to a higher possibility over time that determines his character. This is what led Aristotle to observe: "You are what you repeatedly do." It is not so much that actions define the man, but that repeated actions *show* the man and his spiritual progression or regression. Though this involves intention, it is a matter of *result*. It's *not* the thought that primarily counts, but the deed. Even failed sincere doing is better than the loftiest non-manifested intention.

> *However, sincere actions are not enough. A man's actions must correspond to real provision and elevation for himself and for others.*

A man can do all kinds of actions and make all kinds of excuses for those actions that do not serve others. A man can be a workaholic and rationalize that his addictive removal from his family life is a necessary and noble sacrifice to provide financial support. He can "reward" himself with indulgent vices like gambling, sexual conquest, and drinking alcohol to excess. I am not sure what excuses men are making, but I can practically guarantee that they are convincing themselves they deserve these things.

The realities of infinite spirit expose the deceits of a patriarchal finite world

We men, we humans, "deserve" nothing. Life is not a right. It is an evocative force, calling us to contribute and give of ourselves from a profound level. "Deserving" is of the lower realms of entitlement, and this entitlement without exception is a killer of the spirit. The Golden Boy who can do no wrong, the Guru, whom all others must obey, or the Chosen One anointed to lord over others, cannot help but become corrupt because they are answerable to nobody and they have nothing higher to live for. Because they cannot generate their own energy, they must consume others' energy.

Spiritually confident engagement involves the opposite. It is infinite, ever-creating, ever-giving of itself.

> *Like a rechargeable battery, spirit's increased potential, its capacity to receive, is created through giving. The more I authentically and innately give in spirit, the greater is my polarity and draw for additional spiritual and creative energy.*

By contrast, worldly perspectives, based largely on physical competition over finite resources perceive giving either as a drain or as a ploy to get back more than you give. In the operating principles of spirit, giving creates an evocative force for more energy to come through the giver from higher realms. Here, giving comes with its own intrinsic power and good. In the operating principles of the world, giving creates a loss, a sacrifice, hence concepts like "altruism" which essentially mean sacrifice without hope for material gain. Yet typical understanding of altruism completely ignores the far more precious and powerful in-rush of spiritual energy that comes as a result of wise giving.

> *I say "wise giving" because any giving to a taker, someone who merely consumes our energy as spiritual-physical beings, is not only a waste but an enablement of anti-spiritual power.*

We now have to confront the fact that the vast majority of naïve but sincere givers in this world have given up their sovereignty, choice, responsibility, and power to "takers" guided by metaphors of the finite physical world. On one level, it seems to make sense. I, as a giver, have an excess, and the other as a taker, has a lack or need. Yet when I give to a taker, I am left poorer, because that giving is consumed rather than circulated. When I give to the taker, *he or she is also left poorer* because taking diminishes their ability to give and leaves them even more dependent on and resentful of others to meet their insatiable needs for unfettered power. We have a lose-lose situation.

The opposite is also possible. When givers give to other givers, spiritual energy is drawn into the earthly sphere and circulated. Every "expenditure" of creative or giving energy is neither an investment, nor a sacrifice, but a gift and a testament of gratitude to the very force of life that makes my giving possible at all.

> *I live, therefore I can give!*

A win-win is thus created, not only between givers and givers but between givers and takers. Takers can no longer ignore their spiritual deficiencies. They are invited to learn how to give of themselves, so they can participate in the circulation and utilization of spiritual energy.

One of the greatest lies of patriarchy is that there can be a win-lose, the notion that I can "win" at the expense of another. This is patently false both from a spiritual and practical level. The patriarch claims: "I can plunder the earth of oil or gold. Who cares what happens after I die?" "I can sexually molest a woman. Who cares about her dignity and personhood? I got my rocks off and felt my power, and I got away with it because of my institutional position! Screw others; I 'won!'" *No, you lost.* You destroyed your own character, and you damaged others along with it. Spiritually and practically, there is no win-lose.

> *There is only win-win and lose-lose. We either choose to ascend and make that more likely for others, or we choose to descend and drag others down with us.*

Feminist theorists have made a huge mistake in this regard. They claim that patriarchy benefits men. Quite the contrary, patriarchy destroys men and masculinity by corrupting the very core of masculinity—spiritual character and strength. Except for the most insensible, we all recognize that "gaining the world and losing your soul" is a devil's bargain. Who would rationally (much less spiritually) agree to sell our his or own priceless spiritual capacity for a few material comforts and the aching hollowness of soulless being.

Unfortunately, men by and large have chosen to remain ignorant of this tragic deal. One only has to look around us at the greed, destruction, and selfishness to see which version of manhood has dominated our world history over the last few thousand years. How did we get here and how might we transform life-denying patriarchal world views and training to that of life-affirming spiritual confidence, provision, and strength?

> *How deeply have these patriarchal stories woven themselves into masculinity, programmed so-called "reality," and influenced our understanding of higher truth?*

Why is it that even good men hide from, rather than challenge, patriarchy's dark rule over their identities and the well-being of those they love? How can we collectively and individually break through this patriarchal historical programming and create a new reality of beauty, wholeness, and purpose for men and for humanity?

In the following sections, we will explore the story and choice between the co-creative "provider of the feast" and the patriarchal "ruler on the throne." We will look at their economic, and political, and cultural expressions in our human history including examples from the world's major religions. We will delve into examples of hope and human potential that lead us to the "provider of the feast."

We do not have to wait for some sign. The calling and the capacity are within us.

"Provider of the feast" versus "ruler on the throne"

Dating about five thousand years ago and later, a split between "provider of the feast" and "ruler on the throne" could be detected in early ancient Near East culture and stories. These primarily Mesopotamian and Egyptian narratives pre-dated the Bible and not only served as the template for the "Abrahamic" religions of Judaism, Christianity, and Islam but of Ancient Greek and Roman myths, all of which serve as foundations for Western culture and thought. Each of these societies had their own influential notions of human nature and origins, higher ideals, and even gods transmitted through epic stories that filtered into broad, enduring, and overarching worldviews.

Let me note at the outset, that I am concentrating upon how historical cultural narratives influence our understanding of who we are as humans and what we may be capable of becoming. I am not going to speculate on the validity of a "God" or "gods," nor do I hold a view of a "correct" god. I do, however, make it my business to expose false idols of God, and I will do so in this chapter.

I will say, furthermore, that I believe that all human beings are partial in their understanding and experience, and cannot comprehend nor capture the full scope of the spiritual even in our best representations, our most insightful interpretations, and our highest art.

> *The point is that any spiritual representation, faith, or belief inspires a higher more noble, creative and loving development of our human capability, possibility, and service.*

Each of us has our "greater than myself" "god" of one sort or another. Your god is anything you confer some higher authority or purpose to, anything you look up to, follow, put above yourself, or give your trust over to. For humans, these "gods" could be supernatural beings, religious dogmas, humanistic principles, money, power, work, science, technology, yoga, new-age gurus, ancestors, parents, family, or loved ones, some combination of these, or something entirely different.

We tend to emulate and be guided in life by our "gods." Our life question rests not so much on whether there is a supernatural god in heaven or not, or which gods we choose to venerate, but *what happens as a result of relating to this or that god.* A "high god," for instance, negates its own spiritual authority if it is used to anoint very low deeds. What matters is this: "How do we understand, learn from, and interact with higher wisdom or authority, and how do we act here and now as a result?" Do we end up being a more giving person or a more taking person, a "provider of the feast" or a "ruler on the throne?"

The litmus test: Is your god a higher god or a lower god, a provider of the feast or a ruler on the throne?

> *Any god worth its salt does not mind being tested, because a higher god, interested in spiritual growth and development, understands that **truth tested in experience bears out higher ways of being and acting.***

Therefore, the truth borne out by questioning, employing, and challenging higher "messages" in personal engagement are essential aids to spiritual development for any choosing, thinking, feeling, and learning person.

> *No god worth its salt would ever insist on unthinking obedience.*

Without choice and knowledge, without personal responsibility, any respect paid to a "god" (however that is conceived) would be false, shallow, and hollow. There are no credible arguments to be made that falseness, shallowness, and hollowness could honor anything, much less a so-called "god." What such cross traits do, however, is build a channel of energy to the lower, bringing down a person and feeding lower forms of consciousness.

Cult leaders who put themselves up to their followers as "gods," are perfect demonstrations of false gods. Just as there are certain "tells" in a game of poker that a person with low cards is bluffing, so it is true of lower beings posing as higher beings. If you pay attention to these "tells," you can accurately identify and debunk false gods from a long way off and set your sights on higher and more ennobling influences. These distinctions below work on all levels of refinement and spirituality from "god," to human, to other.

- **Provider vs. ruler:** As mentioned earlier, the higher is a provider; the lower is a ruler. The logic is simple here. If you are truly higher as a person, god, or other, you have no reason to prove your power to others, because you already have it and can exercise it on behalf of a more refined, noble, and beautiful universe. If you are lower, you are required to garner power you do not possess from acolytes or worshippers through some kind of imperative or demand.

- **Producer vs. consumer:** The higher is a producer; the lower is a consumer. This is universally true. The higher has the energy of spirit generating through it. The lower is cut off from spirit and therefore must seek an alternative power source. This alternative source comes in the form of intentional energy drawn or attracted from abused, enslaved, naïve, or openly complicit beings.

- **Love vs. fear:** The higher inspires love; the lower induces fear. There is some confusion here because "awe" is sometimes translated as "fear." I am not talking about fear as awe, a kind of respect for higher ability. I am talking about fear for one's own physical survival and well-being that can induce people to surrender to abuse, inequality, and injustice. Any parasitic extortion of another's energy will be inherently unjust because it is a form of coercion and a violation of free will. This is not something a higher being or principle would ever endorse. Love is the opposite, the unconditional desire for well-being for another married with *their* exercise of choice. We cannot do the spiritual development of other beings. Acknowledging this requires spiritual persistence, courage, and compassion, especially when we see others making choices that adversely impact them and others.

- **Creativity and possibility vs. dogma and "certainty":** For the higher, creativity and possibility reign; for the lower, dogma and certainty rule. Again, possibility requires a confident, creative being. When your life can be anything, when there is no prescription or anchor, you must be secure in yourself. To the creative being, quantum possibility is not seen with terror, but rather fascination. I can be anything! Let's find out what I can be! At this point, those who are of a higher mind go on a journey of delighted discovery, exploration, and learning. The lower shrink from this dazzling array toward "certain" dogmas, because possibility and creativity overwhelm and confuse them and give them a kind of psychic pain.

- **Liberation vs. control:** The higher wants every being to be free to develop, create, and contribute. This makes a richer universe. The lower drives toward convergent control, because possibility is seen as a threat and an invitation to incoherence: "Everything will not be in its place! How do I know what I am supposed to be doing if everything is moving and choosing on its own?" Again, we see the lack of foundation of the lower in its own spiritual core and genius. It needs to compare itself to get a sense of worth because it cannot feel its own internal worth.

- **Responsibility vs. license:** The higher is responsible; the lower is licentious. The higher understands that the root of responsibility is "response." Responsibility is quite literally "response-ability." I could not have any relationship with any other being if I cannot honestly receive them and respond to them. That relationship is too important to sacrifice so I embrace "responsibility," the spiritual notion that every being needs to be inherently recognized and respected. The lower wants its "will to be done," period and to be served hand and foot. The lower sees such responsibility as "obligation" and doesn't want its style to be cramped, nor to acknowledge the consequences of its own actions, so it sets up an operating philosophy of "anything goes" (as long as you do what I say!).

- **Sovereignty vs. slavishness:** Related to the other distinctions, the higher embraces free choice and sovereignty; the lower promotes slavishness. Again, self-rule generates responsibility to the self and to others. I cannot harm myself or others without feeling the consequences. If I am of a higher sensibility, I cannot deny my soul's whisper or give up my autonomy and thinking to some institution without feeling that sickening hollowness and lack of purpose. Being a slave to work, to romance, to religion, even to family, actually tends to erase choice and certain pressures around decision-making, *but it also erases originality and personality.* Slavishness additionally promotes conformity and boredom. This is not a good trade-off for the higher. However, the lower, besieged by complexity, may consider this decision to rid one's self of choice as a matter of psychological coping.

- **Service vs. servitude:** The higher engages in service; the lower capitulates to servitude. There is a difference between service and servitude: Service is something one does willingly and happily as a kind of interpersonal opportunity. Energy flows through me into the enhancement of another. There is a healthy completion of a spiritual cycle between beings, a kind of endless and tableless "pay it forward" which keeps spiritual energy qualitatively circulating. Servitude on the other hand is done under obligation or is seen as a sacrifice. It is quantitative and transactional. One is trying to gain some kind of favor by doing something for another. Flow is replaced by "if/then" conditionality.

- **Embrace vs. judgment:** The higher embraces even that with which it disagrees; the lower judges and demeans even those who provide connection. Again, the higher always recognizes choice as a fundamental operating principle to being. Coercion ruins creative connection by destroying the potential originality between connectors. Failing coercion (forcing another to act or believe as one does), the lower will often resort to judgment, which is casting an isolating and lowering evaluation on another being so as to "banish" them from the club of considered humanity. "You are beneath me," is an expression of this form of judgmental contempt. Again, what are the consequences? Lose-lose. The person judged is assaulted and removed. The person judging denies him or herself an authentic opportunity to connect, learn, and grow.

- **Inclusion, expansion, and deepening vs exclusion, restriction, diminishment**: The higher includes, expands, and deepens; the lower excludes, restricts, and diminishes. The two motivations should be readily apparent to you by now. If you want more and are prepared for the more, then you move to the higher. The movement higher is a movement to the larger, deeper, and more substantial. If you cannot accept this move, you may make a move to the lower. The movement lower is a movement to the smaller, shallower, and less substantial. Each has its "rewards" and demands. Moving higher increases depth and breadth, but also increases complexity and responsibility. Moving lower decreases depth and breadth but also decreases complexity and responsibility.

History tends to go in cycles. From spiritual per-spectives, even a trillion years could be considered a short time, so our perspectives as humans are highly biased toward much smaller time frames because our individual physical lives are fairly brief.

It is clear however that the last couple of thousand years (long by our standards and short by spiritual standards) has been dominated by experimentation in the path of the lower, which I have labeled as "patriarchy."

The male gender has largely perpetuated this, but it is important not to confuse maleness, masculinity, or men's nature and potential with this long and destructive experiment called patriarchy. It is also important to note, as I have in this book, that men can take the path of the higher and undo much of the damage they have caused by imposing the rules of the lower upon the possibility of the higher. As humans, we are a mixture of the two, higher and lower, and none of us is "pure." That is why the dynamic contrast between higher and lower can educate us to confront the lower in ourselves and embrace the higher.

All of us, especially men, must imperfectly but straightforwardly confront the lower aspects of ourselves and make this uncertain and noble journey toward the higher. We are on the threshold of a new rhythm at this point in history. Male subjectivity and wisdom is emerging from this patriarchal experiment into a new era of co-creative responsibility for men and women, girls and boys, alike. It is time for us men to take a major leap. But this cannot be done without understanding human history and, in particular, the history of patriarchy, which slowly and surely legitimized anti-spiritual practices over millennia.

A history of patriarchy and patriarchal gods

In contrast to the procession of tyrannical patriarchs most history books seem to recognize, the world's past does include female leaders and collaborative governance on earth, as well as feminine attributes in human representations of the heavens. Women rulers figured prominently in the First Dynasty of ancient Egypt starting around 3200 B.C.

The Assyrian rulers of northern Mesopotamia in the mid 3rd millennium B.C. onward governed largely by council and not by the mere dictates of a sole king. They worshiped the god Ashur, named in accordance with the capital city of Assur. Ashur was represented in older forms as a winged solar disc, and in later forms as a male warrior only as the culture became militarized.

This same solar disc representation arose in the 18th Dynasty of Ancient Egypt, to denote the primary god Aten, an ascended aspect of the sun god Ra, considered to be both masculine and feminine simultaneously. In fact, scholars in the Hermetic tradition consider the word "Israel" to be derived from the earlier Egyptian Isis-Ra-El or "Mother-Father God." The male ruler of the time, Akhenaten, essentially co-ruled with his wife, Nefertiti, and the two were often pictured in representative art in intimate and affectionate poses with their family rather than distaff and remote "official" poses.

Contrast this history with the dominant emergence of patriarchal images of governance and of gods in the first few millennia B.C. in southern Mesopotamia. The Babylonians of this region worshipped Enlil, a prototype of patriarchal "ruler on the throne" god and human leadership that no longer needed cooperation, respect for the feminine, or any kind of accountability. Enlil was an irresponsible, violent, and punitive god by legend, who raped an adolescent girl and ostensibly created floods and droughts, wiping out whole populations of humans.

Gods, in Enlil's mold, insisted on sole authority and exclusive worship. Council governance and respect for the feminine were erased along with mercy and generosity to be replaced by sheer brutality.

This stark and growing contrast between the "provider of the feast" (God as giver and creator) and the "ruler on the throne" (God as the taker and punisher) is shown in even sharper relief in the first two accounts of God in the Hebrew Bible/Old Testament: Genesis 1:1 – 2:3 and Genesis 2:4 – 3:22 (New Revised Standard translations).

These accounts were written and collected over centuries in the first millennium B.C. and were heavily influenced by divergent Mesopotamian narratives *far pre-dating the Bible*. The biblical stories of Creation, the Garden of Eden, the Flood, and the Tower of Babel descended from the more ancient (and more recently discovered) writings of the Atrahasis, Epic of Gilgamesh, and Enuma Elish.

Few people seem to either recognize or acknowledge the contradictory and incompatible nature of the two rival Genesis visions of God:

The co-creative Provider of the Feast characterization of God in Genesis 1:1-2:3 has God creating earth and heavens out of a "formless void" and distinguishing dark from light. Then God ostensibly creates land, sea, plants, animals, and humankind. All this creation is repeatedly denoted as "good" by God multiple times ending with "very good", confirming the emphatic *original blessing* of creation. (Genesis 1:31: "God saw everything (God) had made, and indeed, it was very good".)

The details of this blessing and its responsibilities were spelled out in verses 1:26-29, where "God" said, "Let us make humankind in our image, according to our likeness; and let them have dominion over (the animals)" (Genesis 1:26):

> *Notice that God here is **plural** not singular, a democratic "we" not a despotic "me." This plural God has made humankind "according to (God's) likeness," not as some cast out or depraved creature, but a beautiful being from the very same spiritual essence as the creator.*

This humankind is meant to have "dominion," which can be best understood as "stewardship" or "responsibility" over the earth and its creatures, that is, someone who will responsively care for its well-being.

> ²⁷ So God created humankind in (God's) image, in the image of God (God) created them; male and female (God) created them. (Genesis 1:27)

This verse is stark confirmation that God 1) was not male, since God created both male and female in God's image, and 2) that females did not come from men or from their ribs, nor does it support any other similarly tilted patriarchal "old husband's tale," where men give birth to women.

> ²⁹ God said, "See, I have given you every plant yielding seed that is upon the face of all the earth, and every tree with seed in its fruit; you shall have them for food." (Genesis 1:29)

This Provider of the Feast God quite literally provides a feast of nourishment for the physical body (and by metaphorical extension, the mind, the heart, and the spirit). *There are no conditions, judgments, or stipulations to this provision.* It is given freely for all time for the creative enjoyment, expression, and thriving of humankind. This passage even suggests a vegan diet for the original humans.

The patriarchal "ruler on the throne" "Adam and Eve" interpretation in Genesis 2:4 – 3:22, is the Creation account most of us have beaten into our heads. These passages paint the creation of heavens, earth, plants, animals, and humans as a paradise ruined by the *original sin* of Adam and Eve. Human life became more like a suffering curse to be endured, once Adam and Eve ate from the Tree of Knowledge of Good and Evil. These passages emphasize *unthinking obedience and acquiescence* as virtues, rather than questioning, learning, risking, and trying.

These passages also communicate *very* different ideas about respect for the divine, the origin of humans, and the relationship between men and women:

> [7] then the Lord God formed man from the dust of the ground, and breathed into his nostrils the breath of life; and the man became a living being…[15] The Lord God took the man and put him in the garden of Eden to till it and keep it.[16] And the Lord God commanded the man, "You may freely eat of every tree of the garden; [17] but of the tree of the knowledge of good and evil you shall not eat, for in the day that you eat of it you shall die." (Genesis 2:15-17)

So now we no longer have a plural God, but rather a singular ruling "Lord God" who created males first (ostensibly in his image, so now God has become male), who sets out stipulations, demands, and judgments. First among these rules, incredibly, is the injunction not to eat of knowledge of good and evil! Isn't that what our very conscience, one of our *highest* spiritual capacities, is based upon? If humans disobey, they are punished with death! One begins to see the notion of tyrannical and jealous petty god emerging, rather than a magnanimous and generous God.

> [18] Then the Lord God said, "It is not good that the man should be alone; I will make him a helper as his partner"… [21] So the Lord God caused a deep sleep to fall upon the man, and he slept; then he took one of his ribs and closed up its place with flesh. [22] And the rib that the Lord God had taken from the man he made into a woman and brought her to the man. [23] Then the man said, "This at last is bone of my bones and flesh of my flesh; this one shall be called Woman, for out of Man this one was taken." (Genesis 2:18, 2:21-23)

Now males give "birth" to females? What a radical change. The human female is no longer co-created and co-creative. The female role is defined as obedient helper to the male, and the male the obedient slave of an overlord male god. This is not going well from the perspective of the autonomy, choice, and creative expression required for authentic, powerful spirituality. This is looking *very* patriarchal and manipulative of sacred narrative.

As punishment to the woman for disobeying and eating from the tree of knowledge of good and evil, this same overlord god says:

> [16] "I will greatly increase your pangs in childbearing; in pain you shall bring forth children, yet your desire shall be for your husband, and he shall rule over you." (Genesis 3:16).

As punishment for the man, this overlord god says:

[17] "Because you have listened to the voice of your wife, and have eaten of the tree about which I commanded you, 'You shall not eat of it,' cursed is the ground because of you; in toil you shall eat of it all the days of your life…" (Genesis 3:17).

> *Now there is no pretense; this is straight up patriarchy: 1) So-called "god" has decreed that males will rule over females as an inherent and original right. 2) Listening to a woman is now a source of evil and error for men, and 3) men are cursed because of women and forced to toil, so really, you know, **men are the victims!***

This serves as a succinct blueprint of patriarchy and the Patriarchal Man: Absolute power over women, absolute right to blame women for every wrong, and absolute lack of accountability for men. This is all *very* convenient. This complete desertion of responsibility would be absurd if it were not such a powerful and lasting habit among men.

> *In the Genesis 2 and 3 ruler-on-the-throne version of God and humanity, women simultaneously come from men, serve men, and are to blame for all men's bad decisions.*

Biblically, starting with Eve, women become the scapegoat for almost everything for which men should be taking responsibility. Women in the Hebrew Bible/Old Testament are almost always cast as deceitful temptresses who weaken and mislead men so that these men can remain blameless for any failure or foul deed they commit. Adam: "Well, Eve told me to eat the fruit from the forbidden tree. I wouldn't have otherwise. It's her fault." Lot: "Well, my daughters got me drunk and seduced me. That's why I had sex with them." Samson: "Delilah (a name that translated actually means "she who weakened") cut off my hair and sold me out to my enemies. That is why I failed."

The term "Jezebel" has been adopted into the English language as an evil, scheming, or shameless woman. Jezebel in the Old Testament supposedly convinced her husband, King Ahab, to abandon the "true" god, Yahweh, and worship another god. For this, she was thrown out a window to her death and eaten by dogs. Apparently, again, Ahab did not have a mind of his own, nor any real responsibility for his decisions.

Muslim religious traditions are not immune to passages and practices which promote the rule of men over women. Many sayings attributed to Mohammad and passages from the Koran, according to Islam scholar Hamdum Dagher, place women firmly under the control of men and give them a lower status as beings.[17] This includes the controversial *Sura 4:34* passage, which seems to countenance violence against women as part of a step-wise strategy to keep women in line.[18]

This unconscionable conception and treatment of women is not confined to the Western Abrahamic religions of Christianity, Judaism, and Islam. It can be found in Eastern Hinduism in a sacred text called the Manusmriti, which among other things proclaims that women ought to gracefully tolerate abuse from a husband, and not work, discern, or endeavor independently.[19] Certain Hindu philosophy and practices, until the 19th century, also accepted and even promoted the practice of *sati*, in which a widow was to be burned alive along with her dead husband. The practice is now banned but continues to this

---

17   http://www.light-of-life.com/eng/reveal/
18   http://www.answering-islam.org/Authors/Arlandson/beating.htm
19   http://nirmukta.com/2011/08/27/the-status-of-women-as-depicted-by-manu-in-the-manus-mriti/

day (though greatly diminished).[20]

In Buddhism, women ordained as nuns are held to be lower than and subservient to males ordained as monks.[21] This has changed in the last couple of decades in some Buddhist orders as some women have become ordained as monks. While traveling in Thailand, I noticed certain Buddhist temples had signs that forbade women from entering. In these patriarchal Eastern examples, as with others in Western culture, the woman is cast as the temptress and held responsible as the holder of virtue for depraved, weak, or even abusive men, who get off responsibility-free simply for being men.

> *One wonders, "Why is the virtue of men, if they are inherently superior, not enough to hold off the 'corruptive' seductions of women?"*

This lack of responsibility for men, even over their own decisions, is the dead giveaway, the supreme "tell" of patriarchally perverted cultural norms. So where are the masculine norms supporting the spiritually confident, responsible alternative?

Hidden but not lost: Re-awakening the "provider of the feast"

Earlier in this chapter, I laid out the qualities of the "provider of the feast." As a species, we humans have become so far removed from these noble attributes that many of us have forgotten that this spiritual and practical potential lies within our present nature, rather than in some idealized or utopian future state of humanity.

---

20 https://kashgar.com.au/blogs/history/the-practice-of-sati-widow-burning
21 https://qz.com/586192/theres-a-misogynist-aspect-of-buddhism-that-nobody-talks-about/

> *We have been convinced over the last few millennia to abandon our choice and our subjectivity in favor of superstition or pseudo-scientific objectivity, a dogmatic religion in and of itself that would have you believe that the cosmos is merely random and mechanistic.*

We have been led to believe that spiritual life force is either a fiction or simply a belief rather than a birthright and a reality. How opportune for those in power. Now we have to find our value, purpose, and affirmation outside ourselves in self-appointed gods, institutions, and laws which coincidentally serve the interests of a small segment of the population.

> *It is time to reclaim the spiritual in its full power and glory while avoiding the distraction, misrepresentations, and outright frauds perpetrated in the **name** of spirit.*

For what church is actually teaching you to discern between the whisperings of the higher spiritual soul and the shouts of the lower animal mind? What classroom is helping you to distinguish between noble and high feeling and intuition versus ignoble and raw base emotion? What economic arena is building into its formulas the rewarding rush of spiritual energy one gains from giving to those who actually appreciate giving? What political forum encourages community members to listen to each other and help each other across ideological lines?

There *are* a few such examples, but they remain all too rare and hidden. It will be of crucial importance for us to more broadly and openly discern and choose between higher mind and lower mind, true joy and passing pleasure, between distraction, drama, and petty power games and an open-minded, full-hearted embrace of the best and highest in one another.

In doing so, we should recognize that we have been trained to buy into patriarchal powerlessness and want.

> *If we take the bait and accept profound spiritual alienation and disconnection, we obsess ourselves with "getting back our lost Eden" through the snake-oil salesmen, self-anointed authorities, and so-called experts of the world.*

Women are taught that they have no power and must get their value and survival met through men. Children are taught that they are helpless and blank humans, with nothing to offer until filled with the propaganda of approved "education."

Workers of the world are told they are worth nothing unless they are slaving away for some faceless corporation. Institutions and media peddle fear, fear, fear, constantly putting the higher human qualities like creativity in subservience to lower human motivations like financial profit. Other supposed "spiritual" gurus and schools of thought make themselves the "only path" and your divine genius contingent upon their approval. *But it does not have to be this way if we learn from our hidden histories and if we begin to look into, reveal, and share the hidden, profound parts of ourselves.*

The patriarchal "ruler on the throne" Adam and Eve interpretation in Genesis 2:4 – 3:22 has largely won out in Western religion, and very few people are even aware of the co-creative "provider of the feast" God of Genesis 1:1 – 2:3.

> *But there are glimmers of emerging hope as a whole new generation of "spiritual but not religious" seekers are throwing off the yoke of an ultimately anti-spiritual patriarchal framework.*

Women are once again re-emerging as spiritual leaders, healers, and prophets, in addition to entering leadership positions in work and broader public culture. We are at a very fertile and intriguing juncture, and the success of a "provider of the feast" way forward will depend in large part on men embracing the co-creative power of women and their own courage to redefine and grow into a new and powerful masculinity.

This is possible because the thread of "provider of the feast" has remained unbroken, even as it has been shrouded over the last 1,700 years. Other ancient traditions and cultures were able to keep elements of the co-creative male/female "provider of the feast" within their workings alongside the patriarchal slant of the "ruler on the throne." The Ancient Greek pantheon had a powerful council of both gods and goddesses located on Mount Olympus. Some of the most powerful forces were represented by goddesses, as with Athena, the goddess of wisdom. At the same time Zeus ruled the heavens, Poseidon ruled the sea, and Hades ruled the underworld, and they were all male. These gods and goddesses were an interesting combination of nobility and power, beneficence, and jealousy.

Even though it was men who owned property and participated in governance, Ancient Greeks still had stories about the Amazons, a fierce all-female fighting force, as well as very real historical examples of powerful, creative, and influential women, like Sappho, the noted educator on Lesbos who taught and wrote love poetry to other women.

> *The "provider of the feast" seems to have consistently found its way into every corner of humanity, even though its presence does not appear as obvious.*

Ancient Hebrew culture was almost entirely patriarchal, yet it gave birth to Jesus, a carpenter, prophet, and teacher, and a revolutionary body of community practices. These new principles and practices utterly challenged and transformed "ruler on the throne" hierarchical values and harsh practices into "provider of the feast" equality and compassion. In Jesus' time, the role of women in religious leadership sprang up again, and spiritual strength was seen in terms of capacity to love, rather than the ability to smite your enemies. Notions of privilege and power were overturned in favor of the "least being the first," "judge not lest you be judged," and "love your enemy."

In many ways the historical "provider of the feast" Jesus was the forebear of anti-sexism, anti-racism, and religious tolerance. This was evidenced in Galatians 3:28: "There is no longer Jew or Greek, there is no longer slave or free, there is no longer male and female; for all of you are one in Christ." Christ here was understood *not* as obedience and worship of Jesus, the figure, but as a body or community of equal spiritual relationship, according no special weight or "chosenness" to one's ethnicity, gender, or political standing.

> *In all three of the Synoptic Gospels (Matthew, Mark, and Luke), Jesus stridently and consistently insisted on abolishing "ruler on the throne" hierarchy in his spiritual fellowship, including **any kind** of subordination.*

Instead, he made the exact opposite, profoundly serving others, a requirement of his fellowship.[22] He often showed this "provider of the feast" principle in striking practical ways as when he reputedly washed the feet of the disciples, which was traditionally the act of a lowly slave, not a most exalted leader.

When Jesus' disciples were quarreling over who would be the greatest disciple in Jesus' eyes, Jesus simply said this:

> [42] ... "You know that among the Gentiles those whom they recognize as their rulers lord it over them, and their great ones are tyrants over them. [43] But it is not so among you; but whoever wishes to become great among you must be your servant, [44] and whoever wishes to be first among you must be slave of all. [45] For the Son of Man (Jesus) *came not to be served but to serve*, and to give his life a ransom for many." (my emphasis, Mark 10:42-45, also Matthew 20:25-28, and Luke 22:25-27)

In this, Jesus "walked his talk." He radically subverted hierarchies between men and women. Here are just a few examples hiding in plain sight even in those gospels approved by the church patriarchy for inclusion in the official canon called the Bible:[23]

- Jesus' inner circle included a number of women, including financial sponsors and those involved in ministry, as well as his mother Mary, and Mary Magdalene, who was the one who ostensibly discovered Jesus' empty tomb and was anointed as the "apostle of apostles" to communicate his resurrection.

22   https://en.wikipedia.org/wiki/Women_in_Christianity
23   https://en.wikipedia.org/wiki/Women_in_Christianity

- Jesus stopped a crowd of men from stoning to death a woman who committed adultery. Jesus confronted these men with an equal definition of justice: "Let he who has not sinned cast the first stone." The men walked away in shame. And yet Jesus also believed in accountability as well as mercy, saying to the woman, "Go and sin no more."
- Jesus allowed Martha's sister Mary to sit at his feet to receive his teachings, a position normally reserved for men.
- Jesus healed a woman who had bled from her womb for 12 years, purposefully breaking Jewish custom by interacting with an "unclean" woman.

In fact, if the Gospel of Thomas is to be believed, it was a woman, Mary Magdalene, who was the favored disciple and with whom he had the most intimate relationship:

> . . . the companion of the [Savior is] Mary Magdalene. [But Christ loved] her more than [all] the disciples, and used to kiss her [often] on her [mouth]. The rest of [the disciples were offended] . . . They said to him, "Why do you love her more than all of us?" The Savior answered and said to them, "Why do I not love you as (I love) her?"[24]

Some consider this text to be "heretical," even though the Gospel of Thomas was likely written during the same time or perhaps even earlier than the other gospels. However, even the "canonical" gospels, or texts approved by the patriarchal Christian Church, give abundant evidence of Mary Magdalene's status *above* the other male disciples.

---

24 http://www.pbs.org/wgbh/pages/frontline/shows/religion/story/pagels.html

"

In Luke 8:1-3 an apparently wealthy Mary Magdalene is listed as a financial supporter of Jesus' ministry. In the apocryphal ending of Mark's Gospel, she is the first witness of the resurrection (16:9). John's Gospel also identifies her in this way. From this material alone, and to say the least, Mary Magdalene was the most prominent of Jesus' women followers. Even more, as the first witness of Jesus' resurrection, she might arguably be identified as the foremost of all disciples, male or female, and even as the legitimate head of the church. This is because ignoring women altogether, the patriarchy's traditional argument for identifying Peter as "head of the church" has been that the risen Christ appeared first to him of all the (male) apostles.

"

Together the "heretical" and canonical gospels suggest a concerted effort on the part of early church leaders to erase the central role of Mary Magdalene and of women in general from the standard narrative about Jesus and the founding of the church.[25]

> *Why was this? You might be wondering at this point, given the overwhelming historical and biblical evidence of Jesus as a radically egalitarian revolutionary, anarchist, and feminist, why and how institutional Christianity completely remade him in its efforts to **uphold** patriarchy.*

---

25   https://www.opednews.com/articles/The-Case-for-and-Intimate-by-Mike-Rivage-Seul-120922-304.html

Much of this turn can be found in the patriarchal background and ambitions for power in his followers, including, most notably Simon Peter, upon whom the Catholic Church was built, and Paul, an upper-class, educated convert from a patriarchal Jewish sect.

Patriarchy reasserts itself

Peter was constantly striving to be Jesus' "right-hand man," a favored son and a high lieutenant in the growing religious movement that came to be called Christianity. Jesus did not look kindly on Peter's penchant for speaking for Jesus, or for Peter's priestly ambitions, and more than once rebuked him:

> [23] But (Jesus) turned and said to Peter, "Get behind me, Satan! You are a stumbling block to me; for you are setting your mind not on divine things but on human things." (Matthew 16:23)

It is no surprise, given the imperial, patriarchal turn of the Christian Church, that its founder, Simon Peter, denied Jesus, not once, but three times in the Bible.

Paul, on the other hand, was an influential early Christian evangelist and former patriarchal Jew. Paul used to be named Saul, and he persecuted and killed Christians before his conversion by a divine vision near Damascus. A great many of the New Testament readings are attributed to Paul, including some egalitarian passages and evidence that he worked favorably alongside female ministers in an early Christian church movement that was primarily composed of women.

However, Paul's/Saul's old patriarchal habits did not take long to reassert themselves in biblical passages that instructed wives to "submit to their husbands," cover their heads, be quiet, and assume no authority over men:[26]

> A woman should learn in quietness and full submission. I do not permit a woman to teach or to assume authority over a man; she must be quiet. For Adam was formed first, then Eve. And Adam was not the one deceived; it was the woman who was deceived and became a sinner. But women will be saved through childbearing—if they continue in faith, love and holiness with propriety. (1 Timothy 2:11-15)

By the 4th century A.D., the Christian Church completed its conversion into a fully imperial, patriarchal institution. Constantine, a Roman emperor and an opportunistic quasi-pagan, felt Christ had helped him win his wars. He made religious tolerance to Christianity his policy, eventually leading to its adoption as the state religion. This did not stop him from continuing to erect statues to himself and to pagan gods. Nor did this cause him to convert to Christianity until he was on his deathbed. His "conversion" at that time was not motivated by faith but was a transparent attempt to be cured of the illness that led to his death by appealing to the Christian god. And, yet, somehow, for this he is considered a saint by the Orthodox Church.

Thanks to various decisions from various councils in the 4th century among other factors, the Church effectively banned women from leadership in the Christian Church. Around that same time,

---

26   https://en.wikipedia.org/wiki/Women_in_Christianity#cite_note-32

the brilliant religious theorist and sex-addict, Augustine of Hippo, provided philosophical and theological support to the "ruler on the throne" orientation with his doctrine of "original sin" and the rest is history.

> *This spiritually ersatz mixture of patriarchy, imperialism, worldly power and religious hypocrisy kicked off a litany of patriarchal abuses by popes and emperors through the next 1,700 years to the present day.*

This includes popes who ordered the murder of rivals, committed adultery, sold the papacy, and promoted torture.[27] The Christian church has largely been an imperial, male-dominated, "ruler on the throne" church, built around domination, fear, and punishment.

If anything, Jesus' crucifixion has been contorted to stand as a deadly warning to any man that might attempt to defy ruling hierarchies, as Jesus challenged in his days the secular Roman officials and Jewish religious officials alike. Jesus' forgiveness, in like fashion, has been contorted into a blank check, a moral get-out-of-jail-free card, for various abuses by patriarchs. No matter how horrific their crimes, they can always be "forgiven" and absolved by a fraudulent notion of Christ which has no accountability and no consequences.

Taking back power— Developing critical mindedness, creativity, courage, confidence, and compassion in the exercise of the spirit

The hermetic tradition, an ancient esoteric body of wisdom that describes the interaction of spirit and the world, articulates the reality

---

27   https://en.wikipedia.org/wiki/The_Bad_Popes

and power of spirit: It is not so much that spirit dwells *in* the world or in the body, but that "matter clings to spirit."

> *Spirit is not opposed to the material Nor does spirit merely inhabit the material. Rather, spirit creates the material, just as intuition creates deeper knowingness and thought initiates everything human-fashioned. Therefore, we do not aspire to spirit; we are born from it, and it is our job to express spirit in the world in progressively more creative, refined, and elevated ways.*

This is the great secret. We are already "anointed" by our spirits to assert ourselves critically, creatively, compassionately, confidently, courageously, and even outrageously. The worldly "powers that be" would have us believe that to do so in a non-sanctioned way would amount to carnality, barbarity, and a host of other ills. *They are wrong.* They are confusing lower animal desire or appetites with desire writ large. What does that say about them? Are they unaware of higher spiritual, creative desire or are they simply terrified by it? It is up to us to share creative spiritual "powers that be" by banding together to confront and unplug from unhealthy systems of thought and to create a new reality in which spiritual confidence asserts itself in how we treat ourselves and one another.

With the rise of feminism in the late 20th and early 21st century, the reintroduction of women's public spiritual leadership, and the major collapses of legitimacy for patriarchy caused by its own actions (i.e., predatory sexual abuse), the world is experiencing real opportunity for human development and growth as well as a spiritual renaissance. By examining the legacy and details of "ruler on the throne" patriarchy and developing a "provider of the feast" alternative, we not only support the re-emergence of a strong feminine but also the birth of a strong and vital new spiritually confident masculinity.

So, let us now take a closer modern look at the dynamics of patriarchy and its spiritually confident alternative.

Dissecting the Ruler on the Throne: Assumptions and practices of patriarchy

For the past few thousand years, *patriarchy*, the notion that humans are to be ruled by the unquestioned emotional and mental ruling dispositions primarily of men has held sway. This "ruler on the throne" experiment (and it is only an experiment) has created several problems from the outset:

1. Patriarchal assumptions about unilateral domination by men contradict natural spiritual law, which recognizes the necessity of *polarity*, the co-equal but distinct participations of male and female in the creation of a healthy and vital life and society.

2. In patriarchy, men largely call the shots, ruling from one pole and *imposing* that pole and its assumptions on the world. This has led to a world in which different men with different assumptions about "what the proper male pole should be" end up warring with each other. This creates a world of destruction and a world in which authority is granted automatically on the basis of physical power and not virtue or care.

3. In other words, patriarchy succumbs to *arbitrariness*, the notion that "what I think" is true, not by inspection, testing, and relationship, but "because I say so." How can human beings spiritually grow and become confident in this kind of emotionally immature, self-glorifying culture? The conversation

has nowhere to go. You either agree with the Patriarchal Man, or you are meant to be damned and destroyed.

4. This imposition of small-mindedness through the use of physical power shrinks human possibility and treats as a threat our greatest spiritual gift—the *power to be creative* and transcend certain rules and limits. (Patriarchy's "rules" are nothing more than restrictions placed to keep this or that arbitrary male ruler in power, limiting possibility for everyone else in the kingdom.)

5. There has to be a higher authority than petty domination. Otherwise, human beings are seriously prevented from growing. *Spiritual authority* can only be accessed by linking to something greater than the self. For everyone, including leaders, to acknowledge this "greater than myself" creative reality is imperative for human progress and elevation.

6. Realizing this problem of a "greater than myself" power, instead of opening up and becoming creatively inspired, patriarchy decided to project itself on the heavens and *pretend* it was following a higher spiritual guidance. This kind of "higher authority" was nothing more than an idol, a projection of patriarchal whims on to the heavens. You can distinguish this idolatry from true spirituality any time you meet a supposed "holy man" who pronounces rather than listens attentively, who gives pre-formed answers rather than asking probing questions, who provokes rather than evokes, and who is asking for obedience rather than helping others.

To overcome the oppressiveness, tyranny, and destruction of the patriarchal "ruler on the throne," modern societies, following 16th and 17th century Enlightenment ideals of intellectual reasoning, individual rights, and scientific method, sought to develop an alternative.

> *However, this more recent variation just moved the oppression elsewhere, abusing Mother Earth as a proxy for women under the male-driven tyranny of technology and consumerism.*

As my wife, Regina says, "Now we had the privilege to be consumer slaves to the elite instead of physical slaves!"

While the hard patriarchy of "ruler on the throne" was driven by wrath, and dominated by jealous emotions, the soft patriarchy of Enlightenment reason allowed "cool heads" to engage in human engineering, creating a passive, but no less corrosive, form of patriarchy—"subjugator of the earth."

> *This soft patriarchy based on exploiting our planet and its resources destroys humanity through a different means by encouraging people to idolize their separated selves and reject greater giving, wisdom, love, or virtue.*

We are fast reaching the limits of our use of the earth's resources for our amusement and distraction. We are being forced to face our choices and to understand fully the systems that have influenced us, honor their lessons, and move on to a new world which encourages every man, woman, and child to contribute creatively and spiritually from the depth of their beings. Of the three orientations, "ruler," "subjugator," and "provider," the co-creative "provider of the feast" is the most viable and elevated way forward for humanity, because it is the only one that actually *includes* the feminine polarity and honors earth's web of life upon which we are dependent.

This extends to an even bolder claim: No authentic higher being or wisdom will *ever* demand obedience and subservience, as patriarchal systems do. "The higher" is wisely a *giver*. The higher "has" so it provides. A higher being's blessings, abundance, and friendship naturally *overflow*. A truly higher being only wants creative overflow, i.e., for *us* to be creative, elevated, and overflowing within ourselves, between ourselves, and in our relationship with our world. This requires full *choice*, not obedience.

The patriarchal "ruler on the throne" and the "subjugator of the earth" *prove their inferiority and weakness* by insisting on obedience, subservience, and worship to false, life-denying idols. *Clearly, they need something they do not have.* These clawing demands indicate attributes and actions of a less powerful, insecure, and threatened lower being, not of a higher being. Therefore, patriarchal gods are inherently false, if we take god to mean "the higher."

> *Patriarchal gods are "gods" only in the sense that we have chosen to worship them as higher, not because they are actually higher. Coercion, judgment, and condemnation are **not ever** the actions of a spiritually higher being. Taking, consuming, and exploiting are **not ever** the actions of a spiritually higher being. Co-creation, giving, and sharing are the actions of a spiritually higher being.*

By analogy, any wise parent serves as a companion, mentor, and uplifting example of giving and creating into the world. The less wise "hard patriarchal" parent demands worship, obedience, and control over the life of the child. The less wise "soft patriarchal" parent is indulgent, cloying, neurotic, spoiling a child with material goods and "all the things I never had." Any respectful, healthy higher mentor or parent will use a "high challenge, high support" approach and will consciously choose neither "tough love" nor indulgent adoration. The harshness of so-called "tough love" crushes the spirit and heart of a child. The learned helplessness produced by indulgence saps the will and courage of the child. Neither helps to create a spiritually confident child.

> *Spiritually confident men, on the other hand, do in fact intervene, disobey, and act up against a system they know to be dehumanizing not only to women and children but their very own spiritual character.*

They do not blame others for their faults, nor do they think misfortune is a sign that God doesn't like them. They allow setbacks and opposition to simultaneously strengthen them and open them to something larger. Their pain allows them to be more compassionate with others. They realize that one of the most damaging myths perpetrated by the Patriarchal Man is that hierarchies of human authority reflect divine hierarchies and that authorities at different levels are meant to play by entirely different rules. The spiritually confident man embraces the golden rule of "treat others as you would want to be treated" and see playing by different rules as inherently unjust and corrosive to human integrity.

The good and bad of patriarchy is that it is collapsing under the weight of its own obsolescence, cruelty, and contradiction. You can be assured that something as arrogant and old as patriarchy will try to commit murder-suicide and take everything with it—the planet, nations, and communities. However, it is up to us to withdraw our agreement from that failed system and create a new experiment, one which includes men and women co-creatively in the building of a new world and one which recognizes and welcomes truly higher and transcendent spiritual principles and influence. We can do this best by understanding the habits we have engrained in our bodies, minds, hearts, and even subconscious from thousands of years of patriarchal rule, not only of physical territory, but also of cultural, mental, emotional, and social space.

The seven C's: Confronting and transforming patriarchal habits

We don't have a lot of training in alternatives to patriarchal principles, norms, and practices. Most of us are still mired in coping and mitigation. We are still trying to clean up the messes created by patriarchal selfishness, environmental destruction, and hard-heartedness.

> *Especially now, as predatory patriarchy is losing its legitimacy in the light of exposure, there is a strong need and opportunity to develop a positive alternative to patriarchy for masculinity and male-female relationships.*

How do we take these initial steps forward? We must *presently* activate and rely on the principles and practices of the higher mind and spirit, instead of seeing them as idealized future states. Throughout history, as I have mentioned, humans have embodied and demonstrated the noble. *When we agree to see only the worst in us, we falter.* By doing so, we adopt the disempowering lens of the ruling patriarchs. Once we make that devil's agreement to view life as a curse, we have only two options: 1) capitulate to and obey patriarchy ("if you can't fight 'em, join 'em"), or 2) escape ("might as well have a (materialistic) good time"). Both of these options disempower human spirit and potential.

> *So, what are some of those high spiritual principles and practices that can help us move forward into a world of collaboration rather than domination, into a world in which the divine genius in every person has a place to offer itself and develop itself?*

In my work in human and spiritual development, I have come across what I call the seven C's, the indispensable virtues of an interactive, vital life: Critical-mindedness, capability, creativity, courage, compassion, community, and cosmic perspective.

Critical-mindedness: Critical-mindedness allows you to analyze context, question your world, and challenge others respectfully. The higher principle that guides critical-mindedness is absolute regard for *truth* and the humility to acknowledge that none of us individually or as a group have a complete truth. That is why human engagement is necessary and desirable. By engaging each other openly and respectfully, we come at a more nuanced, fuller experience and appreciation of larger truth.

Capability: Capability encompasses all those foundational aspects of the self that prepare you to engage more effectively. These aspects include desire, focus, skill, health, discipline, physical training, willingness to learn, ability to risk, "stretching yourself," and so on. The higher principle that guides capability is *excellence*. Capability is driven by the desire to improve, to know more, to refine the being. This operates on two levels: adopting positive traits (like those mentioned above) and avoiding negative drains that get in the way of excellence, like emotional distraction and food that is bad for your body and mind.

Creativity: Creativity helps you elicit and incorporate higher thoughts and feelings into the earthly realm. Creativity is one with insight, finding concrete analogies for abstract ideas, inspired art, and applied spirituality. The higher principle that guides creativity is *inspiration*. Creative actions have the effect of re-ordering assumptions and shaking up the status quo. That is why artists are the most "dangerous" people in the world. Once you change foundations, the ground you are standing upon, then you are no longer living in the same world.

Courage: Courage is one with calling out untruth and injustice, "calling it what it is." We might not desire to see certain unpleasant things about ourselves, others, and the world. Acknowledgment of these things may stress our self-esteem. However, it is the courageous who not only call out the crap of the world but who have the fiber to move into an alternative. The higher principle that guides courage is utmost, transparent *honesty*, piercing the masks and surfaces of things. Certainly, you can see this moral courage, in historical figures like Mahatma Gandhi, Martin Luther King, Jr., and Rosa Parks but courage does not have to be so epic. You can be courageous simply by being willing to stand apart and call out prejudice in any form including those prejudices in your own mind.

Compassion: Compassion has to do with emotionally intelligent openness, connection, and loving-kindness. Compassion means you can be vulnerable, evoke the self, and be empathetically present for the other. The higher principle that guides compassion is *care*. The world matters. Others matter. You matter. Truth matters. Creativity matters. This does *not* mean that others matter more than you or that you have to in any way sacrifice your dignity, authenticity, or sovereignty to attend to another being. Compassion is a choice. Compassion is spiritual solidarity, an affirmation of the high, strong, and tender. Its opposite is indulgence, which reinforces weakness, fear, and arrogance.

Community: Community is personhood shared. The higher principle that guides community is *respect*. Every single person has within them a light to share, a divine genius. This divine genius cannot go out into the world except by community. Others have to be able to identify and recognize the worth of divine genius on some substantive level for it to flourish fully. Yet, we have been taught to distrust each other, to believe that if unveiled, our inner self would reveal only depravity and barbarism. This is the propaganda of those who would have us bow to them rather than call them out as brothers and sisters. Community is embodied best, by this quote from my wife, Regina: "Bow to no one; honor everyone."

Cosmic perspective: With cosmic perspective, one sees not only the trees, not only the forest, not only the seeds which gave rise to the trees, but the very timeless, ageless, and infinite nature of spirit that gives rise to all things. The higher principle that guides cosmic perspective is grateful, expansive *wisdom*. As we live more deeply, we begin to realize we are not the only fish in the universal sea. Our circle of space widens. The richness of our lives grows. As we notice that our lives are continuous with other lives, our horizons of time advance. A calmness descends. We are not alone. We do not simply disappear when we die.

All life is transformation and graduation to greater knowing. What is known cannot ultimately be unknown, despite our greatest attempts to obscure the small but mighty purposes we possess by simply being. There is a persistent larger calling from our souls and spirits. Now it is up to us to do as we will with this deepening and expansion.

This deepening and expansion does not happen in the abstract but occurs in real time in engagement with real issues. One of the most polarizing issues, at least in the United States, is that of abortion. Could it be possible to apply these lofty virtues and principles to an issue so fraught with controversy? Isn't there a limit to how these virtues and principles can be exercised? I do not think so. Let's look at the issue of abortion, with an eye toward applying these virtues and transforming how the issue of abortion is framed and addressed.

The issue of abortion

Why couldn't the desired goal of any pro-spiritual person be that the rate of abortions be 0% and the rate of comprehensive support for women and children be 100%? I have noticed, underneath all the hyped animosity around abortion that we generally share common understanding as spiritual and moral individuals.

Here is what we essentially already agree upon: 1) No critically-minded person is trying to increase the rate of abortions or trying to glorify them as a good thing. 2) No compassionate person is trying to increase the rate of unwanted pregnancy. 3) No person with a cosmic perspective is trying to diminish a woman's or a girl's sovereignty or choice around this very difficult issue.

The first thing one notices when applying *critical-mindedness* is that essentially, no one is "pro-abortion." There is no sane or virtuous person on the planet who claims abortions are somehow beneficial in and of themselves or who treats an increase in the number of abortions as some kind of victory. For modern human beings, abortion is at best a choice for a pregnant woman or girl not to bear a child, necessitated by a host of considerations.

For most people, abortion is a difficult choice in a difficult situation. Access to abortion is maintained, according to advocates, to preserve the sovereignty of a potential mother. In short, we recognize that no one should be forced to give birth if stewardship over one's being is to be honored.

> *Women are not men's properties, not the properties of institutions or societies, nor are they simply incubators. They are sovereign beings whose choices over their bodies and their destinies call to be respected.*

This is linked to the notion of *capability*. If we are moral, we want each person to be able to reach and exceed their potential. *Forcing birth on a mother goes not only against sovereignty but also capability, denying not only her choice but sacrificing her potential to the dictates of others.* At the same time, societies on this globe have not been nearly *creative* enough in supporting *alternatives* to abortion.

> *For just as a woman should not be forced to give birth, neither should she be forced overtly or covertly to have an abortion.*

Across the board, in the U.S. relatively little attention has been given to *compassionate, community-supported* alternatives to abortions for potential mothers. Female sexual pleasure, self-esteem issues, feminine empowerment and other important factors leading to or preventing unwanted pregnancy are either inadequately engaged or not discussed at all.

Social *capability* means putting resources and policies toward the education and development of young men and women. Their sexuality ought to be aware and respectful and not simply repressed. Their knowledge should support healthy life choices and not simply acquaint them with life dangers. Their desire for more creative outlets, so often funneled into sex for lack of alternatives, might be better served by art and music cafés run by young people.

> *It takes **courage and creativity** to break ranks with the identity politics around abortion and develop attractive alternatives. Yes, you can be pro-choice and pro-life at the same time.*

Not everyone is pro-life, understood in its broadest, deepest, and more meaningful sense, as supporting the spiritual integrity and practical upholding of all life. If this were true, then the Patriarchal Man would be in favor of subsidized child care, contraception, women's rights, the empowerment of girls, and a broad list of other supportive measures that would both increase the quality of life for women and children *and* decrease both the number of unwanted pregnancies and abortions. The opposite is typically the case; Patriarchal Men use abortion bans as an enforcement tool of their ownership over women, while at the same time *cutting* support for women so that women's increased need makes them more desperate, pliable, and controllable. It is these contradictions that have to be addressed in a critically-minded, capable, creative, courageous, compassionate, community-oriented, and cosmically-conceived world.

Transforming patriarchal habits in relationships between men and women

> The patriarchal habit can be summarized as "me not you."

This takes on many forms: "either/or," "zero sum," "me against you," "me over you," "you for me," and so on. We can see this habit play out in familiar roles between men and women. The Patriarchal Man is "king of his castle," and expects to be waited on hand and foot for bringing home a paycheck from some industrial white collar job or blue collar work mill. The Patriarchal Man is taskmaster, expert, and authority, anointing himself as the boss in every situation, "mansplaining" things even to people who know more than he does. The Patriarchal Man is the kindly-seeming "father knows best," yet someone who still expects to have his pipe and shoes brought to him. The Patriarchal Man is the "lady's man," always on the make, promising love and fulfillment, while really just trying to get women into bed before he leaves them.

This is not limited to heterosexual men. Gay men have their versions of these Patriarchal Men premised on power, with terms like "tops" and "bottoms" to denote the "man" in the relationship. Obviously, this patriarchal dynamic is changing somewhat given the advent of women in work, the slow and somewhat erratic infiltration of Equal Men into childrearing and sharing household chores, as well as the marrying of gay men and their opportunity for domestic life.

The roles of women have historically formed in reaction to the Patriarchal Man. As a result, many of these roles are simply not that healthy or fulfilling either. The "queen of the house" (or the queen bee of the schoolyard), uses her centrality in family or social relationships to wield a somewhat dictatorial power. The "damsel in distress" who uses her coy weakness and victimhood to entice a white knight to save her. The idolized woman on the pedestal is supposedly exalted for her beauty yet is trapped to live out what others project upon her. The corporate supermom expects and is expected to do everything well—career, children, domesticity, triathlons.

> *For all the talk about equality between the sexes, we still have far to go.*

Equal men are participating in child rearing and household chores, but not as much as you would expect. Pay disparity between men and women for the same job has diminished, but not by significant leaps. We tend to be creatures of habit and simply assimilate and imitate even outdated ways of operating. To change habits, we must consciously and concretely intervene in old relationship roles and "learn into" new ways of relating. In this process, good men and women, even sincere spiritually confident men and women, get hung up.

Patriarchal norms create blind spots and assumptions even among the most aware. When "givers" have generous feelings toward others, they tend to take others at their word, often ignoring their actions. Givers may project love on another person who is consciously or unconsciously manipulating them. A giver might say, "Well, you can't simply use someone if you love them." That's not true for a taker. Takers can and do use someone because "love" to them is a commodity just like everything else.

> *Again, there is no need to go on the warpath against takers. It is time for "givers" to identify "takers" by their actions, withdraw their energy from them, and share that energy with other givers.*

This is the process of being critically-minded without being skeptical or cynical. You are simply seeing what takers are communicating underneath their words and choosing not to participate. It is a form of civil disobedience.

For instance, it is common for a taker to make a little "test comment," a slightly mean or demeaning comment. Givers will often make excuses for them: "Oh, she was just teasing." "Oh, he didn't really mean that." No. That remark is a "tell." Small lies or put-downs should be treated as big neon signs that you are dealing with a taker, grooming you with flattery, only to indoctrinate you with put-downs that get you to scramble for approval and authority. Find another giver and leave this taker.

Conclusion: What is at stake? Only the future of humanity!

The tendency toward patriarchy has always been in the human possibility since the dawn of humanity. Just the very fact that men were built to physically stronger than women, gave them an opportunity to anoint themselves as stronger overall (forgetting that women tend to be stronger and more intelligent emotionally). Likewise, physical survival has always been an important aspect of human existence, but there is no rule to exalt that above all other aspects.

> *Perhaps simple opportunism has gotten the better of men. Men **could** exert their strength over others and enjoy certain perks. Men **could** use physical power over another's survival to get what their lower minds wanted. But there was no injunction, or nature, or law that **made them do that**. **It was a choice, and it can be unchosen, and another choice can be made.***

Even men can now see the full results of this experiment in exploitative opportunism, and it is a lose-lose proposition creating untold cruelty and suffering.

> *The current world demands a new and nobler experiment for men and for the humanity they serve.*

Freedom comes from realizing that we no longer need the old patriarchal system. It is time to unplug and co-create a new, vibrant reality. If we look at the history of humanity, we can glean moments of transcendent beauty and progress, and we can also certainly notice stretches where humanity seems to have descended into a war against itself. It is in this struggle between the beautiful and the grim, between the reality of a spiritual aspect of ourselves (that transcends suffering and endures past our death), and the reality of the animal part of ourselves (concerned with avoiding pain and physically surviving) that we find the richness of the human experience.

Ultimately, we choose how this contradictory and productive dynamic plays out. We humans have sovereignty and choice not only as our birthright but as a requirement of our very existence. We do not have to choose violence and war. It is not our "nature" to choose war any more than it is to be kind 100% of the time. Both of these possibilities are within our nature as possibilities and, thus, choices.

Right now, in human history, we humans, we *men* in particular, are at a crucial decision point. We can either choose "the provider of the feast" and thrive or choose the "ruler on the throne" and bring about our destruction. There is a third non-option that we are entertaining presently—escape. Escape involves the modern delusion that we can simply skip past the choice between "provider" and "ruler" and bask in a netherworld of materialist, consumerist pleasure where everyone is encouraged to ignore fateful choices, and consequences for future generations.

> *We have a choice to make. What good does it do us if we "survive" by leading a life of suspicion and fear, only to die alone and afraid? What good does it do us if we lead a life of enjoyment and pleasure only to find we have contributed and created nothing for others and for this world and the life that has been gifted us?*

However, we have yet to fully embrace *co-creating* (rather than ruling or escaping) and giving our lives over to an adventure of connection, compassion, creativity, and high inspiration.

It is time we start on a new adventure and trajectory, individually and collectively. This begins, in many ways (as shown in the next chapter) with how we raise our daughters and sons to be spiritually confident beings in a spiritually-developing world.

CHAPTER 6

Bringing Home The Harvest—Raising Men And Boys; Opening To Women And Girls

It is very hard to raise a boy to be a man when so many of the men are boys. This is the great ache of our time. All persons desire a man with strength, composure, and grace, but where are these men to come from?

When I speak of "raising" men and boys, I am drawing upon its many senses— "raising the bar" (elevation), "raising the crops" (cultivation), and "raising children" (rearing the young). When we examine current masculinity much of what we see resembles genetically manipulated, waxed, and artificially fertilized tomatoes. They look "perfect" on the exterior, but once you bite into them, you notice a bland, pulpy or woody taste. In masculinity, there is a similar cost for projecting one's outer image at the expense of inner character. A man cannot be all things to all people. If he is to elevate himself and facilitate the healthy growth of the younger generations, then he must concentrate upon the "juice" of life, not a flawless exterior.

This commitment to raising male energetic frequency also

has the benefit of cultivating authenticity over exaggeration. It encourages males to shed their sense of inadequacy when they do not look like a superhero, or they don't acquire the fame of a mega-celebrity. Their "heroic" value has a different basis—engaging the unknown frontiers of the masculine and feminine, rather than reeling under oppressive stereotypes. Such bold and enterprising men reap what they sow and enjoy the benefits of a succulent personal and social growing season.

An opening meditation for men:

Close your eyes and take time to imagine a perfect day when you were a boy. Think and feel through all the things you do, the favorite foods you eat, your favorite activities, the places you go, the friends you meet up with, the people who make your heart skip just a little bit faster. Take some time to live that perfect day. Picture the surroundings. Hear someone saying something nice to you. Feel the sense of limitless joy and exuberance of that boy, where everything seems to just flow. What does it feel like? What effect did this have on you now?

Now imagine an experience when you were put down or treated roughly by other males. Imagine a time when your dreams were smashed, your choices rejected, or when you felt shut down by obligation or punishment. Feel the emotions associated with that experience. Did this treatment continue? Did you retreat, feel humiliated, or angry? Or perhaps you were one of the bullies, and you felt the pressure to be king of the hill? What effect did this have?

Early on, very often, a boy spends time doing things that bring him a measure of joy. Later he begins to feel the small and large traumas associated with being a male in modern society. Coming of age for a male can be an exercise in trying to extend his spirit but getting beaten back and becoming emotionally injured, tired, or confused. A grief weighs on his heart. He is spiritually knocked off his center, finding it hard to recover his footing. His later life becomes an effort to regain what he lost or an attempt to prove himself above it all. The same central challenge persists, however: How might men let go of these compensations and embark on a new and healthy path of masculine development?

There remains a boy in every man, hidden sometimes, which he never loses. In this, we can delight...to an extent. We talk about "boyish charm" and that boyish glow of excitement in a man's eyes when he gets giddy over some new grown-up toy he has received like an ATV or some new gadget for his tool shed. Such a boy-man is irrepressible, hopeful, ardent, and energizing. He has retained some of that creative joy of youth. This is good. But how does he carry his energetic youthfulness forward and yet still grow into mature manhood?

> *What happens when a boy-man refuses amid this boyish flurry to grow wise, tender, and more refined? What happens when a man believes that growing up will strip him of those things he loves, and so refuses to grow?*

What might help a boy to develop into a higher and more fulfilling state of being? What prompts the juvenile man toward vibrant, strong, and reliable masculine polarity capable of manifesting great things instead of merely playing with things?

These are the questions to guide this chapter. We are in a crisis of masculinity. Many men *are* refusing to grow. Many men are raising sons without a transcendent, higher vision of what male energy can contribute to the world, and many are absent from raising sons at all.

There are plenty of new calls for the reassertion of "real men," but these invocations come off more like a retreat to exaggerated representations of by-gone masculinity as we see with professional wrestling. Such overcompensation may help men paper over their insecurities, but it will do little to help men mature.

> *Emotional regression does not solve a man's war with himself and others, nor does it help him connect with his own spirit.*

At the core of this regression and compensation is a lost sense of significance. Loss of male meaning is heavily tied to men's loss of status in society. Having learned to base much of their self-esteem and worth on accomplishing set tasks and holding an honored, recognized status in society, many men lack the wherewithal to reinvent themselves. Under patriarchy, men did not need to *do* much besides be men to receive social standing. Superiority became a sort of birthright, reinforced by fathers, mothers, and society alike.

> *This sense of superiority led to entitlement, and this entitlement has weakened men in a myriad of ways. Once men became entitled, they no longer had to initiate, create, or care.*

The world was simply supposed to serve them. "Let the secretary do all the work while I go out and golf and cut business deals." Men have no enemy but themselves to blame for this pernicious weakening. The collapse of masculine entitlement has caused a crisis in male identity. Universities and increasingly the workforce are now being dominated by women (even though they get paid less) because women are more motivated to advance and provide a living for others. Fortunately, this collapse of traditional sources of male worth also creates an opportunity for men's rebirth and redemption.

What is today's men's transcendent vision or motivation? There isn't a clear candidate. Reasserting the "real man," the wild man, the caveman, even the responsible father are examples of re-casted *roles*. They do not have a creative, transformative, advancing power in them. Men seem to need a jolt, a collective rite of passage out of infantilized and entitled patriarchy. What will lead today's men out of historical adolescence and into a new interactive spiritually confident and productive reality?

Why not ask women? They have struggled, suffered, and fought for dignity under this patriarchal adolescence for millennia. Maybe they know a thing or two! I say this sardonically because it seems as if practically every "men's studies" type of movement just turns back to other men. Not that sweat lodges and drumming circles aren't helpful to a degree. They can be. They simply are not sufficient. The problem with masculinity is *not* simply about men forgetting themselves and needing to remember. It is about men learning, growing, and transforming *beyond* themselves.

If you ask a woman

What is this resistance from a man when it comes to learning from a woman? Does this learning make him less of a man or more of a man? Patriarchy would have you believe that any male interaction with a woman (outside of using her for his own ends, i.e., sexual conquest) makes a man less of a man. There are three "reality checks" to note here: 1) Respectful interaction requires more from a man. 2) Using others is a confirmation of weakness, not strength. 3) Strength can be quiet rather than loud. Who, indeed, is stronger—a man who is prideful, stubborn, and noisy or one who is proactive, appreciative, and engaging?

We know that the magnanimous, spiritually confident male embraces and celebrates others in their own right. He does this partly by learning from others. On the other hand, the spiritually insecure man attempts to dissolve and assimilate others because he cannot handle the enlargement of his world. He needs to remain a relatively larger fish in a small pond because his self-esteem is too fragile to venture out into grander possibilities where, yes, he will become more powerful, but the world around him will also become more complex and spacious.

> *Learning from women is not a "generous" gesture; it can be men's delight and a potent pathway to excellence.*

In learning from a women, men are giving something far more important than attention; they are sharing human and spiritual respect. They are saying in essence, "I honor your person by inviting your experience to affect me." There is a similar difference on the physical level between men "helping" their wives or girlfriends with the dishes, and those who realize that it is not women's job to serve them. Therefore, they choose to be equal partners in household chores. Besides, aren't chores the same as tasks, the things men are supposed to enjoy accomplishing?

Here are some things I've learned from women that I have found to be true and helpful for men. This applies not just to improving relationships between male and female but in strengthening masculinity and healing the damage caused by patriarchal practices and norms *to everyone,* women and men, boys and girls. These invocations are not "demands" from women, but a powerful list of more advanced practices that can aid a man in developing a more spiritually confident commitment to himself and others. These practices invite deeper capability, higher vision, ethical integrity, and greater regard.

- **Listen with an ear toward learning and engagement, without defensiveness or threat.** There is simply no need to deny, dissuade, evade, or project. The person in front of you is not an object to convince. Your spiritual confidence and energy derive from *synergy,* that unpredictable "more" that happens in interactive receiving and listening. A man knows himself and shows himself far better in his capacity to listen than in his capacity to impress.

- **Support others to be their brightest.** Supporting another person is a way of asserting manhood. Support ennobles a man and takes him beyond the boy always needing to be the center of attention. A confident man does not have to be the artificial source of "light" attracting others like buzzing insects. He lets the light from his own heart be known in a relationship and draws the people who are right for his intention and level of development.

- **Relate to others as people not as problems to be solved.** This is a common complaint. Men seem to get nervous when presented with an open-ended situation in which the other person's discomfort or challenge cannot be resolved by traditional means. Why does it have to be resolved? Can't a man simply listen to a woman's challenge, grief, or frustration and work through it with her with questions, rather than attempting to solve it for her unilaterally? Why not allow a genuine conversation to create a pathway toward resolution? This requires patience and humility.

- *Offer* **rather than authorize.** Sometimes a person does not need your help or advice. Sometimes, even if you can help, it is important that you step back and allow someone else to struggle with their challenges constructively. It is better to be a guide and a mentor than a "white knight." This is especially true with children trying to make their way in the world.

- *Confront* **your ignorance and excuses.** Don't make constant excuses to get away from learning or to avoid some consequence! "I didn't know that kind of thing hurt your feelings." Sure, you did. You are saying that to avoid acknowledging you wounded someone you care about. "I wasn't flirting with that woman...That's just your opinion." Really? There was no energy going between the two of you during that hour-long animated conversation? Hey, it's okay, *but be real.* Or how about this one: "Oh *women*, you can never understand them, so don't try." What is more irrational than a woman who holds contradictory feelings? A man who isn't able to recognize that this is normal and dismisses her out of hand.

- *Hold* **yourself to a high standard and act accordingly.** Heed the motto in the movie *The Kingsmen*: "Manners maketh men."

The lead character, played by Colin Firth, uttered this before he elegantly and violently dispatched a group of hooligans. Manners don't make you a wimp, or a momma's boy, and there should be no "manly" nostalgia for rudeness. Manners are an assertion of refined command and generosity of spirit. I've never had a person scold me for opening a door in the thousands of times I've opened doors for women and men because I do not do it to be paternalistic or recognized for my efforts. I do it to be thoughtful, and because it makes me feel good to help others.

- *Show up* and step up. Be a continuing presence. Don't seek to bail when a situation overwhelms you. "Be vividly a man," not a non-entity. When you lose your job, or you fail expectations, be resilient. Take your time. It happens. Take your rest. Lick your wounds. Share your disappointment, and then get up. Let passion be stronger than failure. Rather than, "Hey, I'll never do that again," why not "Hey, I've learned something new today; let's try it another way."

- *Give* without expecting a reward. In the mature man, giving *is* the reward. He sees his generous act as a translation of spirit into the world, and he can feel that flow of energy. He engages on the *intrinsic* joy level versus the *instrumental* got-to-get-something-for-it level. This also takes pressure off the receivers of your giving. They are invited to "pay a kind act forward," rather than wondering what you may want from them. The game of giving is itself the point, not some prize or trophy you get from it. On the other hand, as I have mentioned, do not be a foolish giver to mere takers. Find someone who can respect and appreciate your giving.

- *Stand* up for yourself and be able to stand on your own. There are few things sadder than the beaten-down man, the hen-pecked husband, the bullied sad sack at work or the constantly needy boyfriend who can't seem to decide which restaurant to go to much less what he will do with his life. Such a man is defeated and has agreed to stay down. A man may not know what he is doing. A man may fail. However, the ability to get back up, learn, and make a clear decision guides a man past repeated failures and allows him to show up for the next opportunity. This happens in both saying "yes" to the next moment and saying "no" to what has not worked. There is a difference between stubbornness and resilience.

- *Admit* limitations. The other side of the man with no self-respect is one who constantly tries to be the hero and refuses to recognize his present limitations. A man who honestly identifies limits can share his struggle and his journey. Such a man knows how to rest and reflect instead of desperately prove himself all the time. Such a man asks for help and appreciates such help. There is courage in admitting weakness or inability. This is not forever, and such honesty is critical to mental and emotional health as well as improvement.

- *Be graceful* in victory and defeat. Give it your best and win and lose graciously, whether it be an argument or a sports contest. One of my favorite scenes in real life is when one man says to another man or a woman close to him, "Touché" ("you've scored a point there"). It shows appreciation of skill. The other person in any contested situation can be viewed as a noble adversary, not to be destroyed but to be engaged and even enjoyed. The purpose of this engagement is to invite some higher kind of truth or excellence. Ultimately, for human character, it does not matter who scores the points, but who recognizes the value of engagement and comes to greater wisdom.

- *Risk* yourself emotionally. Thrills are not simply to be found in physical danger, extreme sports, or drunken binges. "Putting yourself out there" emotionally may feel far more death-defying for men. Most would rather risk breaking their necks than breaking their egos! But what is the ego holding on to? An image? A man with spiritual confidence actively wants his image dissolved so he can leave its cocoon. The way forward, he knows, is to share something of himself that he has been hiding or knows little about.

- *Heal* thyself and others. Women I know constantly observe that when men give a back rub, they almost inevitably view it as a prelude to sex. What would it be like for a man to extend a powerful, sensual, masculine healing touch? What would it be like for his hands to gently and firmly channel masculine energy into the body and being of his beloved? Once a man gets out of the "investment" frame and gives something for its own sake without expecting something in return, he is freed to direct his energy in liberated ways. Healing happens when unconditional giving is the intention.

- *Be a rebel* for virtue over vice. Allow a higher vision to get under your skin and into your blood. Challenge meanness openly, firmly, and respectfully. Refuse the patriarchal programming that one never challenges another man in the pecking order. It is in the best interests of men not to kowtow to what other guys want or tolerate their worst behavior. This is not a matter of prudishness, harsh judgment, or control-freakishness, but rebellion against relationship habits that serve no one.

These are not dreary and impossible demands but an actual roadmap for men to become vibrant from their efforts and choices. These choices communicate openness and a real sense of adventure. It's an all-to-common cliché: A typical man in a mid-life crisis ditches his wife or long-time partner for a "younger version." He is hoping to recapture his youth (or beat back his fear of death) by reliving a physically virile past. He does not have to choose to do this. If he is courageous and enterprising, the waning of the physical could focus him toward enlarging his spiritual character. A man is now *freed* to abandon his vanity and acquire depth. Aging opens him to a new basis of significance—seeing through and behind surfaces to the substance of his being and that of others.

A man turned back upon himself: The dangerous alternative to positive masculine transformation

In patriarchal cultures, men have turned back upon themselves, not just in trying to recapture their youth but in rejecting the opportunities brought about by their aging. There is a natural transition from physical to spiritual as a man ages. Physical injuries take longer to heal. Physique, "being in shape," is harder to maintain. Physical erections may become harder to achieve. This progression leads most men into despair because they only see the encroaching blackness of their own death and the fading of their youth. Their old immature competitions and cocksure assertions of superiority are no longer plausible. So now, where is a man to find his sense of worth?

> *What might happen, however, if men could see physical change as a stage of molting, transformation, or even liberation toward a higher way of perceiving and being?*

What if I think about aging differently ¾ that I was once trapped in the body and its ready conceits but am now invited to see beyond its limitations? Might the physical changes in aging help bring on the advancement of growth in spirituality not so tied to the body? You see this in micro form in the practice of yoga. I practiced Kundalini yoga intensively for 15 years. At a certain time in the practice, I began to notice the challenges Kundalini made to my emotions. Fear, in particular, began to give way to more gentle and profound insights as well as more subtle and powerful energy. I was drawn out of alienation with my spirit, developed through the dark night of the soul, and into the realm of the sun, into *connection*—intimacy, spirituality, wisdom, perceptiveness, equanimity, and peace.

Dominance-mindedness, reassertion of the physical, and refusal to let go, on the other hand, reinforce immaturity, negativity, destruction, and cruelty. The sad irony is this: Holding on to past privilege and habits by turning against the world prompts men inevitably to turn against themselves. They age all that much quicker with each hair transplant, testosterone supplement, and arrogant treatment of others.

> *The reverse positive irony is also true: The more a man relinquishes his attachment with the world and develops a relationship with his spirit and the spirit in others, the younger and more vital he looks and feels.*

He is no longer weighed down by the trappings (and traps!) of the world: the dreary burdens of expectations, impressing others and dutifully toiling away for promotion at work. These give way to a man's opportunity to endeavor from his unique divine genius. Instead of competition with others, he is now freed to work with others. Instead of becoming envious of the health and success of others, they give him a sense of joy that the world is advancing in fullness. Instead of comparing himself, he is brought into his originality and can sense the unborn uniqueness of his being coming forward.

When a man ages—this is his time!

This section looks at the harmful consequences of impotent rage, a man turning back against himself and others in avoiding his own aging and death and attempting to control the world. It also examines the healthy alternative—what might happen when a man embraces his own death and his spirit in the service of the world.

> *It is almost as if immature men in this regard feel they owe a certain spite to the world for "setting them up" with a strong body only to cruelly leave them with a feeble body at the close of death. Forget how poorly these same men have treated that world and those people within it!*

Again, this angst around aging is premised upon a lowered conception of power—power in and over the world. As I have said in the introduction, the spiritual man realizes he is master only of himself and no other. The spiritual man derives his power from creative life. He expresses this power in ultimate giving. He fully accepts and appreciates his death, because his life has been such a gift. He has become the "crown" the corollary to the woman who has become the wise "crone."

Our global society is currently experiencing widespread and daunting "macro" historical change, analogous to the micro transition of individuals aging and dying. Old ways are dying, and new "life," in the form of new understanding and practices of masculinity and femininity are beginning to emerge. Our initial impulse may be to either destroy this challenge of change or deny it, yet neither is a viable way forward. We cannot turn back the clock. We cannot unknow what we know.

According to my reading of *Power and Innocence*, a book by the existential psychologist, Rollo May[28], humans, and men, in particular, have three basic responses to challenge and change: destructive aggression, pseudo-innocence, and creativity (which May calls "constructive aggression"). Destructive aggression, the adolescent will to conquer and subjugate, is often exhibited in the conservative elements of society seeking to uphold the status quo and beat back agents of change. Here the tension of change is subverted through some kind of strident protest or actual violence meant to annihilate challenge. This can take the form of setting one's self "apart, over, and against" any force confronting conventional power.

Pseudo-innocence, the childish will to ignore the demands of change and escape learning, is often exhibited in the liberal elements

---

28   Rollo May, Power and Innocence: A Search for the Sources of Violence (NY: W.W. Norton and Co., 1972)

of society. Here the tension of change and the difficulty of the challenge is avoided by denying one's necessary active choice and participation in human development. This can take the form of attempts to create a false "peace" by enforcing passivity or civility through political correctness, self-esteem therapy, drugs, or some other mechanism.

Creativity (or "constructive aggression"), the mature adult will to transform, is often exhibited within progressive elements of society. Here, change and challenge are embraced in a positive rebellion against unjust or constricting norms driven by a desire to innovate. This can take the form of a "velvet revolution," bringing one's self into connection and equality with others while drawing upon individual talents, powers, and gifts to create a new community or society.

I will contend that our world in general and men, in particular, cannot afford destructive aggression or pseudo-innocence. The lower conception of power-as-physical (destructive aggression), leads men down a dark path of militarization/necrophilia, sexism, homophobia, pedophilia, pornography, instrumentalism, and technological transhumanism. The supposedly "neutral" path of pseudo-innocence ends up ceding the reins of power to destructive, aggressive forces to preserve its own "purity" and ignorance. The higher conception of power-as-spiritual (creativity), guides humans toward a path of light—well-being/biophilia, polarity, solidarity, honoring and learning from children, intimacy, intrinsic-ness, and sublime divinity.

> *There **is** a battle going on, but it is not between "men" and others, but between allegiances to the material world and commitments to the non-material spirit **within** human beings, between the destructive and the creative.*

Militarization/necrophilia vs. well-being/biophilia

Inside each man dwells a vital choice to either destroy life (necrophilia) or uphold life (biophilia). I have talked about this earlier as the decision to either "take" or "give."

> *Shall I take from others and the world in resentment that I shall someday die, or shall I give my life in appreciation of that life which has been given me? Shall I rationalize "just" wars in which children get slaughtered, or shall I stand for just treatment where the sick get healed and the poor get fed? Shall I bend to "survival of the fittest" philosophies that allow me to overrun the least powerful, or should I extend a generous and kind hand to those in pain?* **Where do I find my value as a man?**

To the great detriment of human well-being, this internal battle in men between world and spirit, between lower and higher, between destruction and creation, has externally expressed itself as a desire for military control. The dynamic that results is captured well in this quote by Saint Bruno, the 11th-century founder of the Carthusian Order of monks:

It is indeed pointless to attack exterior enemies if we at first do not conquer those inside ourselves. If we are unable first to subject our own bodies to our wills, then it is extremely shameful and unworthy to wish to place under our control any sort of military force... Let us therefore first of all conquer ourselves so that we may then go forth in safety to combat external foes; let us purge our souls of vices before we rid the land of barbarians.[29]

This struggle to become more spiritually confident and competent should not be confused with an idealized state of final perfection. Spirit does not need nor want finality; it wants well-being, growth, and contribution. A desire to achieve (and then impose) so-called "perfection" could only come from a lower, insecure place. In fact, any attempt to coerce and circumscribe the creative growth and choice of another person will come from a lower place. It is the desire to heal rather than hate that turns a man toward the spiritual and to his higher self. And the healing of a man starts with the compassionate, responsible discipline of his vices.

Sexism vs. polarity

When male vices are externalized, we get sexism and a host of other ills. These vices root themselves in resentment against creation.

> *When a man walls off his heart, he cannot create, and he compensates for this loss of power through the inferior power offered by control.*

29   Saint Bruno, Lettres des Premiers Chartreux, 154-61 in Freddy Silva, First Templar Nation: How Eleven Knights Created a New Country and a Refuge for the Grail (Rochester, NY: Destiny Books, 2017) 69-70.

Male-dominated military, political, technological, and economic powers ally themselves to control the sources and bases of creation because they cannot themselves create. It is no surprise, then, that these materialist sources of value and power become anti-women and anti-nature. Women and nature are symbols of organic, natural creation, a birthright and a gift for all humans. Women gestate and birth human life. Nature gestates and births every life upon the face of our planet. Women and nature represent the "wild," unpredictable, and *authentic* sources of creation. Yet this "unauthorized" spontaneous creation is often considered a threat to those who prize control.

What would happen if men recognized that the impulse to control comes from an insecure place and that they could join creation instead of trying to subjugate it? Again, this gets to which "god" a man follows, a destructive, punitive god or a creative, benevolent god.

> *Control is enclosed. It needs no one and nothing else except the person exerting control. "Co-creation," on the other hand, involves another principle or force greater than the self.*

With control, there is no need for vulnerability or listening, only the unapologetic exertion of force. Perfectionism can be imposed on others without feedback to enact a chilling "order." Co-creation demands and desires vulnerability because there is no such thing as self-sufficient creation.

What if men succeed in extinguishing the creative feminine through sexist practices? They would destroy themselves and the whole purpose for their masculinity.

> *Without feminine polarity, there is no place toward which masculine polarity can move and generate a life current.*

If sexism succeeds in making the feminine principle of reception and creation (embodied in the human female and feminized Nature) the inferior "Other," then vital life is imperiled. Male and female principles together create life. Gender equality is, therefore, necessary for the highest and fullest expression of vital masculinity.

Attempting to rid the world of masculinity would similarly bring on self-destruction. Let us be alerted to superficial androgyny, which attempts to dissolve feminine and masculine polarities altogether. Masculinity itself is not evil, but a vibrant and necessary energy. Attempts to criminalize masculinity end up with the same kind of destruction produced by attempts to marginalize and put down femininity. It is all too tempting to make a buffoon out of men or imply that the concept of manhood itself was somehow outdated. *Men need renewal and redemption, not erasure.*

> *Healthy androgyny involves recognizing and developing the best aspects of strong femininity and masculinity within the self. Unhealthy pseudo-androgyny involves trying to erase the poles of gender altogether and abandoning both masculine and feminine energy.*

Homophobia/disconnection vs. brotherhood/solidarity

Patriarchal men who have abolished the feminine in themselves and their surroundings are by definition "homosexual" in its unhealthy sense. They recognize only one sex as having value. Ironically, it is these same men that seem to be the most homophobic toward gay men in the more common sense of homosexuality as sexual orientation.

> *To patriarchal men, gay relationships represent a feminization of at least one of the men, and it terrifies them on some level. They do not want even to imagine the possibility of a man being cast into the role of women, open to abuse and rape.*

The uncomfortable jokes about not reaching down for the soap in prison only begin to get at this fear within male culture. This fear expresses itself as a refusal to be warm and affectionate with other men. ("Hey, I don't want you to get the wrong idea!") Well, why should any guy get the wrong idea? Gay or straight, what's wrong with open affection and friendship between men?

Emotional warmth is superior to stoicism. Emotional warmth binds men together through something far more healthy and productive than the trauma of war. Brotherhood and solidarity demand a different basis for male camaraderie, creating communities of mutual interest instead of being confined to the mindless rituals of drinking and watching sports (not that those don't have their place).

> *It will be the job of emerging men and masculinity to form the basis of emotional warmth and communities of interest among men.*

In keeping with the theme of the spiritually confident "giving" man, why can't men band together to build a youth center, instead of sitting around the den watching football? Why can't men go on an outdoor retreat with a high-ropes course, instead of shooting some deer? Men must reclaim not only lost affection but a sense of adventure and imagination that can lead them beyond their current habits.

Pedophilia vs. honoring and learning from children

In patriarchal cultures, like those of Ancient Greece and Rome, homosexual practices were either tacitly or openly accepted. This drive toward functional homosexuality, even among heterosexual family men, was a consequence, in my opinion, of men *erasing* the feminine in themselves and subjugating the feminine in the world. Men under patriarchal systems cannot relate as deeply to women. Unfortunately, such patriarchal cultures also approve of hierarchical power arrangements that make it acceptable for older men to sexually exploit and steal the innocence of younger youth, thus creating a cycle of emotional theft and sexual manipulation. This domination of the younger male reinforces an unhealthy lesson: Sexual autonomy depends upon the control of others.

> *If a male's innocence is corrupted in a sensitive period of growth, he may become emotionally injured in a lasting way, perpetuating the antispiritual practices of dominance and subordination.*

I believe the patriarchal motivation to become "rulers on the throne," and to take from others, finds its roots in men's corrupted innocence. When men steal the innocence of others through physical violence, sexual violation, circumcision and other similar practices, they become literal vampires of innocence. This is most acutely seen in sexual predators and pedophiles. The sexually predatory pedophile, like a vampire, draws out the blood of innocence through sexual abuse to sustain his own aging body and decrepit spirit. He "grooms" or co-opts these same boys into being perpetrators themselves to normalize his behavior and indict them in the abusive behavior so that they do not tell other people. This move is much like a vampire who turns another person into a vampire by only sucking part of their blood and teaching them to feast on others.

This leads to an important opening principle for all men, especially fathers:

> *No matter how much a man may have been abused by other men it is critical first and foremost that a good man does not pass this abuse along.*

No healthy growth comes from violation of the spirit or anything through which the spirit is meant to express itself freely and vitally, such as thoughts, emotions, or the body itself. A man must choose to be a champion of life in all its forms and not a destroyer of life. *Authentic innocence (versus 'pseudo-innocence') is a vital relationship with the renewing, creative, loving human spirit.* It requires openness to *and alignment with the goodness of spirit.* Far from being weak, such innocence is highly demanding and requires a high level of strength and awareness.

What is the opposite of using and abusing children, especially sons?: Honor and learn from children. Encourage honest emotional expression, including allowing boys to cry. Listen and help to develop creative talents. These are all ways for fathers and adult men to become "immortal" in its best sense, not having a stone statue erected to commemorate some military victory but rather a living monument built through the care and development of the highest aspects and potentials of children.

The issue of male circumcision

One of the most unexamined and unchallenged practices around male initiation into violence, abuse, and trauma involves the barbaric practice of cutting off part of the tiny, delicate penis of a newborn male baby. With all the uproar around female circumcision, animal cruelty, and human rights abuses, where are the voices shouting out for the rights of newborn sons not to have their bodies mutilated in an extreme, invasive, and lasting way?

In male circumcision, the hood that protects the sensitive head or glans of a male's penis is stripped away in the presence and gaze of other men, and this newborn baby's personal instrument of potency and ability to give physical life is exposed and made subject to a cruel, callous regime. Is there any more traumatic way to enter this life? Is there anything more unnecessary to inflict on the helpless?

Not even advocates of male circumcision try to pretend it is not traumatic for the young baby. Attempts to ameliorate this primitive act by applying painkillers do nothing to "solve" its result or to justify the initial ritual. The post-hoc scientific and religious rationales put up for male circumcision do not hold up. Its history and origin have never had anything to do with hygiene or health:

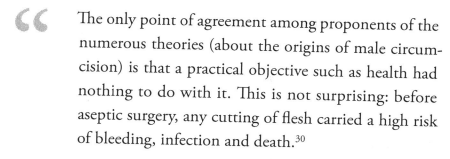

> The only point of agreement among proponents of the numerous theories (about the origins of male circumcision) is that a practical objective such as health had nothing to do with it. This is not surprising: before aseptic surgery, any cutting of flesh carried a high risk of bleeding, infection and death.[30]

> It was only in the late nineteenth century, when mass circumcision was being introduced for 'health' reasons, such as control of masturbation, that doctors sought legitimacy for the new procedure by attempting to explain its origin in terms of hygiene.[31]

What the history of circumcision *has* involved is a veritable "who's who" of patriarchal practices mean to create exclusion, enforce "discipline," reinforce sexism, place young men under the authority of older men, and even purposely diminish male sexual pleasure.

> The Kaguru of central Tanzania explain circumcision (practised at puberty on both boys and girls) in terms of enhancing gender differentiation and social control. They consider the uncircumcised penis unclean because its moistness makes men resemble women, whose wet and regularly bleeding genitals are considered polluting.[32]

30   Robert Darby, "The riddle of the sands: circumcision, history, and myth," The New Zealand Medical Journal Vol. 118, No. 1218, 2005, p. 77. (http://www.nzma.org.nz/__data/assets/pdf_file/0009/17937/Vol-118-No-1218-15-July-2005.pdf)
31   Robert Darby, "The riddle of the sands," p. 78.
32   Robert Darby, "The riddle of the sands," p. 77.

Jewish customs around circumcision do not mention hygiene but stress the religious significance of circumcision as an outward sign of a covenant between God and Abraham and "it persists as a kind of tribal marking."[33] Christians are specifically exempt from circumcision in their sacred texts, and some New Testament passages seem to indicate *non-circumcision* is a sign of faith,[34] yet many Christians do it anyway. There is no mention of circumcision in the Koran,[35] and yet a vast majority of Muslim boys are circumcised.[36] Other actual (versus post-hoc and false) rationales for this grisly initiation include circumcision serving as "'a cultural cosmetic' which enables the older men to impress the young with 'the need for conformity to traditional values and beliefs, and…the superior knowledge and authority of elder males.'"[37]

The real historical origins of the male circumcisions make it quite clear that this painful rite was meant to indoctrinate and subjugate young male children in such a way that their masculinity fell in line with patriarchal norms and social customs. It also appears to be aimed at curtailing the authentic individuality of boys, including personal sexual expression.

It is high time that discussions about masculinity and healing male trauma, include thorough education, serious debate, and active intervention on this inhumane and needless practice.

33   Emily Bobrow, "The industrialized world is turning against circumcision. It's time for the U.S. to do the same," Jan. 17, 2017. https://qz.com/885018/why-is-circumcision-so-popular-in-the-us/
34   Micheal Glass, Answers from the Bible to Questions about Circumcision, 2002. http://www.cirp.org/pages/cultural/glass2/
35   https://en.wikipedia.org/wiki/Khitan_(circumcision)
36   https://en.wikipedia.org/wiki/Prevalence_of_circumcision
37   Robert Darby, "The riddle of the sands," p. 77.

Pornography vs. intimacy

The film *Don Jon*[38] does a great job of portraying the distinction between pornography and intimacy. I consider it required viewing for men. The film examines the issues generated when a basically sweet and sincere guy, who treats women well on the social level, gets hung up on objectifying women on the sexual level. The main character, Jon Martello, is played by Joseph Gordon-Levitt (who also wrote the script and directed). Jon is a very basic "guy-guy." He has a very clear list of aims, not cluttered with nuance: "my body, my pad, my ride, my family, my church, my boys, my girls, my porn."

Like many guys, Jon's world is an objectified one—a list of topics to occupy his time and interest directed by his own unilateral desires. He meets with a "high-class" woman, Barbara (played by Scarlett Johannson) who has all the right curves to meet his objectified world-view but does not have the requisite respect for his flaws nor his deeper aspirations. She judges him for watching porn (since she should be enough for him), and even criticizes him for doing women's work in cleaning his apartment. Barbara vividly demonstrates how women themselves can be "cooked" within a patriarchal culture to reinforce its norms on men.

Jon meets up with an older widow, Esther (played by Julianne Moore) in his night class and begins to have heart-to-heart talks, even about his penchant for pornography. It is this kind of interior honesty that paves the way to a deeper level of intimacy between the two. Esther engages his interest by lending him an erotic video more developed from the female perspective. Jon develops respect for Esther as he learns from her and converses with her. Meanwhile, Barbara dumps Jon over

38   https://en.wikipedia.org/wiki/Don_Jon

his use of pornography and not measuring up to her standards. Jon then goes on the challenging journey with Esther to claim a mutual, intimate sexuality, a sexuality more driven by touch and vulnerability then objects, images, and physical stimulation.

This is not an easy journey for men. Most of our impressions about sex and sexuality are formed in adolescence and molded by the uninformed and counterproductive "locker talk" as well as a wide array of media that emphasize the "male gaze" and looking at women's body parts over receiving the entire person. This, combined with men's instrumental tendency to get worth out of sexual *performance* versus closeness and to concentrate unreasonably on their own parts (i.e., size of their penis, etc.), tends to remove men from a real intimate relationship with women. Again, the desire to learn and open themselves emotionally, seen in "Don Jon," (as opposed to "fake it 'til you make it") may be the most important step toward intimacy from men trying to move on from primitive notions of sexuality.

Instrumentalism vs intrinsic-ness

As we can see with pornography, men and boys have been programmed for thousands of years to derive worth and excitement out of *externalized* or *instrumental* endeavors which objectify others, array every action as a task with a specific goal, and emphasize external triumph or "success." In this programming, there is little to no thought given to the subjective *internal or intrinsic* humanity of that other person or the creativity of the "task."

In short, men have been suckered into believing that if they treat themselves and their various lives as instruments, they can "win" later on down the road. All such men actually end up winning is a booby prize of deferred promises, alienated, temporary pleasures, and an aching knowledge that they have lived their empty lives outside of themselves.

> *For a man to gain real meaning, worth, and identity he must learn to "subjectify" rather than objectify. He must develop the capacity to concentrate on his own and others' intrinsic qualities, rather than their extrinsic traits.*

This can be done by asking curious questions to children (and joining them in their play according to their rules), by making love to his partner in an extended, adventurous, and sensual way, rather than "getting the job done." If learning to fix a car turns into a labor of love, that too could be a form of "subjectifying" one's life. A spiritually confident and joyful man learns how to enjoy the inner radiance of life emanating from its inner qualities.

Technological transhumanism vs. sublime divinity

Transhumanism is the notion that we can "perfect" ourselves and live forever by encoding our consciousness into computers and other machines. Transhumanism denies the spiritual essence of human beings and rejects the possibility of a human soul. In transhumanism, we humans essentially are our brains and our "meat suits." Since the brain and meat suit die, according to transhumanism, immortality is gained by downloading of our minds to artificial memory. We could thus live on as cybernetic organisms indefinitely transferring our data from container to container (hence, "trans"-humanism).

> *This wholly materialistic view of the world, seems to be missing a vital point: What is the source of mind to begin with? Why would we want to live on indefinitely? Why do we live at all?*

Transhumanism does nothing to provide an answer to the fundamental questions of human meaning and significance. Again, we see the compensatory masculine drive to be a definitive "big fish" in a small pond, where we men can simply draw a small circle around a fear, a slice of existence, or an area of interest, and then proclaim we are now masters of the universe!

Masculine notions of divinity are not much better. Too often they are projections of men's megalomaniacal desires to be boss of the universe. Just look at institutional religion, and you will see it shot through with this patriarchal ruling impulse. Anti-spiritual patriarchal religion and anti-spiritual patriarchal transhumanism are two sides of the same coin. Both are aspects of what I call the male "godhood complex." Genuine spirituality, on the other hand, goes beyond such artificial and manipulative man-made constructs. Genuine spirituality emanates from the very spark of life recognized and honored by those who give their life to higher aims. Creativity is spirituality's litmus test.

> *Computers cannot create (though they can sometimes provide convincing imitations). Rulers and ruling institutions do not create; they use the creative energy of others. In true spirituality, everyone creates and is responsible for supporting the creative power of others.*

A journey engaged: Encountering manhood and fatherhood in life's challenges

It is far easier to be a "good time dad" with simple obligations, a decent 9-to-5 job, mowing the lawn, kicking the soccer ball with kids. However, the test of a man is how he reacts when presented with a challenge. This topic hits close to home for me. I am the father of a ten-year-old boy at the time I am writing this. In January of 2008, my ex-wife and I gave birth to a son, Phoenix, in Berkeley, California. Phoenix's first three years were good ones, living in and around Berkeley, where Phoenix had playmates from different cultural backgrounds and plenty of nature, healthy food, clean air, and ethnic diversity.

At the end of 2010, I agreed to a two-year move overseas. My job as a project director at a think tank had ended, and my prospects as an education consultant had suffered in the wake of the economic bust of 2008. I agreed to support my American wife and son as a so-called "trailing spouse" in her work as a microfinance specialist at a development bank in the Philippines. During the next three years, I became the primary caregiver, the "Mr. Mom" taking Phoenix to school, attending school events and playdates, and caring for him full time when his mother took off for international business trips that sometimes lasted up to three weeks.

It was during these alone times with him that I was able to finish potty-training him and wean him from his pacifier. He relied on me, and we developed a caring and tender bond. When he was emotionally acting out, I would encourage him to get at the deeper feelings driving his behavior. Sometimes anger meant he was sad and missing someone. He could cry freely in my presence or express frustration, and I did not try to shut him up. I would just talk with him, so he could understand where these feelings were coming from.

I became the emotional carer and "holder" for both Phoenix and my then-wife. At the same time, I wrote and published my book, *Transforming Economy*, and took up some short-term consulting and tutoring, but primarily there was no fulfilling, appropriate work available for me. The Philippines, for instance, pays its college professors about 300 dollars a month.

My relationship with Phoenix and Phoenix's mother dramatically shifted when she and I divorced, and I was thrust into the role many divorced women are forced to occupy—starting from scratch without a job, without adequate financial compensation, and without a lot of help. So I moved back to the United States to heal and build myself back up. My son was literally half a world away.

My ex-wife did what some patriarchal men do. She increased her work hours to handle the stress and left my son in the care of nannies for longer and longer periods of time. We were not a fit, spiritually and otherwise. After returning to the United States, I was emotionally fatigued, needing to recover my spirit and feel myself again. I moved back to central Ohio with my birth family, wrote another book, worked for my sister at her vegan restaurant, and went out on a total of two "friend" dates in two and a half years.

I met my present wife, and life partner, Regina, while being interviewed on her show "Open Minds" on Gaia TV on my book

Transforming Economy. There was a feeling of familiarity and ease that comes with immediately being able to be me at my deepest and most honest level. Our meeting might be described as "electric warmth." A month and a half earlier, while writing, I had suddenly stood up like a bolt out of the blue and declared, "Enough is enough. I want a spiritual equal. I'm ready." Regina had had similarly prophetic signs, and we have found in each other a spiritual equal and have deepened our relationship ever since.

This does not mean things have been easy sledding since then. Both of us have been tested in the raising of our sons. My son has shown evidence of experiencing harm in the Philippines, leading to an extended court battle over custody and protection. Regina's son engaged in a relationship with a woman that isolated him almost completely from his family and friends. What both of us realized is that our sons do not have adequate supports for learning how to be men in the fullest masculine sense.

Education around masculinity is largely missing. Men are most often assumed to be the center, which does not allow much space for conversation or self-reflection. When they do not know what to do, when they are victimized or make bad choices, there are few options for them within traditional or modern masculinity except faking it or hiding it. Boys and men are trained to pretend to know.

> *If boys and men are constantly apologizing for being male, and if "doing well" means communicating false confidence rather than a true confusion, then how will boys and men learn to tell the truth about themselves?*

Even today, with the advent of "men's studies," most masculine influences are either *inflationary,* prompting boys and men to adopt an unhealthy "pumped-up" version of masculinity, or *reactionary,* prompting boys to reject their masculinity. Teaching our sons to embrace healthy masculinity is a longer-term project, and it requires a critically-minded deconstruction of the current unhealthy messages and an encouragement of alternative practices and way of seeing themselves.

Raising spiritually confident boys: Transforming the messages we are sending our sons

Let's look at the messages being sent to boys and men about what is noble and ignoble for the male of the species. I am told by my son how the heavily muscled fighting men in first-person shooter video games can be heroic because they are defending the land against "terrorists." I notice schools are geared toward well-behaved girls and look down upon "hyperactive" boys that need to move around to concentrate better. It seems like males are beset either by toxic forms of masculinity or efforts to transform boys into honorary girls.

I find that creativity works in my son to both retain his active masculinity and direct it in a constructive manner. There is something about creativity that cuts through programming, even when some violent images may filter into his drawings, for instance. Creativity also encourages Phoenix to move his mind, heart, and body, and to become critically engaged.

When Phoenix writes, the motives of his characters help him reflect upon his own motives. Their subjectivity and choices allow him to reflect upon his own. When I engage in an animated story with my son about the Higher Mind and the Lower Mind, he feels the difference between the animal aspects of himself and the noble aspects of his character. It is this tension between High and Low, well-negotiated and engaged, that raises a boy to a man.

> A "real" and healthy male does not give in to either barbarism or gentility. Healthy males initiate, assert, and rebel and do not simply "behave." The only difference is that a higher boy or man is encouraged to do this *from* himself, through challenge and support, and **not against** others.

In the following sections, I bring forward and debunk some of the implicit messages that alternately disempower and mislead boys and men. I will challenge both misbegotten patriarchal messages and misguided supposedly "feminist" messages aimed at taking down and taking out masculinity altogether.

What our boys are being taught in patriarchal cultures:

- What is "real" is what is concrete. "Feelings" are at best simply vague, passing luxuries.
- Respect means money, fame, and material power.
- Crime pays.
- It's not a crime if you don't get caught.
- "Risk" means having the balls to do something you are told not to do, and "smart" means being clever enough to get away with it.
- If something bad happens, and you are the 'little guy,' then you deserve it.
- Big men are able to avoid consequences, even if these consequences are merited.

- Never admit you are wrong.
- Love means never having to say you're sorry.
- Boys don't cry. Honest emotional expression makes you weak and quite possibly homosexual.
- Other people are meant to be used. They are fortunate extensions of your expanding "kingdom" or empire of personality and charisma.
- "Boys will be boys." It is the nature of males to be irresponsible and the nature of society to excuse males for being irresponsible.
- Women are temptresses. They are responsible for covering their body parts with clothing, and if you violate a female, it is her fault for "pushing your buttons."
- God is on your side.
- Might makes right.

Notice how each one of these messages enforces opportunism, grandiosity, and lack of responsibility. Is it any wonder that boys grow up to men that simply leave their families: "Why not? They weren't serving me like they were supposed to!" There are scores of real-life examples that reinforce these messages. Presidents, whether they be Bill Clinton or Donald Trump, can cajole or assault women with impunity. Religious institutions can be rotted by the perversions of pedophilia yet admit no wrongdoing. The leaders of financial institutions can authorize the theft of hundreds of billions of dollars through "complex" fraudulent schemes and yet assume no responsibility or consequences.

How men are being portrayed

Feminists rightfully refuse to put up with these corrosive messages and examples, yet some all too often make the mistake of blaming masculinity itself for the excesses of patriarchy while reifying feminine essence. This blame and elitism take the form of counter-messages that catch actual boys and men in the crossfire:

- Men are violent.
- Men are oppressors.
- Men do not have what it takes to do the right thing.
- Men quit when the going gets tough.
- Men are filled with fatal flaws.
- Men will only make excuses. Women have to do the work and pick up the pieces.
- Men make it all about themselves. Not everything centers around you!
- Men will let you down.
- When men are nice to you, they simply want something from you.
- Men are crude; they've lost the sense of gentlemanliness.
- Men are hopeless; when are they going to get some courage and take some initiative.
- Men are buffoons like Homer Simpson; women are smart like Lisa Simpson.
- Men are simply concerned with their likes and dislikes; why don't they reach out and share what women like for a change.
- Men are clueless.

The secret to a constructive way forward for both males and females lies in this simple insight: Males have every bit of the same incentive as females to confront their flaws and destructive programming. Contrary to some feminist analysis, it is *not* serving men and boys to follow the negative stereotypes of maleness. Whatever benefits boys and men might gain in terms of unwarranted privilege, increased economic leverage, social standing, or political power, are more than outweighed by the damage patriarchy inflicts on their sense of worth, nobility, and justice. However, men *do* have to stand up and be counted.

> *This is where the feminist critique is right on target. If men refuse to unify against destructive, patriarchal messages and examples that take men collectively to a new low, then they tacitly agree to their own debasement.*

Real men's studies are not an extension of women's studies or a reinforcement of "men's rights" (as much as that may be needed in certain areas like child custody), but are commitments to deeply investigate the nature, subjectivity, and experience of manhood, call out that knowledge, and set men on a path of supportive yet disciplined development. Men have to take responsibility, and this starts with how men account for and conduct themselves, how men stand up to other men, and how men raise both boys and girls.

Raising boys according to the seven C's (critical-mindedness, capability, creativity, courage, compassion, community, and cosmic perspective)

There is much work to be done when it comes to how men raise boys. Today's boys need a whole lot more than a sex education class, a tour with the Boy Scouts, and a weekend spent hunting, fishing, or kicking the ball around with dad. Today's boys need to develop emotional intelligence, empathy, conviction, resilience, and adventurous humor, curiosity, and creativity. Boys need to learn how to be receptive as well as enduring, enterprising as well as dedicated, and affectionate as well as competent. This is aided by responsible mentoring where the father figure learns alongside a boy. The boy's interests and questions are drawn out in dialogue. His perspectives and skepticism are met, rather than ignored, evoked rather than denied.

Here is how I experienced the 7 C's with my son, Phoenix:

Critical-mindedness: When Phoenix was six, we visited a Walgreen's in South Carolina. I happened to notice a whole row of boxes of "fruit strips," the kind that come in a roll to peel off and eat. The boxes were decorated with images of fresh fruit, making them seem as if they contained healthy, natural food. Yet the side of the box said "0% fruit," yes, 0%. I pointed out to this deceptive tactic to Phoenix and observed also that the row of boxes was placed at his eye level to get him to notice it. He was very intrigued and kept coming back to his inside knowledge of this scam.

- *Principle: Boys can learn to be critically-minded detectives piercing the ruses of society if we teach them.*

Capability: In the summer of 2017, my mother provided Phoenix with a cheap little trick scooter at the skateboard park. He'd been having serious problems with his self-esteem, claiming he couldn't do anything well and constantly comparing himself to the competitive boys at his school. I took him to a skate park in Sedona, Arizona. As soon as he hopped on that scooter, he seemed to have a preternatural grace and skill as if he'd been on it for years. His joy was there as well. He didn't criticize himself one bit. The "skate culture" of the park was very supportive, promoting collaboration on how to nail a trick rather than emphasizing competition.

- *Principle: Every boy has something in him he is good at, and through experiment and support can find a way to be high-performing as well as fulfilled.*

Creativity: In the same summer of 2017 in Sedona, AZ, I was having trouble redirecting Phoenix' habits away from simulated violence in play and in video games. Regina, and I set some consistent limits, chief among them that he takes any imaginary shooting and violent play outside. However, this was not adequate. As I began to share with Phoenix my creative process when I write and, as I praised him for his creativity, he began teaching himself how to make and edit videos about the family on his iPad, complete with text and background music. He started fiddling with composing music in the Garage Band app.

- *Principle: Given an opportunity, boys can be drawn toward creative production and away from violent consumption.*

Courage: That summer, Phoenix and I got a membership at a nearby water park. One of the fastest and scariest rides was one where you stood in a vertical tube, and the bottom dropped out, and you accelerated straight down before curving. Phoenix really enjoyed the first few tries and then bumped or scraped his elbow and developed a fear of trying it again. I tried to challenge and cajole him and even allowed him to initiate a bet with me that he would do it again. Each time he decided not to try. I got upset because I thought it was a failure of courage. Upon talking with him, I noticed he had to make this journey himself. I look forward to future summers and seeing how he has grown.

- *Principle: Rome was not built in a day, and neither is a boy's character. No need to panic. If a boy has the desire, he will eventually find a way to face his fears and feelings.*

Compassion: As insensitive and mean as young boys can be, it piqued my interest when Regina, my son, and I went to see our friend, who is an historian and impressionist. Before we met him, Regina asked Phoenix to be sensitive to the man's rotund size. Phoenix asked, "Why is he so big?" Regina said, "Because he has low self-esteem, but he's also really smart." Phoenix replied, "Why does he have low self-esteem?" Regina: "Because his mother kept telling him he was stupid when he was young." Phoenix replied, quite moved and disturbed, "Why would any mother tell her son he's stupid, especially if he's smart?" He continued asking us this question many days and weeks after this meeting— I saw this same empathy and care in Phoenix's playfulness with our two small dogs Ernie and Angel.

- *Principle: When a boy is given the opportunity to care and empathize, this experience can be quite natural and powerful for him.*

Community: Around Christmas, 2016, my brother, Apollo, Regina's son, Stuart, and my son Phoenix got together with Regina and me for extreme adventure four-wheeling over the red rocks of Sedona. There was palpable energy between "the boys," at experiencing this adventure together. There was a place where you could take a picture lying on a rock sideways that when rotated looked like you were hanging off a cliff. (This caused equal measures of alarm and laughter when we posted it to friends and family.) It's this kind of simple, back-to-the-earth camaraderie that boys so enjoy.

- *Principle: "Guy-time" bonding and back-to-earth camaraderie are important, and they can be enhanced rather than diminished by having a woman along.*

Cosmic perspective: During that fateful summer of 2017, Regina also got a psychic "bleed through" a tremendous intuitive sense that Phoenix was a reincarnated, "Wolf on Wall Street" broker or trader who got shot in a robbery and who had never learned to respect women or higher principles in that life. It became an interesting conversation piece between us, and when we shared this story of reincarnation with Phoenix, it seemed to broaden his curiosity and horizons. He began to see reincarnation, in his own words, as a "hypothesis," and whether he seriously entertained reincarnation, discussing it seemed to awaken a notion in Phoenix's mind that his being might go beyond the merely physical. (It certainly helped put his adult-like obsession with time and money in context!) This, in turn, expanded his understanding of the choices and factors that guide his life from mere "lower mind" concentration on money to "higher mind" focus on finer human spiritual and character qualities.

- *Principle: Discuss the higher virtues of humanity as real and concrete, rather than abstract. Engage how different human motivations create different life consequences.*

There is hope: Standing up for our daughters and sisters as well as our sons and brothers

It is not just boys that men must raise and mentor as fathers and advocates, but girls as well. It is time that men and boys recognize and appreciate strong women and girls, not only those who stand up for themselves, but who work day in and day out to hold up the world until men and boys can learn to listen and once again break through to their true leadership and their hearts.

It is the mark of an honorable man to take profound inspiration, teaching, and faith into his own heart and actions. Too many men seem to be caught like a deer in the headlights in the onrush of a fast advancing society. Others become belligerent because they are no longer the top dog calling the shots. However, there is a much nobler, co-creative path forward—solidarity with women and girls. Men and women, boys and girls can help each other get both stronger and more delighted by life if we champion one another if we appreciate the co-creative miracle of healthy masculinity meeting healthy femininity.

In 2002 I had the honor to support a strong and vital femininity by aligning with women's groups to preserve Title IX protections granting equal opportunities for girls and women in sports and education. My sister, Athena, was executive director for the National Association for Girls and Women in Sport. She was part of a coalition of groups that successfully defeated federal administrative efforts to curtail Title IX. From a masculine standpoint, it was inspirational to see how many fathers across the moral and political spectrum refused to let their daughters get sidelined. Conservative, liberal, and progressive men alike were not going to allow retrograde policies to steal opportunity from their daughters.

I testified at the Secretary of Education hearing on the matter at the

Drake Hotel in Chicago, noting that much of this effort to undermine women's participation in sports and education was driven by certain men's desires to re-establish patriarchal authority and superiority. I asked the question: "Is Title IX being attacked for its success, rather than its perceived problems... (and for) the implications, strengths, and challenges (this) presents (to men)?"[39] I went on to comment that female strength and flourishing should be welcomed by males who consider themselves strong. This is an important and irrefutable principle: "Real men and boys need real women and girls."

> *No one is ennobled by the subjugation and repression of other people.*

Everyone is lifted by mutual thriving, yet insecure habits still linger in persons who base their worth on relative comparisons rather than absolute good.

And it is not just heterosexual women and girls that "real men" are asked to stand by, but lesbian women and girls as well. It may seem contradictory that two of my most significant philosophical influences were Friedrich Nietzsche and radical, lesbian feminist Marilyn Frye and her book *The Politics of Reality*, which developed powerful and practical theories about power and access. Both were foundational to discovering my own distinct masculine subjectivity, awareness of sexism, and fruitful support for masculinity and femininity alike.

No real man would condone bullying because of a person's sexual orientation. In Chapter 4 on the Emerging Man, I talked about the film *Moonlight*, as an excellent example of the resistance and violence

---

39   http://webapp1.dlib.indiana.edu/virtual_disk_library/index.cgi/5584563/FID907/Hearings/02_Chicago/sept17.pdf , p. 286-288.

generated by heterosexual boys and men in the face of one male's genuine love for another male. Why is this so threatening to heterosexual men? Another boy or man is my brother, period. As spiritually confident men, we are asked to defend our brother's right to choose to form a union with another person, regardless of gender. This comes from the very same courage, compassion, and commitment deployed to defend boys and men from being sexually preyed upon by other men.

> *One begins to see the moral consistency here: Love wins, and predation loses, no matter what the form, who does it, and to whom it is done.*

Life is a creative conversation: "Task" and "relationship"

Research concerning men's and women's identity, note that men gravitate toward tasks and women toward relationships. Stereotypically, men like to share experiences, and women love to share conversation. Here is the missed opportunity in these observations, however: Men do not have to solely direct themselves toward objectified tasks, just as they don't have to objectify women. Men can "subjectify" what they do, by connecting what they do to a bold and imaginative spirit. Tasks can stimulate the mind and turn up the passion in a man toward greater relationship with his world including other people.

Matthew Crawford discusses this distinction in his book *Shop Class as Soulcraft: An Inquiry into the Value of Work*.[40] He contends that much of what estranges men in the world is their incremental removal from physical engagement with tasks that elicit their interests, their minds,

---

40 Matthew Crawford, Shop Class as Soulcraft: An Inquiry into the Value of Work (New York: The Penguin Press, 2009)

and their passions. He calls for a reassertion of skilled manual labor as a way to reconnect men to their primal roots in an increasingly abstract world dominated by knowledge workers. Crawford walks his talk. As a philosopher and mechanic, he works at a think-tank while operating his own independent motorcycle shop in Richmond, VA.

I agree with much of what Crawford puts forward. Men do need some sense of concreteness in an increasingly abstract "post-modern" world. But this concreteness does not mean that men have to be anti-intellectual troglodytes.

> *Work understood as "soulcraft" can connect a man with the finer aspects of his being. He becomes not just an alienated worker pounding out the widgets in a factory but an artisan, having a living relationship with the objects of his work.*

This respect, appreciation, and aesthetic sensibility lends itself well toward a man having an honoring connection to other human beings. Similarly, women do not have to turn every relationship to an exchange for exchange's sake. They can objectively come up with some tangible ends in conversation in order to involve the man.

Going along these line, if "relationship" for a man is a "subjectified" rather than an objectified endeavor, he is less apt to talk about his "old lady" as a "ball and chain" and he is less likely to see her need as an eye-rolling obligation.

> *One of the greatest complaints I hear from women is that their men are trying to "fix them" as if they were objects rather than listen to them as subjects.*

Many men I know just think that woman want to vent and use them as a dumping ground for their emotions. These men deal with this by pretending to be present while thinking about something else. What would it look like for men and women to break through this dynamic and actually learn together to reach the heart of their engagements with tasks and with relationships?

Refusing to sell out our sons and daughters

A final word about the betrayal of the younger generations by older men and women alike and our need to collectively heal and redeem connections between the generations. Our world is racking up loads of environmental, economic, political, and cultural debt for younger generations. Global climate change is upon us. Well-paid satisfying jobs are drying up. Young people have limited say in governmental policies and decision-making. The world is being besieged by a manipulative form of social media that often takes the authenticity out of interaction and reinforces the consumption of ideas rather than the passionate exchange of meaning. Boys are still sent off to war by the fathers. Girls are still made to tend to the families by the mothers. We remain stuck in the objectification mode created by the Industrial Age (which I call the Second Dark Ages).

It doesn't have to be this way. We have reached the end of the road in terms of instrumental and "objectified" thinking, which is a form of taking and treating others like tools. By scrambling to get our needs and deficits met and by using other people for own ends, we have made things worse for ourselves. We are like the old tale about a journeyman visiting two groups of people with long-handled spoons around a communal porridge pot. In the first group, it was every man and woman, boy and girl trying to awkwardly feed him or herself. For this group, almost all the food spilled out before eaten. In the second group, everyone was well fed and happy because they fed each other.

That is an apt meditation and metaphor for our current age.

> *We can be every man and woman for him or herself and set our interests against each other, or we can learn to work together to feed each other.*

We can ignorantly act as if every generation exists for itself and not care what happens after we die, or we can nurture succeeding generations in a world of giving and enhancement of the future. It is a choice each of us makes over and over again, a grain of gold added to another grain of gold until a golden pyramid arises.

CHAPTER 7

Lighting The Fire, Providing The Feast— Developing Spiritual Confidence

It is time to prepare the food, light the stove, and serve the meal. Growing is not complete until one rejoices and revels in its sharing. And why not? We are continually being led around by advertisements and our anxiety to see growth as always shooting for that next horizon. We seldom take the time to appreciate what we have harvested, which invariably leaves us "on edge." A hearty, savory spiritually confident meal is an excellent way to celebrate breaking out of the constraining boxes of outworn masculinity and femininity.

This means holding our cups high to the possibilities and bounties of the spirit. With humor and nostalgia, we can look back at our foolishness with gentle wisdom and forward to new adventures with rapt anticipation. Our imperfections are what have allowed us to experience and grow, so they too should be honored and remembered. What need is there for perfection? We inhale and exhale, eat, and drink, converse and grow amid the glow of spirit.

S PIRITUAL CONFIDENCE REQUIRES A certain genius of the heart, a certain poignant coming to terms with our frailties and a willingness to surrender pretenses. Let's set the table for this chapter with an opening reflection on philosopher Friedrich Nietzsche's "Genius of the Heart" passage:

 [T]he genius of the heart who silences all that is loud and self-satisfied, teaching it to listen; who smooths rough souls and lets them taste a new desire—to lie still as a mirror, that the deep sky may mirror itself in them—the genius of the heart who teaches the doltish and rash hand to hesitate and reach out more delicately; who guesses the concealed and forgotten treasure, the drop of graciousness and sweet spirituality under dim and thick ice, and is a divining rod for every grain of gold that has long lain buried in the dungeon of much mud and sand; the genius of the heart from whose touch everyone walks away richer... newer to [themselves] than before, broken open, blown at and sounded out by a thawing wind, perhaps more unsure, tenderer, more fragile, more broken, but full of hopes that as yet have no name... [41]

41   Friedrich Nietzsche, "The Genius of the Heart," Beyond Good and Evil: Prelude to a Philosophy of the Future, passage 295, trans. by Walter Kaufmann, Vintage Books, First Thus edition, 1966

It is time to open and connect our spirits, our hearts, our minds, and our bodies. We can no longer deny that the Animal and the Spirit in us is inextricably bound in the Human and that we are a beautiful and challenging hybrid of the two.

On the vertical dimension of being, a vibrant reality beckons us to fully unite and express our bodies, minds, hearts, and spirits. On the horizontal dimension of becoming, a new resonant possibility emerges that male and female energies, masculine and feminine polarities, can join and manifest in co-creative, deeply-honoring relationship.

How, then, might you and I, men and women, boys and girls, transform the realities of our relationships and bring new, healthy, spiritually confident possibilities into the world? How do we all become "providers of the feast," rather than "rulers on the throne" or "hiders in the dark" or a thousand other fruitless efforts to escape or compensate for what we miraculously are and who we generously can be? The way forward will both confront and confirm our child-like dreams of spirits liberated to play in the world. There is much work to do to face and engage our darker, more jaded and more self-destructive "adult" habits. There is much we can enjoy by opening toward a flowing peace and power from which arises innovation and solidarity.

What are some key principles, questions, and answers from the standpoint of a Spiritually Confident Human? How *do* we embrace the multiple aspects of being and becoming—of Animal and Spirit, of body, mind, heart, and spirit, and of male and female?

Principles of spiritually confident living

- Spiritual confidence *increases* your responsibility, rather than diminishing it. Spirituality is response-ability.

- Spiritual confidence involves conscious, informed *choice* and exercise of *sovereignty* from your being. No god or alien is going to save you from yourself.

- Spiritual confidence requires *authenticity.* There are no short-cuts spiritually. "Looking good" and appearing to be pious do not cut it.

- In spiritual confidence, your being and your life are an *original blessing,* not an original sin. You don't have to make up for being born.

- Spiritual confidence means *a different kind of honoring.* No higher power or spiritual being worth its salt would ever demand obedient worship.

- In spiritually confidence *truth is the deciding medium.* Knowledge is the paramount *virtue* and leads to health and refinement of the spirit. Ignorance is the paramount *vice* and leads to breakdown.

- Spiritual confidence means *"no excuses."* Deal with what is in front of you. If you hurt someone, recognize it. If you failed, learn from it.

- Spiritual confidence always requires *rebellion*—against our prejudices, our comforts, our platitudes, our assumptions, our devolutionary social norms.

- Spiritual confidence is not just the "inner" but the *inner meeting the outer.*

- Spiritual confidence requires *discernment,* not moralistic judgment.

- Spiritual confidence is *intrinsic rather than instrumental, non-material rather than material, absolute rather than relative, unconditional rather than conditional.*

What are some tips to develop spiritual confidence in myself and others?

Believe in yourself as a spiritual being and not simply a body walking around other bodies. This means you have the power to create, to love, and to engage.

Do not allow others to pass sentence on your soul. If anyone seeks to put you down, rise even higher.

Step up. Men, don't give yourself a pass on ignorance, and women, don't allow men to get away with it. Men are no longer children, and they need to learn to take care of themselves and others.

Understand the difference between compassion and co-dependence. Compassion means connecting with another human being and supporting their development. This contrasts with co-dependence, which is handing over your sovereignty to another human being and doing the work they need to be doing on themselves.

Believe in the capacity of another person to improve and grow. However, get rid of the notion of "saving" another person. If you present yourself as the "white knight" or the "good woman" that is going to turn that other person around, they will either take advantage of you or disappoint you. Saving is not your job. Engaging is. This advice also holds with the brand of soft egoism called "saving the world."

Be too lazy to lie. Lies are complicating, toxic, and draining. For all its discomforts, the truth is simpler, purer, and more fulfilling. Truth is worth the investment.

See yourself as a conductor or channeler of light rather than a container of good and bad. If you are screwing up or if you have wronged someone, don't hide. Invite light of truth, love, and higher wisdom *through* you. Sincerity is an underrated element of spiritual confidence. If you don't know something, then learn. If you wronged someone, apologize.

Call others out when they do something crappy, tasteless, or unjust. Too many times, men, in particular, turn a blind eye when other men are causing harm or being idiots. Think of it as reminding someone when they have their zipper open or some food hanging on the side of their mouth.

Find and apply your best and highest insight to any situation. Too often people know how to be gracious, but short-sell themselves. "Oh, that's pie-in-the-sky." "That person will make fun of me." "This place is too unenlightened to respect my ideas." *Offer your best anyway.* In spiritual confidence, the best is not contingent on conditions. You make a practice of doing and offering your best despite the reception it might receive.

Take time and clean out your psyche when you need to. Renewal and restoration are critical to spiritual strength and confidence. Whether it be meditation, a quiet walk, an early bedtime, or something else, sometimes the best "accomplishment" is taking the time to do nothing, so that you are energized when the time comes to do something important.

Listen to your intuitions. To use the example of my wife, Regina, if there is a sign asking for help in staging the school play, and a little voice inside yourself says, "Do it," then why not do it! Instead of always slighting the intuitively important for the practically urgent, why not "give" in to a higher enjoyment?

DARK AND LIGHT, GOOD AND BAD

*How do dark and light operate in this world, especially
between male and female? Are "good" and "bad"
boys and girls two sides of the same dark coin?*

> *The dark will never stand up and say, "Yeah,
> I'm evil and unhealthy; so what of it?"*

The dark works by obscuring and creating deception. It cannot contend with the presence of spiritual light. It can only offer its substitutes, its own artificial "lighting" in the form of false promises. Therefore, it is the purpose of dark to challenge light with deceptive ignorance. The dark is very clever. It will set up a world of "good" and "bad" in which both ends of the spectrum are without light. You see this false spectrum in modern models of the "bad girl" and the "good girl," in notions of the "bad boy" and the "good boy," which shroud, rather than reveal, our highest potential.

The "bad" girl and boy are more obvious representatives of dark masculinity and femininity. They are unapologetic takers and manipulators. They don't care who they hurt or use. It's all a game, played for advantage or kicks. The "bad" girl is the exotic, seductive, rule-breaking, femme fatale. She wants to push the edge and challenge society's every rule. She promises a certain alluring insanity that seems to drive guys wild even when they know they are going to crash and burn. The "bad" boy is the symbol of erotic danger, the charismatic and utterly unrepentant rascal. He winks and implies that he is amazing in bed, but if a woman chooses to sleep with him, it will be over in thirty seconds. He'll be asleep by the two-minute mark.

> *The "good" girl and boy are more subtle representatives of the dark. Both have given up sovereignty for approval, or to be seen as moral people, or to get into some mythical heaven awaiting people who do nothing more than follow other people's orders and expectations.*

The "good" girl is often forced to provide primary care for her birth family especially if she is the oldest daughter. She is dutiful, overwhelmed, but optimistic because she wants to believe in the goodness of the world, even if she does not experience it in her own heart. The "good" boy is everyone's friend, the nice guy, the designated driver, helping others out but secretly wishing to go beyond his own backyard and be as popular as the bad boys of the world.

Both "good" girl and boy lack creativity, as do the "bad" girl and boy. They all work according to formula. They all tend to be unaware of any true rebellion they can wage against the inhuman habits of their world. They are simply playing role-driven variations against a spiritless background. The "bad" girl and boy escape into vice, and the "good" girl and boy escape into pseudo-innocence. All four are cut off from their deeper and higher selves.

They often find each other, to share their loneliness. When you see the descriptions and dynamics of the "bad" boy and girl and the "good" boy and girl, you can see the allure they have for each other, as incompatible as they may seem on the outside. The "good" girl can redeem the bad boy, or at least feel something for once, and momentarily break from her chains of obligation. The good boy can save the bad girl, or at least temporarily escape his self-conscious bubble and play along the edges of forbidden territory.

> *This is the dark Disney-fied present reality in our world. Both the good and wicked, the Cinderellas and Cruellas, are upholding a dynamic in which innocence swallowed by the dark. Evil is only vanquished by some imaginary prince or other idealized symbol of the good, not by brave ordinary people.*

This black-and-white story does not reflect the spiritual mixed bag most human beings embody. There are some exceptions: In fact, I was drawn to the story of the *Beauty and the Beast* precisely because it goes against their simplistic black-and-white construct. A smart, strong, courageous girl meets a former bad boy prince whose enchantment as a beast has taught him humility, sacrifice, and longing for love.

In the world of light and spirit creative actions are always some kind of rebellion against the dark desire to enslave the transformative, uncontrollable spiritual aspects of the world. *Politeness is laudable, but it is no substitute for virtue.* Brashness may help one stand out, but it is no substitute for courage. That which is bad or evil is that which tries to oppress the human spirit. That which is good is that which exalts the human spirit. The light of spirit is co-creative and illuminative; it is neither obedient nor abusive. We do not so much have to *fight* the dark as we have to *light* the dark.

Dark is but a call to light. We may not have an external savior, but we have grace, and we are lifted up by the whisperings of our souls. Low is but a call to high. Injustice is a call to justice. It is up to us. We have each other. We have higher guides and living principles. We do not have to "save the world." We need to pierce the darkness in ourselves and light the fire.

Why do we get duped by the lower aspects of existence and remain blind to the higher?

We keep getting fooled because we keep surrendering ourselves to the more obvious remedies of the world instead of welcoming the far more subtle but powerful rays of spirit. In short, we have a problem with nuance.

> *We keep allowing ourselves to believe in promises that we know inside can never pay off, because we have learned to distrust our intuition and deeper knowing.*

Perhaps we are afraid to advance upon our own choices and beyond the promises of others. Their assertions relieve us of responsibility even if we experience the consequences of their ineptitude, humiliation, or abuse.

How many times does an abused woman believe her abuser is "really sorry" and "will never do it again" only to be hit the next day. At that moment, she probably senses his sincerity. Perhaps she is afraid that she cannot make it on her own or that an uncertain future is scarier than a violent present. This trauma makes her even more impressionable and malleable. Caught in the web of lower realm thinking and acting, she is trained to adopt this abuse as her world of possibility. She learns to adapt and rationalize. The man does the same but in reverse. Perhaps he is sincere, but now he rationalizes his abuse. The next time it comes up, abuse is somehow different and warranted in his mind. Besides isn't she still staying around? Maybe his intimidation is "working." Now he doesn't have to face his fear that she will leave him.

It is easy to be reactionary and seduced. We let another person or advertisement set our baseline reality and range of choices. Should I get this awful generic laundry detergent or this other sparkling happiness-inducing laundry detergent that costs twice as much? "Well, I want to be happy, don't I? So maybe it's worth it." But where does the lasting happiness of joy come from? Not from laundry detergent or any element of the world.

> *You cannot expect light and lasting happiness from the dense world of our animal impulses and our material practices. You are asking that world to promise transcendent states it can never deliver. So it has to lie to you to get your attention.*

The feelings and effects of the dense and material world are easier to apprehend and feel on the physical, and even the mental and emotional planes. Hate feels more "solid" and easier to grasp than airy love. Certainly, an addictive drug like cocaine can seem to offer clearer and more immediate benefits than an organic green salad. But here is the catch: By investing ourselves in the material lower realms over and against spiritual higher realms in our being, we lower our frequencies. We become addicted to the effects of the lower, and our choices become compulsions. We lose our sovereignty. We can control material effects to a certain point, whereas spiritual good always seems to come from beyond us. We can take a pain reliever to relieve physical pain. We can attempt psychotherapy to relieve emotional pain, but this will never be a sufficient replacement for spiritual inquiry, courage, and a certain amount of discipline.

The green salad enhances our health and clarity and ability to contact the higher. Cocaine destroys our health and replaces our ability to reach the higher in ourselves. Shortcuts like artificial sweeteners may have no calories, but, it turns out, they can cause cancer and have other disruptive effects on the being.

> *Any time we are greedy to "get away with" something in the material world that is exactly what we will do: "get away" from spirit and our deeper, higher selves.*

We are saying in effect: "Life is too hard; I just want to be a spectator and a consumer. It's easier. I can have the fun without the responsibility to contribute and create. So what if its shallow?" It reminds me of the fellow who betrayed his comrades in the film *The Matrix*: He knew the taste and sensation of the steak he was eating was fabricated, but he did not care. He was tired of the struggle, so he sold out.

But there is hope. Eating a green salad is not just something you can learn to enjoy. It is something which provides spiritually-directed nourishment from Mother Earth herself. We can experience a different kind of high when we treat our beings with respect and give freely to each other. This "high" is not based in self-interest, but from a palpable flow of feeling and energy that comes through us when we treat ourselves in a healthy manner and give to someone who gratefully receives.

VULNERABILITY

Why am I terrified of vulnerability, and how can I transform this fear into something constructive?

Our collective and individual fears of vulnerability are hurting our relationships, particularly those between men and women. This fear appears to be attached to an unconscious survival impulse. We can know this by looking at the fear itself. In modern and post-modern times, humans usually experience aversion to vulnerability as fear of "what can happen," rather than a response to a real and present threat.

Perhaps this is best shown by the many examples we have all heard from friends where they were either rejected by someone in a romantic relationship or, in fact, rejected someone "before that other person could reject me." We see in this example a strange fear of vulnerability that is so strong and preemptive as to sabotage "the best thing that ever happened to me." Why do we have a fear of success? It leaves us vulnerable to increased expectation and a potentially bigger fall from grace if we fail.

Do you see the craziness in this? All of our present, beautiful life is not only being lived in the future but in an ugly and anxious future. In short, our fear of vulnerability on an imagined level (and our desire to avoid that imagined threat) is what makes us less protected and aware on the real level.

By contrast, engaging and conquering fear requires us to be "real" and transparent about our feelings, which requires real sensitivity to identify those hidden aspects of ourselves that go against our higher mental, emotional, and spiritual instincts and capabilities.

Think about how many times we are inundated by all kinds of media, social media, news, commercials, etc. that make us afraid of everything from an "embarrassing" stain on our clothing to a mass shooting. The more we respond to and re-imagine these stories in our brains, the more stressed and keyed up we get. This is especially potent because modern media is designed to get around our perceptual filters. These messages are engineered to use threat to garner our attention and stimulate an emotional response, which can be "cured" by a pill, a stain remover, or an alarm system that the same media is selling. This identical technique is used by many self-help and enlightenment vendors:

> "Are you lacking meaning in your life?" "Is anxiety taking over your world?" "Do you want to be successful? ... Well, we have just the thing, the one thing, that will solve your problems for you."

> *Lesson one in developing a vibrant vulnerability: Do not listen to anyone claiming to solve your problems for you.*

Anything that takes your responsibility and choice from you is a false god. Not only is this person assaulting your spiritual sovereignty, but he or she is also removing your ability to grow upward. True spiritual illumination and maturity *always increases your responsibility.* Increased responsibility (ability to respond), is a requirement to increase our power in connection (where all real power originates).

Let's say a woman is in a vulnerable romantic relationship with a man. Let's say that she reveals a deep wound from her childhood. Almost certainly, this will create initial discomfort in a typical man. This discomfort may even lead him to try to quickly "solve" the problem by trying to make it go away. Yet, if he simply listens and empathizes, rather than viewing her emotions as a problem, he can more keenly call forth and express the manly parts of himself: listener, protector, provider, advocate, warrior, confidante, constant and steady companion.

Her vulnerability becomes a gift to allow him to be more deeply present to her and to exceed himself. He can affirm in this sensitive moment that he likes what he sees and that he loves her all the more for her emotional honesty. He can choose to melt and become purified by her vulnerability like precious metal in a crucible. Now he can flow brilliantly and form any durable shape from this molten precious spiritual and emotional metal.

> *Vulnerability is not, nor ever can be, a role. It arises from the desire to connect. It is a necessary and unavoidable state in the process of spiritual and emotional growth.*

Most people mistake the *feeling* of vulnerability with weakness or exposure or dependence. Some may see it as an invitation for other people to "stick the knife" in them and dominate them in some way. That is why it is important to discern between the traumatic negative Animal experience of vulnerability leading to physical and emotional injury and Spiritual vulnerability used to open up and connect positively with others and with larger wisdom.

> *In pure relationship, you and I must agree to*
> *bring all our attributes flowingly to the table, not*
> *all at once with a splurge of confession, but with*
> *an eye toward the seasons of our growth and with*
> *a mind for what we and others may be ready for.*

For men and women, this means sharing the wounded child who needs nurturing, and a sacred agreement to provide this nurturing rather than avoiding the other person or attempting to "toughen them up." By mutually agreeing to be vulnerable, you and I become more aware of ourselves and more capable of both spotting and addressing potential abuse. Truth is the mightiest weapon, and there is no truth without mutual acceptance of our inherently interdependent and vulnerable state of being.

This mutual agreement to be vulnerable allows a parent to enter into the world of the child, allows the child to care for the parent. This mutual agreement allows a man to be with a woman rather than "solving her problems," and allows the woman to discuss a man's doubt without feeling this is a threat to stability. In mutual vulnerability, there is neither victim nor victimizer. There is a mutual acceptance and advocacy of the strange and challenging situation called being human. Isn't it our greatest wish that we may all be in the presence of another in which we can be our full and authentic selves, all warts and wonders exposed and embraced? Isn't this vulnerability and imagination what a child shares with an imaginary friend? Why can't we make it real? Why, indeed!

TRUST

So how about trust? When should i trust someone with my deeper self? How do i know if that other person will honor me and treat me with respect?

Trust is not merely something you surrender to someone else. Trust is a bridge well-built between you and another person. Trust is inherently relational. It is learned rather than earned. We have all had the experience of someone who has been unequal to the trust we have placed in them, not because they were evil or manipulative, but because they were immature or unready or unable to follow through on the invitation that trust creates.

> *Trust is not a contract or a thing; it is connecting energy that takes time to establish.*

This establishment of trust is a continuous part of growth and learning for all humans. Parents may grant the opportunity to their teenaged children to come home on time from a night out or trust them with the opportunity to make good judgments around consuming alcohol. Not that the child will always "do what I say" (or what I deem responsible), but I "trust" that they will do their best and trust their intuitions and their judgment not to hop into a car with an intoxicated driver. Trust does not always guarantee a favorable outcome, but it provides grace. It gives the teenager the opportunity to call late at night if there is real need or danger.

Trust between men and women, likewise, does not guarantee a trouble-free relationship or "happily-ever-after" but it provides a necessary foundation for deepening connection and reliance upon one another.

Trust is not so much a prerequisite to a relationship as a valid *expression* of genuine relationship. Trust does not entail reading the future but dealing poignantly and honestly with the present. In developing a present-minded trust, we begin to know ourselves more, know the other person more, know the world more, and know the relationships between each of these. Ironically this allows us to see the future more clearly. We can see what another is capable of holding and what the world is capable of receiving at this point in time. We can see if we are a fit for another person.

> *Trust is not a possession. We cannot confer it on someone else. Trust is an expression of genuine relationship.*

If you are head-over-heels in love with someone, you do not have to hold your cards close, nor do you have to give yourself away. *Take time.* Open as the relationship allows. Notice everything as it happens, not as you would fear it might happen or wish it would happen. Do not project your desires on the actual reality of the relationship. Be intent, interested and even fascinated by the unpredictable and creative directions a mutually-vulnerable and mutually-learning relationship may take.

Let yourself be shown and keenly observe what the other person shows. Look through them, not merely at them. Simple things are confirming signs that this person is not as he or she seems. If people tend to belittle you about small things now, they will almost inevitably belittle you about big things in the future. If a person is pressuring you to have sex with them, he or she is essentially demanding that you give yourself away, without any complementary vulnerability on their part; he or she is using you. Healthy sexuality at the start is always mutually disclosing and considerate. It allows for mutual ripening. It does not demand or pressure. It recognizes the fragility, sensuality, and sacredness of sexual union. It is neither prudish nor pornographic.

Trust is about mutual presence and transparency. It is a reality, not an aspiration. Again, trust is patient and increasingly solid as it forms a bridge between people on the foundation stones of their truer, deeper selves. If a person's present self is immature, then trust can offer support for that person to mature. If that person refuses to learn and grow, then the trust process is broken, and the relationship is bound to end.

> *Trust does not demand immediate excellence, but it does demand willingness to grow.*

Trust asserts itself most amid change. It never demands that a person stop changing. How many people have said this: "You aren't the same person that I married?" For better or worse, of course, that person is not! Now evaluate what this means. Has your partner-in-trust retreated emotionally from you and their growth or are they simply growing apart from you and failing to meet your expectations? If the person is in retreat, is there a way to support them to steady and advance? If the person is not meeting your expectations, is there a way for you to question your assumptions and develop your own empathy, generosity, and growth?

Remember that healthy trust always serves mutual connection. It does not demand that we martyr ourselves for another. Rather it is a spiritual conduit, allowing us to see each other authentically, care for each other, and even let each other go. One of the most powerful and beautiful forms of trust is spiritual self-trust, trusting the most vital part of ourselves, and forming a mutually-respectful relationship between the Animal and Spiritual aspect of the self. It is unlikely you will have a deeply fulfilling relationship with another until you are willing to start on the journey to deep spiritual self-trust.

You say to spiritually "trust yourself on your deepest and highest level". That seems so abstract. What does that mean? What does that look like?

First, trust does not mean being without doubt. You may have doubts about yourself, what choices to make, and what life means. But this does not make you untrusting. Trust of yourself, at its core, means embracing the opportunity to experience what life offers to its fullest. Well, what does this mean? First, it means recognizing that the gift of life is one of grace. We have received the gift of life without any merit on our part.

> *To take up life, therefore, cannot involve "deserving" but rather curiosity and a willingness to engage life on co-creative terms, rather than telling it what to do.*

In short, trusting life and trusting yourself mean expressing gratitude for having been given the opportunity to live.

This is a big step for many who might say, "Life does not seem to be a gift. It seems like a constant struggled riddled with suffering and only a few glimpses of joy." "It is not so much that I don't trust myself; it is that I do not trust the world and I do not trust others. They let me down constantly." And, yet, what really has the world let down? Your pre-fabricated notions of the "good life" as one of milk and honey, leisure and money, of freedom from want or care?

Would that really be a good life? You might initially think so but look more closely. A life without effort and challenge is a life without choice, creativity, and appreciation. Does such a life sound good to you? Of course not. We are tempted to imagine the care-free as inherently good without understanding the cost. A life without effort and challenge sounds good only as a reaction to a life of drudgery and pain.

But a very different notion of good life forms when we are open, proactive, and respectful of the greater gifts of life. If we decide not to dwell in the sewer of discontent, we realize that spiritual trust is not built on the fulfillment of mentally pre-formed notions of what it means to "live large." Most of these notions, like that of "success," are simply social programming that has no room for our contribution, uniqueness, or expression. (This is proven by all the unhappy, so-called "successful" people out there.)

True spiritual joy, "life flow" (versus "lifestyle") has no condition, except being alive and desiring to express the energy of life. Trust in life and one's self as a child of life is expressed in refinement, joy, and creativity. Self-trust involves a necessary self-empathy for being "flawed." A flaw is a divergence from formulaic perfection and is necessary for creativity.

> *Life is not a formula. It is an improvisation.*

One of my favorite wry observations of life is this simple observation: "How does one develop good judgment? Experience! How does one develop experience? Bad judgment!" The point of life, and trust in life, is not to merely concoct and pursue a goal you *think* will give you happiness (usually based on other people's advice), but to *feel* deeply what gives you joy in a lasting way and to *explore* that feeling and *experiment* from that feeling.

INTIMACY

Why do men send mixed messages, especially around intimacy? Where do men find their deep worth? Why are many men afraid of commitment?

Why is it that heterosexual men, in particular, rely so heavily upon a women but, at the same time, hide from women? Why is it that so many men seem to want women that will challenge them to keep things interesting, and yet get angry and insecure when women exceed them? Why is it that men are so willing and able to accept sympathy but so unable to hand it out?

> *It's almost as if men are willing to take emotional energy to lift themselves up but see that same emotional giving to others as pulling them down.*

Men typically have been trained in comparative and individualized self-worth. They have been taught see themselves as endpoints. These are not helpful or healthy teachings when it comes to spiritual and practical growth and development. Instead, these habits prompt a man to claim himself king no matter how small or humble the realm.

A spiritually confident man sees the expanding cosmos itself as his domain. He is a growing soul in an ever expanding and deepening universe. He knows that the universe grows faster than he grows and is glad for it. He will never run out of possibilities or things to learn and explore! So, he looks at himself, not in comparison, but in absolute terms: "Am I stronger, wiser, more open, than I was yesterday?" "Have my relationships grown healthier?" "Am I doing my life's work, and if not, how can I come closer to my dharma?" With this mentality, a man can feel a sense of accomplishment in his understanding and correspondence with his spirit.

Typical men are always looking outside themselves for validation. This makes it difficult for them to give, so desperate they are to receive this validation. Many will seize that validation with whatever power is at their disposal.

> *And this is what is at the core of men's problems with intimacy: If they are revealed to be empty frauds in a very fragile and tender sphere, then they believe they will have no one to believe in them, especially (and devastatingly) those closest to them. The strategy seems to be: Hold others at arms-length enough so they won't see the fraud; bring them close enough to provide validation and emotional energy.*

Ironically, the pressure to become more intimate, which happens when a partner or companion wants to get closer and become *more* understanding, is what causes many men to leave the very person trying to support them.

> *This answers the question, "Why do you see so many men throw away or sabotage relationships with good women?"*

These women are getting too intimate and being "too good to be true." It's easier to manage a demanding woman. There is no threat she'll get too intimate emotionally. Because men have been trained to view intimacy as a threat, they largely become estranged from the world, because fear and inability around intimacy usually overflow into alienation in other areas of life. They begin to tell themselves that no one wants them as they are, even though they rarely share the authentic, flawed side of themselves.

There are those men that take the opposite tack: Spread themselves around in polyamorous sexual intimacy. Here no one woman can make an "inordinate" demand like total commitment upon him. When did avoidance of intimacy become the motto of a man? I'm not sure. But I am sure that men need to re-engage and learn intimacy again.

There is another aspect of men that prevents commitment to and respect for a good woman. *Men have been weaned to respect the demanding and cruel, not the supportive and kind.* "If someone is kind, aren't they giving something to me for free?" "I didn't earn it, so clearly its worthless." This tough love = value equation is complete crap. A kind woman is a miracle of grace. I would advise men to respect kind women and forsake the thrill of a hunt which lands them with a manipulative woman.

Why do men often find emotions painful? Why are they threatened by "fuzzy" vs. defined emotions?

This is related to the previous question. Men typically have a problem with "fuzzy" emotions versus "tangible" ones. Their more basic, tool-oriented, task-oriented approach to life makes ambiguous emotions like love seem disorienting. There is not a straightforward use or definition for love as there is, say, for anger. Ambiguous feeling without clear-cut rules invites vulnerability and uncertainty. Sure, this ambiguity and its multiple possibilities are what makes creativity possible, but that means a man is no longer self-sufficient. He needs to improvise with others, and who knows what they will do! They could mess things up or attack him or ignore him! Again, men have been taught to center too much upon themselves and their control. They fail to see where real power resides—*between* themselves and others.

> *Men find emotions painful because they personalize them, instead of decentering them in "betweenness" in relationship with others.*

Picture man's brain being like a computer, and him trying to stuff the entire Google search function on his hard drive, instead of accessing the internet (which is the "cloud" or the connected "betweenness" of cyberspace). He'd soon get overwhelmed. Picture the situation of a man's heart trying to do the same thing, managing and controlling all these feelings and emotional demands coming from everywhere. He would very soon become exhausted and wrung out!

> *It is no wonder why so many men try to rise above these emotional demands, escape them, become stoic, freeze up, shut down, or stonewall, given their outdated emotional operating system. Complex, ambiguous emotion has become for many men a warning trigger to overwhelm, trauma, and pain.*

I want to say to these men, "You don't have to stuff every bit of mental and emotional information on your personal hard drive!" If you do, you are going to break down and not be of much use to you or anyone. Trust intimate betweenness to hold the emotional energy and simply be yourself! Don't be a master of your domain; be a collaborator, sharing your unique perspectives, deep loves, and interests, and let the "work" be done by the search engine of betweenness. That's why men don't ask for directions; they feel "less than" if they don't already possess the knowledge in their brains. Well, that is ridiculously unreasonable especially with society's exponential increase in information.

I am alternately amused and alarmed by all the ways men are trying to reclaim a specious control, reassert dominance, and throw themselves "back to the basics" of defined masculine emotions and roles. To these men, I say, "Hey, don't you remember those video games like 'Pong,' you know, Atari's first system in which you had two moveable line segments operating as paddles, and you whacked a pixelated dot back and forth across the video monitor? Those were simpler, basic times! Why don't we just go back to that!" There is not a guy who would take me up on that. They'd all be screaming for their multi-terabyte game consoles and hyper-realistic war simulation games. *Yet when it comes to emotional development men go back to Pong and "tough love" and self-sufficient manliness more appropriate to the 19th century than the 21st!*[42]

> *The real source of wisdom for men is the soul connected to the cloud of spirit, not the brain, the human computer hard drive, with all its limited powers and prejudices.*

---

42   http://www.artofmanliness.com/2014/06/09/semper-virilis-a-roadmap-to-manhood-in-the-21st-century/

This spirit is refracted through a man's masculine polarity and unique divine genius to create and offer worth. Therefore, worth is not something a man has to prove but to *birth* from the cloud of spirit, through the soul and higher mind, into the body and the world. This is inherently a co-creative versus formulaic process. Hierarchy has no place in this.

The future "real man" will be an active philosopher and an applied psychologist. He will honor that which is presented to him instead of trying to conquer it. He will regard emotion as an opportunity for discovery, *as a curiosity rather than a threat.* The future spiritually confident man *will* still destroy, *but* this will involve the creative destruction of his old prejudices and outworn habits in the project of co-creating new life. He doesn't have to defeat the other or slay the dragon of uncertainty, because change does not cause him fear. Possibility is an ally, not a threat.

STAYING YOUNG IN SPIRIT

When they age, why do men go for the 'younger model' of women?

One has to look at the reasons why men dispose of a wise, strong, and caring woman their same age for an often very much younger woman. There are rare occasions when this is merely a matter of falling in love and little else. Most often, however, it has its roots in insecurity, a misbegotten notion of power, or a desire for revived youth and adventure.

The insecurity and panic part is easy to explain. The spiritually inse-cure man's sense of identity (in patriarchal culture anyway) is attached to physicality. As he ages, he feels he is literally losing himself because he is losing his physical vigor and what he feels is his "mojo" attached to the physical. This creates a challenge to his identity and a kind of desperation to prove he is still a player on the world's stage rather than a has-been. A younger woman who adores his wisdom and financial wherewithal can feel like medicine, making him feel temporarily whole again, addressing the symptoms of aging without getting to the root.

The reason for men going with younger women in later life almost always follows the same script. "Hey, I'm the top dog. I can get any woman I want, so I'll buy one." I won't waste the reader's brain space on this, except to simply note it. The healthiest and most understandable reason why a man pursues a younger woman in later age is that a man wants a revived sense of youth and adventure. He simply wants to feel "young again," dare again, and feel significance with someone who is "into" him. Too often long-married couples do get comfortable and even complacent. For many couples, this is entirely acceptable, and they like that kind of ritual steadiness. Other couples part over this issue. One (either man *or* woman) wants adventure and a second life, and the other wants to go gently into that good night.

This is the time to embrace nuance and expand the sense of adven-ture. It doesn't mean men have to tour around doing extreme sports. Why not adventure into deeper reaches of emotional intimacy, mentor-ing young people, and volunteerism, taking time to enjoy the energy of learning? What do men have to lose? What excuse do they now have against being spontaneous? Why not leave it on the table?

There is a scene in the film *Love Actually* that illustrates this issue and always moves my wife to tears. The long-supportive wife in the film, Karen, played by Emma Thompson, finds what she thinks is a gift to her, an expensive necklace with a heart on it, in the pocket of her husband's coat. When she gets a compact disc of Joni Mitchell as her gift, she knows that the necklace went to the young siren at the office who has amorous intentions toward her husband. Karen confronts her husband, played by Alan Rickman, and he begs forgiveness, but he has made a mockery of their marriage, and something is irretrievably broken.

> *When a man is attached to the physical and bases his virility upon the physical, it is understandable that he would feel abandoned by aging and death. However, spiritually confident manhood is not based upon the physical, but the opposite, the surrender of the physical as a basis for meaning in the development of a higher, more refined spiritual adventure and daring.*

Now a man can bungee-jump off the cliffs of his own emotions into the rushing air of intimacy rather than shrinking from that challenge. Now he can see where his intuition might take him, rather than posturing and proving. He becomes affirmative rather than reactive. He deepens into something beyond his own physicality. He becomes multi-dimensional rather than a one-dimensional version of himself.

This does not mean a spiritually confident man abandons physical health or dietary concern. In fact, the opposite occurs. He realizes how smart exercise and diet support his spiritual health, precisely because he is aging. He no longer can go on a drunken binge and other unwise behavior and recover his well-being as quickly as he did when he was young. His energy has a different source, the spirit, brought through his body in fuller maturity and awareness, and this expands and deepens his higher powers.

A man then has a new question, *not* "Who will make me feel young again?" (because he doesn't want a return to immaturity) but rather "How will I engage myself and who will engage me to be the higher, more powerful man?" More often than not, the answer to the latter question is someone who knows him well, someone who is steady and wise and has stuck by him in trying times as well as pleasant. That same person is likely to be open to a renewed sense of this man's power and adventure. Few are the women (or gay men) who would say, "I want *less* passion and adventure in a man as he gets older." And if she or he does, then that is on them. If both the woman and the man are lacking a sense of adventure, that can be relatively easy to cure if both desire and open to new life.

> *The spirit will find a way if the desire is there.*

The practical aspects of later life are favorable for adventure. The kids are going out into the world, off to college, and so forth. There is some financial security and time in retirement. Why not learn new things, volunteer, and experiment with life like a child in a sandbox? This is the time to rebel, explore, surprise yourselves rather than settle in for a long winter's nap. This adventure, however, will probably look somewhat different than it would in youth, inviting greater sensuality and depth.

> *Middle age and beyond is the time to open up the carburetor rather than close up shop.*

For a man, this means exerting spirit in the face of death. This is the ultimate act of rebellion and the true sign of virility for a man: To lose his life (physical trappings of power and reputation) to gain it (life force, a flow of creativity). *To be present rather than dominant is the essence of manhood.*

FALSE GURUS AND MATERIALISM

Why are there so many male false gurus and charismatic jerks out there?

Men are used to being followed and feeding off the belief of their followers. The "leader" gets more self-assured and energized by belief placed in him and the followers sense this energy and conclude that he must, therefore, be a messiah. In the end, what followers really want is affirmation on some level, and a false guru is able to provide that affirmation by linking their identities with allegiance to him. Now they *have* to believe in him or admit that they are failures for having trusted him in the first place.

Given how many times these so-called spiritual gurus and Jim Jones-like cult "leaders" have been debunked, I am not sure why so many keep falling for their schtick. Whether hawking a "can't miss" investment "opportunity," a wonder diet, or a "can't fail" formula for enlightenment, white guys do have a gift with making even manure seem like it's solid gold. I think part of the problem around people falling for their snake oil resides in the scarcity of opportunity to directly develop spiritual capacity and intelligence.

We live in a scientific materialist age which seems intent on dismissing the spirit altogether and offering up pipe dreams of eternal life, worth, and enjoyment in the form of technology.

> *When consuming technology proves a failure, many people turn to a leader and "consume" him.*

And that is the key. It is our own alienated consumer impulse that sets us up to give our sovereignty up to a false prophet. We feel we cannot do it ourselves, and, frankly, we cannot. We do need others to grow and learn, but instead of going with the quiet, giving mentor we are attracted, like children, to the blare and flash of those charlatans promising the heavens. Once we develop a sense and respect for subtle wisdom, more of us will unplug and leave these swindlers in the obscurity they deserve.

ANGER

Why is anger such a motivating emotion, especially for men?
In a world in which men feel they cannot express themselves in traditional ways, and in a world in which they have not learned new, satisfying, and socially acceptable ways for men to express themselves, a sense of pent-up frustration and anger is likely to mount.

> *The best approach to this topic, for men is not to ask, "Who's to blame?" but rather, "Why am I angry? Why am I frustrated, and how can I find an authentic, significant and fulfilling way to express myself?"*

In general, open anger is still tolerated as an expected masculine emotion. Its cathartic clarity fulfills a need for men to release pent-up inactivity or frustration. Unfortunately, however, it also alienates others and can harm relationships. This situation with boys and men is not helped by the increasingly sedentary nature of work and schools.

Transforming anger centers upon understanding anger itself, divining its sources and motivation, and finding effective alternative forms of expression.

The "chemistry" of anger

- Anger arises out of *a sense of threat*, of one's self or group being thwarted, denied, diminished, slighted, put down, insulted, and/or degraded, leaving what feels like a deficit, an injustice.
- Anger tends to bring about an unreflective or *reflexive/automatic* desire to respond *immediately* (without a pause) to correct the perceived imbalance, deficit, or injustice. In other words, it feels like there is "no time to think, no time to wait."
- Anger *does not gather information* and look at the other party's intention to check *or communicate* whether or not the slight was an accident or merely an unthinking blunder.
- Anger tends to *escalate*. Anger informs the other party of their alleged offense (whether they meant it or not), usually with a little extra force to give them "special" warning to emphasize not to do this in the future.

- Anger tends to gain *momentum*. This creates a new injustice, a perceived imbalance, a disproportional response, which invites stronger anger and a sense of injustice by the other party. A negative feedback loop establishes itself.

Why does anger feel so motivating?

1. Anger involves a *sharp sense of urgency* to initiate an action to correct a perceived threat: "I have to engage/strike back or else." This is not typically the case with sadness (which is vaguer and fosters a reflex to withdraw) or fear (which is clear but fosters a reflex to actively avoid or run away).

2. Appraisal is inherently *"built into"* the anger response rather than being a separate conscious act. Ex. "He did this to me!" or "She should have known better!" These are evaluations that "believe" they are inherently right and, therefore, are not open to correction.

3. Anger *concretizes*, simplifies, and gives meaning to ambiguous, complex emotions like sadness, confusion, and anxiety. Shades of "gray" become black and white. Example: A child misses his mom who has gone on a business trip (sadness) and acts out his sadness and anxiety as anger or crankiness.

4. Anger *offloads* emotional responsibility, burden, and distress (caused by shame, guilt, failure, insecurity, low self-esteem, etc.) to temporarily alleviate emotional pain and uncertainty. A continuing cycle of anger (resentment) can keep this pain at bay, much like an alcoholic can avoid a hangover by staying drunk. Example #1: Racial resentment and police brutality: Why doesn't the shame of public video exposure of police brutality suppress behavior instead of increasing it? Exposure

causes shame, which translates into motivation to offload shame through anger and re-establish authority, leading to more abusive behavior. Example #2: Blaming foreigners and economic distress: Why are Mexicans being blamed for job losses when this situation is caused by concentration of wealth, automation, and outsourcing exploited by hyper-wealthy, powerful individuals? Additional fear and anxiety are generated by challenging someone more powerful than you, so distressed people offload their anxieties, through anger, on to the less powerful. This is like a man who kicks his dog after his boss gives him a hard time at work.

5. Anger *sends a signal,* sets a boundary, for future actions and relations. This emerges from fear of consequences down the road if one does not establish a precedent. Example: A teacher may think, "The students will walk all over me if I don't show toughness in my first few weeks."

6. Anger can be *pre-emptive* in nature, intending to send a protective warning to "leave me alone" in a way that can be read as aggressive, again resulting in escalation of tensions.

7. Anger is *social in nature* (rather than anti-social like sadness), magnifying implications for social pecking order, hierarchy, territory, relationships.

Given this analysis, we see that male anger is not strictly unreasonable. It may be primitive, but it serves, albeit poorly, real underlying needs. What strikes me when looking over this self-created list of sources and motivations for anger is how often even fairly minor things are seen as a threat by angry men. So many of these alleged threats are simply generated by impersonal changes in the world that angry men take personally. They get ratcheted up and find no place to put these hyped up feelings except into anger. "If you touch my emotionally sensitive or sore spot, you are an attacker. I am just defending myself! I'm the victim!"

The curse of male privilege

> *It is ironic that the same thing that allows men to be the center of everything, patriarchal privilege, is also the same thing that traps them into facing responsibility for failed leadership.*

When the chickens come home to roost on a man's failed proclamations and assertions of power, that man is left with himself, and no way out... He doesn't have the emotional equipment to take responsibility, thanks to his entitlement, so he must make it someone else's fault. You see this in so many of the so-called "hate radio" programs, crawling with disenchanted men trying to find a way to blame everyone and everything else for the world's messes without once taking responsibility for themselves.

A spiritually confident man, says, "Okay, this is the situation, and this is my part in it. Let's get to work." Regardless who "started it" or who is ultimately responsible for the mess, a spiritually confident man knows he is part of the solution. Therefore he "softens and leans into the point," as the Buddhist phrase goes. He finds an alternative cathartic expression for his pent-up frustration, for example, through intense exercise, experience in nature, or creative activity intended to solve a problem or express a desire. In these, he can feel a sense of intrinsic power, joy, and significance. It takes the edge off his restlessness because he is not only venting but venturing forth into new realms, an archetypally satisfying endeavor. Now we just have to encourage men to do so without expecting or proclaiming they are masters of their new domain, but rather citizens!

FAITH

What is faith for a man?

To me faith means letting go of myself to be called beyond myself. This means utter honesty, transparency, and vulnerability from the spiritual on down.

> *There is, in a man's life, those rare opportunities to step up to the plate and give in to the promptings of his spirit and follow its whispers even when his body, mind, and heart rail against such a decision.*

This is a man called to his higher self. Maybe it comes when he breaks through his bravado and apologizes for being mean. Maybe it comes when he finally hears the plea of his son to play catch through his haze of workaholism. Maybe it is a cry to protect and care for a child when he feels at his weakest and most stretched.

A man surrendering to faith submits to a higher authority not "out there" but "in here." He is a man of active and strong conscience but ultimate receptivity. Such a man, again, "softens and leans into the point." He does so naked to his own spirit. He chooses to take off his armor. A faithful man is willing to let go of all he has built to co-create anew. His reputation is surrendered, his traditional fighting tools are laid aside. He relies upon the equipment of his heart for a confrontation with his smaller and lower self. He acknowledges his childlike emotional body wandering afraid and confused in the wilderness. He lets go of the mental body's obsessive analysis of the world and its pitfalls to allow the emotional body to grow into adulthood.

A faithful man does not have the luxury of cynicism, of disenchantment, of "being right." He is drawn to be good. He is asked to be strong in a different way like a tensile strand of hair, which is sturdy and pliable, rather than stone-like. A faithful man is permeable. He can hear, and feels, the cries of another as his own cry. He is broken open to the suffering and the beauty of the world. He embraces his next journey and chooses to go on the more difficult one at the crossroads. He has been an uncertain man, and now he stands as a man beyond the need for certainty. He aspires to be a greater man, even as he has discovered that the "greatness" in his soul exceeds and leads him in a far different direction than what is taught by school, society, and community. *He now conquers himself rather than the world.*

We do not have to know where this new spiritual journey leads or how it will turn out. This is the step of faith. We know where we are beginning. We know what we are surrendering. We are open to the future. We are listening to the past. We stand ready and alert in the present. We know this is a time of significant transformation and learning for men if we gallantly take up the challenge and invitation to be new and better men. We know we are born to do this, for this is the real adventure of a man, the real seed he gives. Faith. Surrender. Transformation. Rebirth. Life.

Very few people understand that Jesus did *not* utter on the Cross, "My God, my God why hast thou forsaken me?" (Matthew 27:46 KJV). That is a King James mistranslation of the original Greek and Aramaic. The correct translation has a diametrically opposite meaning: "My God, my God for this I was born/kept!" (Matthew 27:46, trans. George Lamsa).[43]

A present-day man can take a faith lesson from this corrected translation.

> *Instead of seeing the world as abandoning him and against him, today's man can choose to see his challenges as something he was born for and **entrusted with** because the cosmos and his own spirit have **faith in him!***

Why not take up *that* invitation as men. It is certainly more empowering and redemptive.

By contrast, the messages we receive from patriarchal institutions are manipulative and disempowering, meant to keep us controlled, down, and doubting. False kings and idols of this world are terrified that we men will discover a new power of spirit and abandon not God, but *them* and the false gods they represent. If we men faithfully recognize an empowering spirit that generously embraces all people including the "least" of us, then the power of hierarchy crumbles, and we come to a new earth. Let us choose to do so and courageously engage our manhood in a new way.

---

43   https://wahiduddin.net/words/forsaken.htm

EMOTIONAL WELL-BEING

*How do we create relationships and communities
that support emotional health and well-being?*

"Bow to no one. Honor everyone."—Regina Meredith

Why is it that people who have been betrayed in a close relationship (for instance a spouse who has been cheated on), will take on the guilt and responsibility for that action? Why do they frequently say to themselves: "What did I do wrong to allow this to happen?" And why is it that the people who betray others will often rationalize the action and experience with no guilt at all? There is something strange going on in this emotional jungle.

> *It is as if emotional and moral responsibility and reality have been subverted to put the blame on the innocent person and lift it from the truly guilty party.*

Why is it that people who were taken in by a lie, or who were taken advantage of, feel shame and chastise themselves with "I should have known better." Yet, the person doing the exploitation or abuse of trust seems to have no shame at all? Why is it that we commonly get embarrassed *for* someone else when they are having an awkward time public-speaking? In each of these cases, it is almost as if empathy has gone so hyperactive that a non-responsible party takes over responsibility for the sins or anxieties of others.

In my studies in self-esteem, I found that women (more attuned to relationship) were far more likely to be beset by *self-doubt* and take on responsibility, even for those things they should not have to be responsible for, and men (more attuned to task) were far more likely to embody *self-deception* and offload their responsibility on someone else, even for those things that are clearly their responsibility. In short, females tend to internalize responsibility for emotions and males tend to externalize this responsibility. The point of emotional intelligence and courage is for both men and women to support one another and re-balance this dynamic.

We all have a stake in going beyond mere emotional coping, survival, and blame games toward mutual empowerment. This is especially urgent in a time in which virtual reality and social media are making the distinction between a lie and a truth almost indistinguishable.

> *Fake news, fabricated memories, the "selfie culture" in which people put out unreasonably happy edits of their lives, have muddled the necessity of "being real" with each other and with ourselves.*

We are facing a social reality of rhetorical support for emotional transparency and honesty that is actively discouraged in practice.

How many of us have experienced our parents admonishing us to "be nice" and "pretend you are having fun" to that annoying aunt who treated us like a perpetual three-year-old or that somewhat creepy uncle who seemed to hug us a little too tight? How many of us have noticed that instead of acknowledging grief, anger, and frustration, we are typically socially taught to deny uncomfortable emotions so other people will not feel uncomfortable? When we do "slip" and express these uncomfortable emotions, others usually try to jump in and either "solve" them with clichéd advice or ease them out of the picture by making light of them. These are essentially tactics of avoidance and suppression, in other words, lying by omission.

There has to be something more than image control introduced into our perception if we are to interrupt artificial realities and become more emotionally honest. With virtual reality and social media, we are becoming too successful manipulating our own feelings to support an unreasonably rosy "fake it 'til you make it" view of ourselves and our world. If we aren't letting emotions run wild, we are suppressing or controlling them, or we are transfiguring emotions to suit any desire or self-image we wish at a given time! *We need to develop much more sophisticated craft understanding of how to creatively explore and constructively express our real emotions.*

PEACE AND JUSTICE

How do I gain peace and justice?

First, one must recognize what true peace and justice are. Peace is not merely the absence of worldly conflict, and justice is not merely worldly equality. On the spiritual level, peace is creative flow unimpeded. Peace is an acceptance of growth and the inevitable flaws in the creative procession of life. Our sense of justice is based on the intuitive rightness of this peaceful, creative flow and on an acute awareness of the consequences of thwarting of this peaceful flow. Fighting injustices often comes out in the form of fighting inequities precisely because these inequities oppress others, prevent their access to those resources and recognition, and therefore obstruct them from being fully realized, contributing members to the creative flow of life.

> *In a truly peaceful and just world, all people would be sharing their divine creative genius, and there would be universal respect and space for this endeavor.*

However, we live in a world of competing notions of power and worth. The spiritually immature believe that they can attain an alleged peace, power, and worth by controlling others, and by being the ones who give orders over and against others. Obviously, that strategy does not embody peace or justice. In fact, this strategy does the opposite, compelling a person toward paranoia, addiction, and entitlement in ways that make peace and justice nearly unattainable both for themselves and for others.

In the peace of creative flow, yes, cessation of open destructive conflict is helpful and even necessary. However, creativity always requires open, *constructive* conflict, like that dynamic that plays out in the debate between two contrasting philosophical notions of the good.

> *It is by enjoining contrast, constructive conflict, that we learn and grow. This kind of conflict is necessary to real creativity, peace, and justice.*

Having your beliefs challenged is not the same as having your person violated, even though the two can feel similar. A mature spiritual person does not want another to merely be a mirror of themselves.

A mature person enjoys the dynamic of difference and has gratitude for the learning and creative power generated by contrast. If both contenders over some issue have respect for each other, then both will go away richer, fuller, and even more peaceful having formed a basis of appreciation for the "opponent." What looked like competition on the surface was actually more akin to a creative collaboration underneath. This latter understanding is what the Ancient Greeks refer to when they talk about a "noble adversary." In some ways, I can learn from and respect my "enemy" and even learn to love him or her. Certainly, this book could not be written without respect and attention to those I disagree with.

> *Even a powerful inspirational idea is a "threat" in the sense that it threatens to dissolve your world in the light of transformation. If you act on this inspirational idea, you will not be the same person. You are "risking" a new life.*

Again, so much of people's lack of peacefulness has to do with their fear of conflict and death, yet both are necessary for the goodness in this life. We have to confront our small or lower selves to rise higher both within ourselves and in our society.

We have to "die" to smaller, more timid versions of ourselves to expand, deepen, and grow braver and wiser. *Peace involves that compassionate acknowledgment of painful internal struggle that gives rise to our fear, violence, or anger in the first place.* Peace and justice involve binding ourselves to the thread of life and appreciating its challenges as the painter appreciates the colors, textures, and viscosities of his paints. He couldn't paint without those paints. We cannot live a meaningful creative life without contrast, and we cannot have peace and justice without appreciation and engagement of difference.

PLEASURE, HAPPINESS, AND JOY

What is the difference between pleasure, happiness, and joy?
Pleasure is a physically enjoyable sensation. Happiness is the mental or emotional equivalent of physical pleasure, where the feelings reside in the more non-material realms of the mind and the heart. Women tend to be driven more by emotional happiness, boosted by relationship and intimacy, which allow them to connect with others. Men tend to be driven more by mental happiness, gravitating toward activities which allow them to "figure out" or "master" the world and feel a sense of corresponding power.

Joy is basically spiritual happiness. It is more subtle and transcendent than physical, mental, or emotional forms of bliss, due to its higher frequency. Joy is felt within the physical, mental, and emotional realms, but is not limited to these realms. Joy has a way of radiating out past the individual and into the surrounding environment and relationships. Joy is, in short, infectious. Unlike happiness, joy is not conditional or instrumental.

> *You can try to "make someone happy," but you will be unable to make someone joyful. Joy is a result of the walls tumbling down and that cathartic release of oneself into the essence of things.*

Joy is an end in itself, like the joy of being alive. In many ways, joy is a pure expression and pure connection that exceeds the body, mind, and heart.

We can see the difference between pleasure, happiness, and joy within a sexual act that encompasses both sexuality and sensuality. (The book "The Joy of Sex," should probably have been more accurately titled, The Pleasure of Sex" or, at most, "The Happiness of Sex.") The pleasure of sex is rather obvious. Intense arousal and release can cause waves of physical pleasure, which wash over the shores of the mental and emotional. The stimulations, imaginations, touching, and connections in good sex can trip every mental and emotional trigger in a person, lighting them up like a Christmas tree and easing them down the other side into a warm untroubled relaxation. That is sexuality—sharing and pleasure that is both intense and warm from the essence of intertwined persons.

> *Sensuality, however, transcends the person and the couple, it involves a subtler, more spiritually powerful fusion experienced by two persons joining. It is an aesthetic, creative energy that leaps outside the boundaries of skin and draws in otherworldly energy.*

In sensuality, one "feels into" the essence of connection itself, dissolving the self. Perhaps this is the origin of the French term for sex, "le petit mort," the little death. In sensuality one loses oneself to a larger wave, only to be rewarded with a more intense experience of oneself. By feeling the skin or feeling the sight of another at its essential level, energy courses through your being, and you begin to know the "other" as you.

GENDER POLARITY

What is the difference between what you call "polarity" and gender roles?

Note, again, the false dichotomy: "Conservative" people are trying to reinforce rigid and sexist gender roles, and "liberal" people are androgynously trying to get rid of any distinction whatsoever between male and female under the rubric of "equality." Depending on which side you are on you can argue that you are good and the other is evil. You can argue that liberals are trying to corrupt the so-called "natural" differences between male and female. You can say the conservatives are despotically imposing sexist norms on women. Both approaches are intensely partial and misleading.

> *From time immemorial there has been polarity, the notion that male and female offer different but complementary essences.*

One is not bad and the other good. Nor is the difference between male and female bad or good. It simply is. Yes, these male and female energies have been weighed down and overlaid with gender images of how a real man or woman "ought" to behave. That is a superficial argument.

The yin-yang symbol represents well the female and male principles: The receptive female "yin" represents the dark womb-like hidden origin of birth from chaos, and the active male "yang" represents the penetrating ray of light that sets creation into motion. Each has an element of the other in them. The yin-yang symbol has white within the black and black within the white. So, women are not prevented from asserting, and men are not prevented from receiving. In fact, for exchange to occur at all, there must be some feminine in the masculine and some masculine in the feminine, otherwise there could be no reception and translation of the other's energy.

Furthermore, there exists a wavy border between the two elements of yin and yang, suggesting flexibility in the boundaries between the two, not a rigid straight line. Yet both masculine and feminine are still distinct and contrasting, which they need to be to have anything to offer and to create the transformative power of thesis-antithesis-synthesis. True and healthy androgyny should not be this sexless mixture of feminine and masculine exterior styles, but the accentuation and development of the best and highest feminine and masculine interior attributes within the body and being of a man or woman, boy or girl.

The active masculine principle doesn't mean that it is weird or unnatural for a woman to initiate, to embody male elements, or assert herself. Vice versa, the feminine, receptive principle doesn't mean that it is weird or unnatural for a man to be receptive, embody female elements, or demonstrate sensitivity. In addition, the *way* men express their initiative can be through giving and supporting, and the way women can express their receptivity is by evoking the truth of a situation rather than passively agreeing to immature behavior.

Another way to understand this difference between weak and superficial androgyny and vital androgyny is by understanding the difference between a stereotype and an archetype. A stereotype is a convenient or oversimplified idea mapped on the world to get the world to conform to a particular pattern. It is, therefore *convergent*, self-certain, and constricting. You see stereotypes evident in prescribed gender roles in which women are forced to be in the home and "barefoot and pregnant" because that is asserted to be their "natural disposition." However, the same use of stereotype in reverse is asserted by so-called proponents of "women's liberation" in which women are forced *out* of the home and into work to supposedly combat sexism. Both rely upon prescribed roles of what women "ought" to be. Neither respects the choices of a woman to be in the home *or* in work.

Archetypes, on the other hand, are *divergent*, generative, and expansive. *Archetypes are prototypical starting points, rather than prescribed stereotypical endpoints.* What you *do* with a masculine or feminine starting point is up to you, just like what you do when you juxtapose red paint next to blue paint on a canvas. And, yes, you can mix masculine and feminine qualities and come up with purple. The point I am making is that we be careful not to make a regime of our art. If our gender art is to be authentic it will be an organic, outgrowth of our individual and collective creative journey of self, not some trendy, pseudo-rebellious, glomming on to the gender identity style du jour.

> *Stereotype emphasizes the object—categorize the other and imprison them in your concepts to reinforce yourself and your sense of superiority. Archetype emphasizes the subject—access ancient energies, models, and spiritual symbols as sources of empowerment to transform yourself and your sense of creativity.*

You can feel the difference between a lecherous stereotypical man at work and an honoring archetypal man. Both can put their hands on the shoulder of a female co-worker in what looks to be identical ways.

Yet the same woman will receive the former touch as sexual harassment and the latter touch as comforting. Why? Because a touch is not simply a touch; it is a powerful communicator of energy and intention.

> *If you are objectifying someone and want something from them, it will come out in your touch. Just that little ounce of extra pressure by one of the fingers communicates, "I want you to be an object for me" rather than, "I acknowledge you, and congratulate you."*

Men pretend ignorance on this, and now even use the supposed threat of being accused of sexual harassment to lock women out of male professional networks and perpetuate sexism in another form. Women aren't stupid. They have had millennia to decipher a respectful touch from a disrespectful touch. It's now up to men and women both to learn appreciation and respect for each other and communicate that in their interactions.

What does it look like for a giver man to get together with a giver woman and not only challenge patriarchal habits but develop spiritually confident, honest, and intimate ways to relate? There is something about a giver coming together with a giver that is so beautiful, especially after it has come on the heels of "giver-taker" relationships and experiences. There is a real lasting appreciation and a mutual choice to explore frontiers together. There is an opportunity for the man to liberate himself from the false polarity of patriarchal norms and give himself to the true polarity of his co-creative masculine nature.

For the co-creative, spiritually confident man, giving of himself is not an obligation or a "watering down" of his identity. It is the very completion of his identity, and as this giving transforms him, he experiences the birth of another higher identity, and another higher identity beyond that in escalating cycles of new beginnings. Instead of his self-esteem and confidence resting on defending things as they are, the spiritually confident, giving man is excited about seeing what can develop creatively, what can emerge beyond his expectation.

UNLEASHING

How do I give myself completely over to life?

The spiritually confident person is broken open. This body cannot contain the spirit. This spirit can travel in realms unseen. It can surprise. It can create. It can surpass even the most outrageous imagination in connection with the soul. The spirit connects to the "cloud" of intelligent universes born past, present, and future. Spiritual connection can bring access to literally everything. That interaction with the unique divine genius in you, that unique individuated ray born from a hidden sun, refracts through your being and creates.

Now give yourself to life by understanding that you have nothing to lose and nothing to hold back. You are given this life to create. So use it!

> *Life, in this understanding, is not a finite quantity ending on the day you die, but an overflowing bonus streaming forward since the day you were born.*

Yes, human life can be complicated and confusing. It is easy to feel fear or vertigo when there are so many contradictory aspects of existence. Take the time to slow down and breathe. Realize that most of the pressure and angst we experience is created by us artificially. Let that pass and hold high the miracle of life. Get up in delight and create again. Life is not a hoped-for future; it is a present invitation.

So let life overspill from your being. Let yourself be uncontained. Feel the eternity of your infinite spirit in your finite body, and delight in the contradiction. Now you have both time and timelessness in your being. You have more to create with. You have all the time in the immortal universe and, yet only a window of bodily mortality. Everything you are is quantum—"already *and* not-yet," both definitive and possible, both identity and something far beyond identity. Radiate pure essence, light, kindness, courage, and presence in the face of everything seeming to affirm your worthlessness. Your worth is assured by the fact that you are alive. Playfully engage. Experiment. Leave nothing behind. Invite the future as a friend and co-conspirator in creation.

Wholeness

The end is the beginning. I wrote this book for a beleaguered generation of men and boys in the hopes of pointing to a new path forward that might both open men and boys up and stimulate their collective nerves for adventure. This adventure does not just occur within a man, and between men, but in a community of human beings embarking on a wiser, more honoring, more creative enterprise. The field is open for spirit to come to earth and for spiritual confidence to be the accepted principle rather than an exceptional example.

> *The work and the fun begin now. We can no longer unknow what we know.*

So let us dedicate ourselves "whole-heartedly" to active conversation and transformation. This whole-hearted dedication is the motivation of the spiritually confident man and woman, and it is the basis for their choices. They trust the intimate and ultimate wholeness of their hearts. They know they cannot dedicate themselves entirely if they are emotionally or mentally fractured individuals and if some of their parts are warring against the others. They must be willing to be committed co-creative apprentices in a growing universe.

How does the spiritually confident man become a committed apprentice?—by understanding that his biology is not his destiny. "Who a man is" is not a given; it's something he grows into. Healthy masculinity is more like epigenetics, the well-established scientific concept that we can turn on and off the expression of our gender "genes," our biological tendencies and social possibilities, by our life choices and practices.

A whole man, for instance, includes and honors the feminine parts of himself, like his capacity to experience and express feeling. He critically disagrees with phrases like, "Boys don't cry." Boys and men should and do cry as a show of feeling and honest engagement with the world. He can be frustrated and defeated, and he can show it. Afterwards, he picks himself up, gets back on his feet and resolves once again to succeed, including asking for help if he needs it.

Without authentic wholeness, and social support for that wholeness, boys, in particular, alienate themselves from their own spirits, and they compensate for this alienation with tribal affiliation—like joining a gang—in which the very worst tendencies of maleness are amplified and made the requirements of fraternity. I do not need to tell you what kind of destruction and havoc this has caused the world—posturing and dominance that boils over into full-scale world wars that kill tens of millions of people.

This pervasive need for a boy or a man to feel like a whole person emerges as a consistent theme in books and movies, and, indeed, in life. Fragmented, competitive "ruler" masculinity leaves shattered lives, self-destruction, and grief in its wake.

Fragmented men and boys often feel they are not allowed to be a whole person. They don't feel as if they are allowed to be both weak and strong, emotional and physical, intuitive and intellectual, uncertain and certain.

Instead, fractured males encounter a great deal of pressure to fake strength they do not have, withhold feelings they do have, and pretend they already know something they do not. This becomes a real problem when learning about and relating to a girl or a woman.

Because men and boys are generally not encouraged to express their feelings or admit they do not know, the resulting anxiety has no way to be expressed or shared, further disconnecting men from others. Instead, they shut down or engage in risky behavior to avoid feeling the anxiety and to override the accompanying insecurity and alienation.

In such a state of things, honest conversation and experimentation with new forms of masculinity become strained and turned against themselves. Purpose becomes edged with a kind of neurotic and narcissistic desperation. Time and space become things to dominate and take over like seized territory. This leads to the problem of "misplaced men."

Resolving the problem of "misplaced men"

In this era of increasing regard for equality, it is no longer appropriate for men to compensate for their anxieties in the old inequality-producing ways. For men across the globe, it is becoming less and less acceptable and coherent (if it ever was) to be the cave man, the singular "stand apart" hero, the world-beater.

Yet taking the opposite tack does not seem to be working either. Acknowledging the destructive reality of active machismo (with its emphasis on "taking"—competition, imposition, control freakishness, conquering, possessing), many men have overcorrected and run in the opposite direction. They have silenced themselves and abdicated their own initiative, *forgetting that the new spiritually confident forms of men still require wise assertion, risk, and sacrifice.*

> *The spiritually confident man, on the other hand, embodies both worlds. He mixes assertiveness with openness, seriousness with humor, endurance with care, and emotional toughness with emotional vulnerability.*

A man with the old physical purposes of dominance is doomed to destroy others. A man with no purpose (or a purpose that simply imitates women) is bound to lose his polarity, his distinctness, singularity, and drive, and dissolve himself.

A spiritually confident man is not a "rock". Nor is he a "wet noodle". He has a fiber given in the very uniqueness of his life, his "divine genius," something he alone possesses and which he relies upon and trusts. This reliance is necessary so that he can more deeply share his potent, distinct, creative energy and not simply hold it to himself.

> *There is no formula for the spiritually confident man. Ultimately, he operates on faith, a willingness to risk where the spirit will take him in intimacy as well as aloneness.*

A faithful spirit

This faith in one's spirit is a sign of gratitude for having been given life at all. What risk is there to life really? The spiritually confident man and woman, boy and girl, recognize that they have been given a blessed opportunity to live. Their only question is whether they will live deeply and authentically from the roots of their spirit as expressed through their bodies, hearts, and minds.

> *Spiritually confident persons, therefore, find no lasting comfort or meaning in roles they adopt but in the beings they are becoming.*

This is crucial to understand: When an opportunity arises that beckons spiritually aspiring persons beyond themselves, they give themselves to life from their bodies, minds, hearts, and souls. They hold nothing back, because life itself resides in giving. If they are fortunate, they will meet another person who will give all of herself or himself. This is spiritual sharing— giving to another in a way that transcends the narrowly confined individual interest, and that manifests as a higher "fusion," a co-creation which lifts people beyond their present expectations, imaginations, and horizons.

This is the vision upon which this book is based: Pioneering a new frontier of co-creative masculinity that honors and embraces femininity.

Respect each other. Love each other. Learn from each other. Go forth and create together.

Printed in Great Britain
by Amazon